[illegible] would have
This far
[illegible] you!
Love,
Deborah

Modes of Seduction

Modes of Seduction

Sexual Power in Balzac and Sand

Deborah Houk Schocket

Madison • Teaneck
Fairleigh Dickinson University Press

Associated University Presses
2010 Eastpark Boulevard
Cranbury, NJ 08512

The paper used in this publication meets the requirements of the American National Standard for Permanence of Paper for Printed Library Materials Z39.48-1984.

Library of Congress Cataloging-in-Publication Data

Schocket, Deborah Houk, 1969–
Modes of seduction : sexual power in Balzac and Sand / Deborah Houk Schocket.
p. cm.
Includes bibliographical references and index
ISBN 0-8386-4043-5 (alk. paper)
1. Balzac, Honoré de, 1799–1850—Criticism and interpretation. 2. Sand, George, 1804–1876—Criticism and interpretation. 3. Sex in literature. 4. Seduction in literature. I. Title.
PQ2184.E76S36 2004
843'.7093538—dc22

2004009526

PRINTED IN THE UNITED STATES OF AMERICA

To Andy

Contents

Acknowledgments

I am deeply indebted to Lucienne Frappier-Mazur, who expertly guided my work in the early stages of this project, as well as to Charles Bernheimer and Gerald Prince. I would also like to express my gratitude to Isabelle Naginski for her attentive reading of the manuscript and helpful suggestions. I thank the editors at FDU Press and AUP for their assistance. Numerous mentors and colleagues have given me inspiration and encouragement over the years, and I especially wish to thank Deborah Harter, Becky Brown, and Marcia Stephenson. For their love, support, and belief that I really could write this book, I thank my parents, Rob and Lyn Houk, and especially my husband, Andy. I am also grateful for Sophie, whose imminent birth spurred me to stop procrastinating and complete the manuscript. I have received generous financial support from the Mellon fellowships program at the University of Pennsylvania, the Jacob K. Javits Fellowship Program, and the Purdue Research Foundation Summer Grant Program.

I gratefully acknowledge permission to reprint material, in modified form, from the following articles:

"Domination and the Ends of Seduction: Comparing Sand's *Leone Leoni* and Balzac's *Un Prince de la Bohème*," *George Sand Studies* 19 (2000): 62–74.

"On the Margins: Social and Political Identifications in George Sand's *Horace*," *Romance Notes* 39, no. 3 (Spring 1999): 257–64.

List of Abbreviations

All translations are my own, unless otherwise indicated. Quotations from the works of Honoré de Balzac and George Sand are cited in the text or notes with the abbreviations listed below.

Balzac:

- *B* — *Béatrix*. In vol. 2 of *La comédie humaine*. Bibliothèque de la Pléiade. Paris: Gallimard, 1976
- *FYO* — *La fille aux yeux d'or.* In vol. 5 of *La comédie humaine*. Bibliothèque de la Pléiade. Paris: Gallimard, 1977
- *IP* — *Illusions perdues*. In vol. 5 of *La comédie humaine*. Bibliothèque de la Pléiade. Paris: Gallimard, 1977
- *PB* — *Un prince de la Bohème*. In vol. 7 of *La comédie humaine*. Bibliothèque de la Pléiade. Paris: Gallimard, 1977
- *PC* — *La peau de chagrin*. In vol. 10 of *La comédie humaine*. Bibliothèque de la Pléiade. Paris: Gallimard, 1979
- *PG* — *Le père Goriot.* In vol. 3 of *La comédie humaine.* Bibliothèque de la Pléiade. Paris: Gallimard, 1976
- *SMC* — *Splendeurs et misères des courtisanes*. In vol. 6 of *La comédie humaine*. Bibliothèque de la Pléiade. Paris: Gallimard, 1977
- *SPC* — *Les secrets de la princesse de Cadignan.* In vol. 6 of *La comédie humaine*. Bibliothèque de la Pléiade. Paris: Gallimard, 1977
- *TVE* — *Traité de la vie élégante*. In vol. 12 of *La comédie humaine*. Bibliothèque de la Pléiade. Paris: Gallimard, 1981

Sand:

- *CD* — *Le Château des Désertes*. Meylan: Editions de l'Aurore, 1985
- *CTF* — *Le compagnon du tour de France*. In *Œuvres complètes*. Vol. 12. Paris: Perrotin, Editeur, 1843
- *H* — *Horace*. Meylan: Les éditions de l'Aurore, 1982.

Ind *Indiana*. Coll. Folio. Paris: Gallimard, 1984

I *Isidora*. Paris: Calman Lévy, 1880

L *Lélia* (1833 version). Edited by Pierre Reboul. Paris: Garnier Frères, 1960.

L II *Lélia* (1839 version). 2 vols. Meylan: Editions de l'Aurore, 1987

LL *"Leone Leoni" et autres grandes histoires d'amour.* Paris: J'ai lu, n.d.

M *La marquise*. In *Nouvelles*. Paris: Des femmes, 1986

Modes of Seduction

Introduction: Balzac, Sand, and the Conduct of Seduction

Seduction. The word fascinates the imagination, conjuring up notions of unbridled desire and power unleashed, of alluring bodies and devious minds, of misled maidens abandoned by seducers and enchanting seductresses overpowering men's will. As a space where the forces of desire, power, and sex converge, seduction provides a productive site for examining issues of subjectivity and the ways in which private erotic relations are inextricably embedded in social and political structures. While factors such as social class, economic status, and gender shape the identities of the seducer and the seduced, their relationship does not necessarily replicate the hierarchy of the social order. The present study analyzes representations of seduction in the novels and short stories of Honoré de Balzac and George Sand, and also draws from theoretical works on seduction, psychoanalytic and feminist perspectives on desire and subjectivity, and cultural and historical studies of postrevolutionary France.

Literary critics have rarely paired Balzac and Sand, and yet this coupling makes sense on a number of levels. Both writers began to publish their major novels in the 1830s, and their years of productivity overlapped quite closely (although Sand outlived Balzac and continued to write long after his death in 1850). Despite their divergent backgrounds—Balzac with his bourgeois origins and aristocratic aspirations and Sand with her hybrid peasant and noble parentage—and their different political and social agendas, Balzac and Sand admired one another, maintaining a friendship through social visits and correspondence. Their letters both to and about one another display a respectful, if not always perfectly harmonious, relationship. Sand's words from an 1833 letter to Laure Decerfz characterize the way in which they appreciated one another despite their differences: "Je ne vois plus Balzac, il m'ennuie trop, d'ailleurs nous sommes bons amis et nous nous grattons de loin."[1] [I no longer see Balzac, he bores me too much, moreover we are good friends and we scratch each other from a distance.] We know that they read and commented upon each other's works, and their personal and professional interactions helped to create the sense one gets today of a spirited dialogue existing in the material of many of their novels.

Juxtaposing Balzac's and Sand's writings provides several advantages for approaching the subject of seduction. Because power inequality, which is one of seduction's founding characteristics, is conjoined with the inequality of the sexes in the social order, comparing a male and a female perspective is particularly illuminating. But I have not posited these writers as a mouthpiece for their sex and their works as essentially male or female versions of seduction. Rather, the most productive aspect of this comparison lies in the possibility of observing the intersections as well as the differences in their representations of seduction, variances I account for not only as a product of sexual difference but also as stemming from the distinct ideology that underlies each one's worldview and, hence, his or her conception of the novel as a literary genre. The primary mode chosen by each writer—realism for Balzac and idealism for Sand—implies the very different vision Balzac and Sand had of their respective writing projects. While Balzac, casting himself as a social observer, wished to create a fictional world reflective of contemporary society, Sand took a moral and didactic approach, giving her fictional universe a utopian outlook. She usually preferred to emphasize more egalitarian, republican, or idealistic communities and relationships than the ones she actually observed around her. These writers' different ideas about what the novel should do and be had a profound effect on their representations of seduction. Thus, the vantage point gained by comparing a large number of texts written by a man and a woman can avoid the pitfalls of blindly attributing a writer's perspective and attitude to sex alone.

Furthermore, my choice of Balzac and Sand was informed by a desire to examine representations of seduction created during the early-to-mid nineteenth century, the period in which these writers lived and wrote. Whereas past studies of seduction have focused on literature written during the ancien régime (in particular, seduction novels of the eighteenth century), this study takes postrevolutionary society as its focus. With only one exception taken from Sand's works, the texts analyzed here were written during or set in the periods of the Restoration (especially the 1820s) and July Monarchy (1830–48).[2] During this time, French society witnessed profound mutations in class relations and the increasing importance of money—as opposed to birth—as a signifier of power. This historical phenomenon prompts the question of whether representations of seduction evolved along with the instabilities and changes in class structure. To be sure, seduction is not the property of any class. However, ancien régime literature portrayed two divergent contexts for seduction: fiction represented nobles with no pressing occupations engaged in the "art" of seduction in the same way medieval knights proved their reputation by combat, while in the bourgeoisie seduction appears as a useful tool for social mobility. In particular, rich bourgeois men and women who aspired to marriage with an aristocrat, or at least the social influence of a liaison, found seduction a powerful means by which they could gain entry into higher social circles. Although nineteenth-century literature did not usher in any radically new forms of seduction, a significant development manifested in the works of Balzac and Sand is their tendency to draw on both literary traditions, creating fluctuating, hybrid modes of seduction that, indeed, could be said to mirror the shifting power dynamics in society at large.

The Legacy of *Les liaisons dangereuses*

Perhaps the single text that shapes today's ideas about seduction more than any other is Choderlos de Laclos's epistolary novel *Les liaisons dangereuses* (1782). With the multiple film versions of the novel that appeared at the end of the twentieth century, this vision defied boundaries of the French and the literary and went on to reach the wider audience of people who view American films. In this story, the letters exchanged between Valmont and Merteuil, plus those written to and by the other characters affected by the two libertines' seduction plots, constitute an insightful meditation on the principles and techniques of seduction. Balzac's familiarity with Laclos's novel has already been proven in an informative article by Rose Fortassier that notes both direct references to *Les liaisons dangereuses* and situational similarities.[3] As for Sand, the connection is less obvious. Her texts do not contain the kind of close references to Laclos's novel that one finds in Balzac's works; instead, she preferred to evoke the mythical Don Juan as her prototypical seducer. Nonetheless, the cold-blooded manipulations of Sand's eponymous heroine Césarine Dietrich reflect a will to power and a dominating sexuality of a nature similar to that of Merteuil, and one could also hypothesize that Horace's recounting to the old libertine Marquis de Vernes that his mistress Marthe committed suicide after he seduced her stems from an imagination filled with images like the death of the Présidente de Tourvel over Valmont's abandonment of her. Then as now, it would be hard to think about seduction without *Les liaisons dangereuses* running through one's mind.

Laclos's novel provides an ideal backdrop for defining what seduction involves, how it works, and what constitutes its specific nature as opposed to other erotic relations. Seduction, as we will see, involves more than pure sexual desire or attraction to another person, for it is also inextricably bound up in a subject's need to experience a sense of power and agency. When Valmont explains to Merteuil why he prefers to pursue the Présidente de Tourvel over Cécile de Volanges, his line of reasoning underscores that the difficulty presented by a particular "victim" determines the value of a seduction: "Que me proposez-vous? de séduire une jeune fille qui n'a rien vu, ne connaît rien. [...] Vingt autres peuvent y réussir comme moi. Il n'en est pas ainsi de l'entreprise qui m'occupe; son succès m'assure autant de gloire que de plaisir."[4] [What are you proposing to me? to seduce a young girl who has seen nothing, knows nothing. . . . Twenty others could succeed at it as well as I. Such is not the case for the enterprise that occupies me; its success assures me as much glory as pleasure.] Valmont's words highlight how seduction thrives on the challenge of an obstacle to overcome, and his term "entreprise" suggests the notion of a self-conscious plan that distinguishes seduction from relationships ruled by the heart rather than the head. Further, Laclos emphasizes the search for personal glory as a key motivating factor.

As a type of relation based more on artifice and calculation than on authenticity of feelings, the act of seduction relies on transposing principles of theatricality to amorous settings. Laclos's epistolary novel cogently reveals how the libertines Valmont and Merteuil rely on skills of dramatic representation, for their letters themselves are employed as a stage for identity construction. Merteuil thus instructs her "pupil" Cécile about letter-writing techniques: "Vous voyez bien que, quand vous écrivez à quelqu'un, c'est pour lui et non pas pour vous: vous devez donc moins chercher à lui dire ce que vous pensez, que ce qui lui plaît davantage."[5] [You see very well that, when you write to someone, it is for him and not for you: you must thus seek to tell him less what you think than what will please him most.] Designing the self to fit their audience, Valmont and Merteuil appear one way to each other, and another way entirely to those they wish to seduce or to other friends and relatives. Seduction thus demands that one present oneself as an image of the other's fantasy, a paradoxical situation (explored in detail in chapter 2) whereby to satisfy one's desire one must first be sure to appeal to the other's desire. Moreover, Laclos uses the very structure of his novel to highlight the extent to which the seducer or seductress's identity is a role, a strategic mask, by juxtaposing Valmont's letters of seduction to the Présidente de Tourvel with his candid evaluations of those same letters, written this time to Merteuil. In one such instance, Valmont tells Merteuil of his *mise en scène* of an act of charity in which he helps a poor village family with a donation of money. This "charitable" action is specifically staged for the benefit of a servant the présidente has sent to observe Valmont, and it is designed to make him appear an *honnête homme* in her eyes. The subsequent letter reveals just how well this ploy has worked, as the présidente relates her version of this event to Madame de Volanges, suggesting that Valmont's behavior puts into question his reputation as an unyielding libertine.

Seduction must disguise the power game at its core so that the seduced person does not realize he or she is being manipulated. Thus, Valmont takes care to write love letters to the présidente that appear written with all the abandon of someone innocently in love, even though this strategy represents a calculated act on his part. Furthermore, because sexual activity constitutes the endgame but not necessarily the primary excitement or interest of seduction, the seducer may postpone achieving his conquest so as to savor the evidence of his power over the other. Thus Valmont posits that his delay in possessing Madame de Tourvel has nothing to do with weakness and everything to do with increasing his pleasure.

The power motive in seduction can also take the form of seducing someone to achieve an ulterior design. Some chose seduction as a way to boost their standing in society by becoming associated with a social superior, while others might be motivated by rivalry, using their victim as a tool for hurting a third person. For Merteuil, seduction is a tool of revenge. She arranges Valmont's seduction of Cécile so that Gercourt will not receive the pure convent girl he thinks he is marrying. Her seduction of Prévan is also motivated by a desire for revenge, for she conceives her plan upon hearing that this man dared to question her virtue in public. She thus has the power to affect other's lives. Nevertheless, the fate Laclos assigns Merteuil at the conclusion of his novel—disfigurement from smallpox, public humiliation resulting from Valmont's and Danceny's publication of compromising letters, and the loss of her court case—suggests that in a male-dominated society, female revenge is only allowed to go so far. Appropriating what society considers the "masculine" power of active, desiring sexuality, the seductress threatens the normative assumptions of patriarchal structures. As Roy Roussel writes in his analysis of Laclos's novel, "Merteuil's success would reveal that the assignment of qualities of masculine power and feminine sensitivity to the male and the female, respectively, is only conventional. The recognition of her power would involve the impossible public recognition by convention of its own arbitrary nature."[6] In the end, then, Laclos bows to social conventions and orchestrates the downfall of the female character whom he had represented as more powerful and skilled at seduction than his male seducer. Valmont, too, is punished for his use of seduction, as he suffers death in his duel with Danceny. The conclusion of Laclos's novel thus corroborates the interpretation that Laclos, à la Rousseau, set out to condemn the decadence of this society. But it does not erase the subversiveness of the libertines' acts, especially the seductress's. We will see that Balzac's and Sand's narratives also reflect an awareness of seduction's subversive potential and, more often than not, of a need to contain it and maintain order.

Gender and Seduction

Seduction raises complex issues for the study of gender, as this site reveals the problematic association of set sexual behaviors with each sex. To characterize seduction accurately, then, a model must be developed that recognizes the fluidity of sex and gender roles within the relation of seduction.[7] As opposed to biological sex (male and female), masculine and feminine gender is defined in relation to social conventions. Traditionally, masculine and feminine have been placed in a dichotomous relationship where certain qualities are exclusively assigned to each gender: men have been considered the active, desiring subjects of the sexual relation, while women have been deemed passive objects of male desire. Ironically, while masculine seduction tends to be supported by an ideology that views men's domination as natural and reinforces the vision of feminine submission and surrender, it coexists with representations of female seduction that belie patriarchal assumptions by granting women like Laclos's Merteuil a decidedly "unfeminine" active role. Thus, depending on whether it is a man or a woman who initiates the seduction and what strategies that person uses, seduction can alternately support and undermine patriarchal assumptions of male dominance.

Seduction, then, as an uninstitutionalized relation (unlike marriage or American-style dating) is not governed by the same rules that prescribe masculine and feminine attitudes in other arenas. Yet, just as conventional notions of passive, demure femininity exist, so too is there a type associated with the female subject of desire, and chapter 4 shows how representations of the seductress often cast her as a diabolical figure—precisely because her display of power and desire threatened the very foundations of the patriarchal social order. The seductress experiences sexual agency and enacts her desire to master and control, thereby evoking the possibility of a "masculine" woman while simultaneously emasculating the male victim. This figure of the phallic woman remains sexually identified as a woman, but all the while adopts behavior conventionally designated as masculine. The split representation of women as either desexualized angels or desiring whores was particularly prevalent during the nineteenth century. In fact, the nineteenth century marks a period of great importance for erecting gendered public and private spheres—and relegating women to domesticity.[8] Further complicating this gender scenario is the fact that some of Balzac's and Sand's seducers and seductresses do not correspond to traditional portraits of male and female seduction.

Seduction presents a kind of gender conundrum of the type that threatens those invested in the patriarchal social order while providing critics such as feminists reason to feel vindicated in their assertion of the constructed rather than natural condition of social roles. While seduction is undoubtedly a power relation based on dominant and submissive roles, countless examples in literature and in life show that one's sex does not predetermine which role one will play: women can embody the active desiring position just as well as men. Further, while authors often represented women as seducing through use of their physical allure or by more passive means, such is not always the case. Thus, while we use the terms seducer and seductress to identify the sex of the person who initiates a seduction, these labels tell us little about the actual methods and strategies men and women will use. By creating seducers and seductresses whose behavior ran contrary to conventional social roles of the time, authors like Balzac and Sand questioned the assumptions on which the social order was erected, revealing the inconsistencies of roles and relations that society took for granted. In effect, Balzac's and Sand's seduction narratives alternately corroborate and subvert the social agenda of domesticating and disempowering women, as chapter 3 will show. In the realm of seduction, the relation male/female has no fixed correspondence to dominant/submissive or active/passive behavior (discussed in chapters 3 and 4). Instead, the oppositional dynamics of seduction allow for men and women to play either role.

Conduct Books: From Libertinage to Postrevolutionary Seductions

Between Laclos's 1782 novel and the nineteenth-century works by Balzac and Sand, the literary landscape, and indeed society itself, witnessed a profound revolution that turned the world as libertines knew it upside down. The groundwork for the shift between the ancien régime's separation of bourgeois and aristocratic spheres and Balzac's and Sand's tendencies to draw upon both these traditions can be seen by examining the genres of arts of love and conduct books—early examples of what today's bookstores categorize as "self-help" literature—that flourished in the postrevolutionary period. In presenting advice on all varieties of intimate relations from how to seduce a woman to how to please one's husband and on the question of the woman's proper role in the home and society, the authors of these manuals had to come to terms with the ways society had changed since the end of the ancien régime. In particular, conduct books and arts of love written from the 1820s to the 1840s—during the Restoration and July Monarchy—show that in the early nineteenth century seducers and seductresses adapted to the changing social scene and made class mobility, that *non-dit* of eighteenth-century France, one of their primary motivations. These nonfiction texts provide a historical context and will serve as a basis for analyzing the social and political dynamics present in the fiction of Balzac and Sand.

The discourse found in several nineteenth-century arts of love attests to the continuing influence of ancien régime notions of worldly society during the postrevolutionary period. In Louis de Saint-Ange's 1825 text, *Le secret de triompher des femmes et de les fixer*, one finds examples of vocabulary that would be familiar to readers of someone like Crébillon fils, since the author uses terms like a man of "bon ton."[9] In *Les égarements du cœur et de l'esprit*, which I will analyze more fully in chapter 1, the Count de Versac lectures the young Meilcour at length on the importance of *bon ton*, that indescribable quality separating aristocrat from commoner. The type of advice found in *Le secret de triompher des femmes*—with its emphasis on knowing the ways of the (aristocratic) worldly society and on the use of *bon ton*—suggests that such notions still carried weight in Restoration France. A few years later, the anonymous author of *L'art de rendre les femmes fidèles* speaks of upper-class women in a way that recalls the privileges enjoyed by the great ladies of the ancien régime: "[C]'est surtout parmi les femmes riches que l'infidélité est commune; [...] parce que dans la haute société, il y a une espèce d'honneur qui autorise la galanterie, et oblige le mari à la souffrir pour ne pas se donner en ridicule."[10] [It is above all among rich women that infidelity is common; . . . because in high society, there is a type of honor that authorizes gallantry, and forces the husband to put up with it in order not to appear ridiculous.] This author is suggesting that adultery was not only more widespread but also better tolerated among the upper classes. Significantly, though, he speaks of infidelity in terms of rich women, rather than defining high society as a matter of birth. Thus, notions of how the upper echelons of society behaved remained constant even if the definition of who makes up that privileged class had evolved.

Nearly a decade later, in 1837, the anonymous author of *L'art de faire la cour aux femmes et de s'en faire aimer* makes a direct reference to ancien régime literature when he recommends that suitors study novels by Marivaux, Prévost, Crébillon fils, and Rousseau in order to find models of eloquent discourse they could use to captivate a woman.[11] Although the author initiates his readers to techniques of courtship through ancien régime literature, he has nothing positive to say about the art of seduction so often represented—and at times even glorified—in texts of that period, where seducers use "un art perfide" [a treacherous art] and "se font un jeu de l'honeur, de l'amour, la plus sainte des passions"[12] [make a game of honor, of love, the most saintly of passions]. Referring to literary and historical examples of well-known libertines, he advises young readers to steer clear of the models of Lovelace, Don Juan, Richelieu, Rochester, and Faust because "[d]ans la société [...], on ne gagne rien à jouer le jeu de ces messieurs"[13] [in society . . . , one gains nothing from playing the game of these gentlemen]. Whereas Crébillon's Meilcour was expected to establish his reputation in worldly society by developing talents as a seducer and essentially learning to be like Versac, his model and initiator to society, in *L'art de faire la cour aux femmes* the author explicitly entreats young men to avoid the famous literary seducers' libertine games. The invocation to read eighteenth-century novels, including Crébillon's *Le sopha* and *Les égarements du cœur et de l'esprit*, thus exists in a context hostile to the spirit of these texts. In serious arts of love (as opposed to parodies of the genre), the libertine pastime of seduction and abandonment has been replaced by a program of captivation that leads to marriage. Such a shift in attitudes about male sexual conduct fits into a larger societal phenomenon: the reaction against the moral decadence of the eighteenth-century aristocracy with the growing ascendancy of the bourgeoisie in the nineteenth century.

By the late 1820s and certainly in the 1830s and 1840s, arts of love reveal the existence of a conscious sense that some great threshold had been crossed and that society's values and morals no longer resembled those of the ancien régime. The author of *L'art de faire la cour aux femmes* offers one of the clearest examples of this value shift when he writes: "[N]os mœurs d'aujourd'hui n'offrent plus cette corruption qu'on trouvait aimable il y a cent ans, et on n'éprouve plus que de l'horreur et du dégoût à lire les scandaleux mémoires de ce terrible maréchal de Richelieu, dont on admirait les vices précoces."[14] [Our morals today no longer offer that corruption one found so likeable one hundred years ago, and people no longer feel anything but horror and disgust in reading the scandalous memoirs of that terrible Maréchal de Richelieu, whose precocious vices people used to admire.] Even as he accords eighteenth-century literature certain merits, the author's preference for nineteenth-century society is clear in his discussion of conversation. Taking exception to the generalized belief that the art of conversation has died in the new century, he claims, "[C]e langage dégagé, vif et pétillant du dix-huitième siècle n'existe plus, mais la conversation de nos jours est plus vraie, mieux sentie, sinon plus rillante qu'à cette époque."[15] [This free, lively, and sparkling language of the eighteenth century no longer exists, but the conversation of today is more true, better felt, if not more gay than at that time.] For this author at least, nineteenth-century life might be less vivacious, but it offers significant improvements in the moral realm.

Not only were writers aware of a change in the moral climate early in the nineteenth century, but also these texts signal a shift in class consciousness and class hierarchy that reflected the increasing importance of the bourgeoisie. In proclaiming the disappearance of the Paris/Versailles opposition that had governed ancien régime society and marked the superiority of the aristocratic court society over the bourgeois city, Jules Janin observes in his 1841 introduction to *Les Français peints par eux-mêmes*: "[C]e monde-là s'est perdu; il s'est évanoui dans les révolutions et dans les tempêtes."[16] [That world is lost; it vanished in the revolutions and storms.] In a commentary that shows how deeply society has been transformed, Janin remarks that even the idea of what it meant to be rich had changed. Before, he says, to be rich was to eat fine foods, to have a palace in the city *and* in the country, and to have a duke in your family. In the postrevolutionary period, however, the rich are those who play the stock market, live on the third floor, attend a theater performance with a complimentary ticket, and marry their son to a moneylender's daughter. Putting it succinctly, he notes, "L'homme d'argent a remplacé le grand seigneur."[17] [The man of money has replaced the noble lord.] The terms of Janin's opposition suggest that he believes in the superiority of the old-time *grand seigneur* over the new class of moneyed elites.

Janin is not the only writer for *Les Français peints par eux-mêmes* to speak of bourgeois ascendancy in disparaging tones. Balzac contributed an article entitled "La femme comme il faut" to the volume, and in his text this nineteenth-century female type appears unfavorably compared to the great lady of ages past. According to Balzac, to be a *femme comme il faut*, an honorable and upstanding woman, does not even require *esprit* (intelligence and wit), one of the defining traits of the great lady. Further, his comments underscore that the aristocracy could no longer afford the libertine excesses that some found so charming: "L'aristocratie en entière ne s'avance plus pour servir de paravent à une femme en faute. La femme comme il faut n'a donc point, comme la grande dame d'autrefois, une allure de haute lutte, elle ne peut rien briser sous son pied, c'est elle qui serait brisée."[18] [The entire aristocracy no longer comes forward to serve as a screen to a dishonored woman. The honorable woman thus does not have, like the great lady of ages past, an allure of intense struggle, she can crush nothing under her foot, it is she who would be crushed.] The anonymous author of the article called "La grande dame de 1830" explicitly condemns the new power structure of class relations for the passing of the great lady when he says that the true lady of ages past could not exist in this new era of "fusion," which he prefers to call one of "deplorable or grotesque confusion."[19] For Balzac and many of his contemporaries, then, the blurring of class distinctions marked a social decline. In their eyes, bourgeois attempts to imitate aristocratic style invariably led to a loss of style and grace—in effect, the passing of *le bon ton*.

Others, however, recognized changes in class structures as an opportunity for social climbing, and some conduct books from the early nineteenth century read as a lesson in how to benefit from new possibilities for class mobility. The 1829 edition of *L'art de briller en société; ou, Manuel de l'homme du monde* contains chapters on such wide-ranging practical subjects as social conventions, cleanliness, clothing, politeness, and salutations, and it instructs its readers how to behave on social visits, at balls, or at the theater. Going into great detail, the author tells his uncultured readers: "Un homme propre ne s'habille jamais sans avoir battu son habit, son pantalon, son chapeau, décroté ses bottes et levé les taches qu'il pourrait avoir attrapées la veille."[20] [A clean man must never get dressed without having beat his frock, his pants, his hat, scraped the mud off his boots, and removed any spots that he might have got on him the day before.] Those who were born into high society could simply learn social graces by observing their elders the way Crébillon's Meilcour of *Les égarements du cœur et de l'esprit* learned the ways of the world from the Count de Versac and his mother's friend Madame de Lursay; they would not have needed such a manual, which suggests that this text was written with social outsiders in mind. It served as an instrument abetting the process of *arrivisme*, as members of the bourgeoisie strove to cross barriers that had formerly excluded them from the elite inner circles of society when membership had been based more squarely on noble birth.

Other guides are much more explicit in their appeal to readers with arriviste aspirations. In the 1826 *Art de réussir en amour, enseigné en 25 leçons*, the author offers a complete step-by-step manual on how to seduce a woman, and, as Catherine Nesci has noted in *La femme mode d'emploi*, this particular text parodies the genre, which was more often directed toward socially sanctioned aims such as finding a husband or wife. Like so many other guides aimed at instructing men about how to attract women—for marriage or any other purpose—this text emphasizes the importance of identifying a woman's personality type and tailoring one's advances accordingly, since, for example, a sentimental woman would be susceptible to a different approach than a coquette, or a prude. In addition, the book's third section categorizes women according to social class and profession, recommending different techniques for women who are noble, bourgeois, writers, artists, or working girls. The writer makes direct references to the postrevolutionary class turmoil of his society when he remarks to his reader, "Mais quels obstacles tu auras à surmonter, toi qui ne peux te réclamer que d'un nom sans illustration, qui sembles encore un vassal à la femme dont le père était seigneur, et qui ne peut s'accoutumer à l'égalité qu'un nouveau siècle a mis entre elle et toi."[21] [But what obstacles you will have to overcome, you who can only lay claim to a name that is not illustrious, who still seem a vassal to the woman whose father was a lord, and who cannot accustom herself to the equality a new century has placed between her and you.] Thus, even in the postrevolutionary period and even when armed with the expert advice of this manual, social climbing through seduction remains difficult. While emphasizing the obstacles, the author nonetheless takes an optimistic approach when, a few pages later, he encouragingly notes that many upper-class women are willing to overlook differences in rank due to birth when pursued by a man of talent and intelligence.[22] This comment shows that bourgeois notions of judging someone based on personal merit rather than on birth rank were becoming more accepted by society. The message to the aspiring social-climber was clear: the old barriers to social success were no longer insurmountable.

Though class distinctions posed less of a problem to the aspiring arriviste than in the previous century, certain barriers between the bourgeoisie and the aristocracy remained. As the author of *L'art de faire la cour aux femmes* told his readers in 1837, a commoner seeking to improve his social standing through marriage would find that "on n'attachera aucun prix à votre origine; la fortune et le mérite seront les seules distinctions dont vous pourrez vous honorer"[23] [people will attach no value to your origins; fortune and merit will be the sole distinctions with which you may honor yourself]—unless, that is, he had his sights set on a noblewoman. A noble family would demand that the daughter's suitor supply a title, an illustrious family, and a historical name, which is precisely the stumbling block Balzac's Lucien de Rubempré encounters in his failed pursuit of Clothilde de Grandlieu in *Splendeurs et misères des courtisanes*. This chapter of *L'art de faire la cour aux femmes* nevertheless ends on an encouraging note as the author concludes, "[O]n peut obtenir les faveurs de ces dames, à titre d'amant, sinon à titre d'époux, et [...] le premier est de beaucoup préférable au second."[24] [One can obtain the favors of these ladies, as a lover, if not as a husband, and . . . the first is much preferable to the second.] Thus, the most inner circles of the old aristocracy remained tightly closed. And, as the author's remarks about lovers suggest, even a liaison with a noblewoman could improve a young man's social standing, perhaps even marking a first step into high society that might later result in a marriage.

The conduct of seduction as presented in these two nineteenth-century arts of love thus differs starkly from the libertinage of the previous period, as these guides are clearly written for non-noble readers full of ambition to crash the gates of elite society. In nineteenth-century France, young men like Stendhal's Julien Sorel used seduction to achieve their arriviste goals, whereas libertine seducers of the previous era already belonged the elite social class. However, many aristocratic elites found themselves in a very different world after the Revolution. The aristocracy was less able to turn its nose up at new members of the power structure in France, because so many noble families had lost their wealth as a result of the Revolution. Faced with poverty, an aristocratic family was more likely to consider seriously an alliance with a social inferior if that person had money to bring to the marriage. This phenomenon of marriages between wealthy bourgeois and impoverished nobles contributed to the blurring of distinctions between the two classes.

The presence of such an extensive number of self-help manuals from the Restoration and July Monarchy suggests that the public was trying to adjust to new rules of interpersonal relations in the new century, and Balzac's and Sand's novels also respond to this societal concern. In the chapters that follow, we will rediscover many issues and themes found in these manuals, and we will use the lens of seduction to examine the particular ways Balzac and Sand viewed French society in the postrevolutionary period.

This book follows a thematic organization based on different modes of seduction, defined by the primary motivations that drive the seducers and seductresses, as well as the strategies and techniques they use to ensnare their victims. Despite these differences, however, certain fundamental threads will be shown to interweave successive chapters, uniting them all. Indeed, some texts appear in more than one chapter—approached from a specific and limited angle in each case—

because they contain multiple facets that highlight more than one aspect of seduction. Together, the representative group of sixteen texts by Balzac and Sand offer a picture of the players, rules, and contexts of seduction in French literature of the early nineteenth century.

Chapter 1 demonstrates how seduction can act as a kind of sexual politics whose stakes extend to the socioeconomic realm. In a number of texts, Balzac and Sand created scenarios that embedded seduction in the shifting class dynamics of Restoration and July Monarchy France: Balzac's *Le père Goriot* (1835), *Splendeurs et misères des courtisanes* (1847), and *Béatrix* (1839), and Sand's *Le compagnon du tour de France* (1840) and *Horace* (1841). This chapter pinpoints certain continuities and rewritings of prerevolutionary seduction narratives, using Crébillon fils's *Les égarements du cœur et de l'esprit* (1736–38) and Marivaux's *Le paysan parvenu* (1734–35) as ancien régime examples for comparison. Balzac and Sand manifest divergent attitudes toward the sexual politics of social mobility, yet these differences stem more from the two authors' very different conception of their writing than from a masculine versus a feminine perspective.

In chapter 2, I will establish a general framework for describing the theatrical context in which seduction operates. In effect, the seducer or seductress performs an identity designed to appeal to the other's fantasies, and when the other accepts that identity as real, succumbing to the seduction, the situation inaugurates a new—and often somewhat illusory—reality. The primary texts analyzed in this chapter all contain seductions that highlight the key role played by theatrical behavior: Sand's *La marquise* (1832) and *Isidora* (1846), and Balzac's *Les secrets de la princesse de Cadignan* (1840) and the second part of *Splendeurs et misères des courtisanes* (1847), entitled "A combien l'amour revient aux vieillards." Asking whether the act of seduction takes on a different signification depending on the gender of the players involved, I will also investigate the authors' divergent attitudes regarding the artifices of seduction.

Chapter 3 explores the question of how the distribution of power in seduction corresponds to—or conflicts with—male and female positions in the social order by examining texts whose representations of seduction foreground the issue of sexual domination: Balzac's *La fille aux yeux d'or* (1835) and *Un prince de la Bohème* (1845) and Sand's *Indiana* (1832) and *Leone Leoni* (1834). Significantly, these works do not present a hegemonic view of masculine power, for the narratives that do depict a traditional configuration of male dominance and female submission exist alongside others that reverse male domination or display an alternation of sexual power. An element that remains constant, however, is the power asymmetry on which seduction thrives, opposing seducer and seduced, pursuit and resistance. To better understand seduction's dual relation to the patriarchal power structure—its paradoxical ability to act as a normalizing or a subversive agent, depending on the context—I turn to psychoanalytic and sociohistorical analyses of gender and power in intersubjective relations. My aim is to identify and compare Balzac's and Sand's attitudes toward the power displayed in seduction, as well as to explore the ideological function of these varied representations.

Chapter 4 examines two social types prevalent in Balzac's and Sand's representations of seduction: the coquette and the dandy. After comparing female characters in Balzac's *La peau de chagrin* (1831) and *Béatrix* (1839) with Sand's *Lélia* (1833 and 1839), the chapter explores the nineteenth-century phenomenon of dandyism as embodied in Balzac's *Illusions perdues* (1843) and Sand's *Le Château des Désertes* (1851). Coquettes' and dandies' personalities are characterized by a strong narcissistic impulse. In order to understand how this psychological constitution plays into their seductions, I turn to psychoanalytic theories of narcissism, which underscore the narcissist's split between a fragile interior and a seductive exterior persona. In addition, these narcissists' seductions frequently rely on mimetic desire and rivalry, a dynamic I explore by drawing on the work of René Girard in *Mensonge romantique et vérité romanesque* and *Des choses cachées depuis la fondation du monde*, as well as Sarah Kofman's *L'énigme de la femme*. Finally, the conjunction of seduction and narcissism poses interesting questions for the study of gender roles, as this site allows for a breakdown in the traditional association of men with the active pole and women with the passive pole. Because active and passive bear no stable relation to gender in these texts by Balzac and Sand, I propose the gender-neutral terms *l'être séducteur* and *l'être séduisant* as the best means of describing these narcissists' behavior.

In multiple contexts during the course of this study, I am constantly asking how Balzac and Sand represented what is at stake for the men and women involved in seduction—psychologically, sexually, and socially. The analysis examines the subjective makeup and desires of both seducer and seduced, as well as their social position and the larger context in which a seduction takes place. In exploring nineteenth-century understandings of seduction, this project reveals the intersections of sexual politics and ideology and analyzes sex and gender roles as they relate to power, both sexual and in the social order. Furthermore, this comparative study provides insights into the affinities and singularities of Balzac and Sand as writers, for reading them together effectively brings out the uniqueness of each one.

1
Seduction and Society: Balzac's and Sand's Sexual Politics

How did the 1789 Revolution, and the changes it created in relations between the classes, influence the conduct of seduction in postrevolutionary France? For French society of the early nineteenth century, nothing could have weighed more on the collective mind of the people than the Revolution. But rather than marking a watershed moment when the relative power of the aristocracy and the bourgeoisie suddenly shifted places in the hierarchy of class identity, the Revolution only brought into the open and into public discourse the effects of a long-term evolution the old ruling class had simply avoided facing. In toppling the preexisting political system, the Revolution materialized an ideological revolution and reinforced shifts in power, allegiances, and values that had actually already been developing during the course of the eighteenth century. Class mutations became an unavoidable issue in nineteenth-century life and fiction, and sexual politics proved to be a fertile site on which novelists could stage the dynamics of shifting power in society.

This chapter will examine the interplay between strategies of seduction and sociopolitical maneuvering in some of Balzac's and Sand's novels where the historical setting during the Restoration and July Monarchy plays an important enabling role in diegetic events: Balzac's *Le père Goriot*, *Splendeurs et misères des courtisanes*, and *Béatrix*, and Sand's *Horace* and *Le compagnon du tour de France*. While close connections exist between the material circumstances of postrevolutionary France and Balzac's and Sand's fictional representations, the modes of seduction they envisioned also share certain ties with their ancien régime predecessors, and this chapter will explore some of the continuities and discontinuities between representations of seduction in the eighteenth and nineteenth centuries, drawing on the prerevolutionary examples of Crébillon fils's *Les égarements du cœur et de l'esprit* and Marivaux's *Le paysan parvenu*.

The competing and shifting class interests at work in contemporary society are issues Balzac and Sand explicitly address in their fiction, although the two writers' different social preoccupations set them apart in important ways. Both construct plots that interweave seduction and social climbing, sex and payoffs, honor and merit. While the politically motivated pairing of economic and sexual concerns hardly constitutes a nineteenth-century innovation and certainly did gain representation in some veins of prerevolutionary fiction, it is only in the postrevolutionary era that a full range of social forces and perspectives comes to play a widespread role in fiction and gives rise to explicit commentary. Priscilla P. Clark suggests it is the totalizing vision Balzac aimed for in *La comédie humaine* that accounts for his wider viewpoint : "Balzac's goal of portraying a total society virtually forced him to acknowledge the significance of the bourgeoisie as the dynamic element of French society, a significance willfully ignored by more selective authors."[1] Sand also contributed new social perspectives to the contemporary fictional scene. With her espousal of republican politics, her admiration of the common people, and her belief in class and gender equality, her narratives give voice to otherwise underrepresented elements of the social fabric of nineteenth-century society. At the same time, the postrevolutionary attitudes and situations encountered in Balzac's and Sand's works mingle with clearly identifiable ties to specific types of eighteenth-century literature.

In its purest form, seduction is a game whose ritualized behavior of pursuit and resistance, of captivation and submission to desire, constitutes an end in itself, providing satisfaction that is not only sexual but also an affirmation of the seducer's or seductress's sense of agency. The libertine tradition of the eighteenth century produced seduction narratives that—even today—remain our point of reference. As Laclos's novel *Les liaisons dangereuses* and its many screen adaptations convey so well, there is something about the privileged and wealthy class that makes its members particularly suited to idle pursuits like seduction. Yet, to view seduction as a strictly nonutilitarian relation, completely divorced from economic or social interests, provides only a partial perspective that limits one's understanding of seduction's multiple uses and historical roles. As we will see, even during the ancien régime, literary traditions other than libertinage portrayed materially motivated seductions. During the postrevolutionary era of the Restoration and July Monarchy, modes of seduction became even more diffuse and more inventive—particularly with *La comédie humaine*. In a world turned upside down, the literature of seduction no longer showed the same face as it had in the dominant aristocratic tradition of the ancien régime. While perhaps less of a pure art form than the aesthetically motivated libertine seductions, seductions based on pragmatic calculations of material gain still display the key components of theatricality and the creation of a self-referential reality based on the seduced person's belief in the seducer or seductress's performed identity.

SEDUCTION *À L'ANCIENNE*: *LES ÉGAREMENTS DU CŒUR ET DE L'ESPRIT* AND *LE PAYSAN PARVENU*

During the ancien régime, class differences tended to be more pronounced in literature than in actual life, particularly in the aristocratic vein of fiction that strove to preserve the vision of a fixed class system with the nobility safely ensconced at the top of the social hierarchy. The libertine tradition that flourished during the eighteenth century with writers such as Crébillon fils, Denon, and, of course, Laclos portrayed an aristocratic way of life that would no longer exist in quite the same way after the Revolution. In libertine fiction, seduction played a largely aesthetic role and served as a way for idle aristocrats to pass the time. Yet multiple modes of seduction existed even before the Revolution. During the seventeenth and eighteenth centuries, writers of the comic and picaresque traditions such as Sorel, Scarron, Restif, and Marivaux paired strategies of seduction with their characters' material concerns and desire for social mobility. For these protagonists, a successful seduction could provide not only physical pleasures and a boost to one's ego but also entry into a more exclusive social class, with all of the possibilities for status and wealth that this association included. The eighteenth-century examples by Crébillon fils and Marivaux will help to underscore attitudes toward class and seduction during the ancien régime, providing a base of comparison from which to view Balzac's and Sand's treatment of the theme of seduction and initiation into *le monde* of high society during the nineteenth century.

The relationship between Crébillon's first-person narrator-protagonist, Meilcour, and his mentor, the illustrious seducer Count Versac, illustrates how seduction functioned among members of the aristocracy as a noble art designed to create distinctions of reputation among social equals, all of whom were privileged by birth and wealth. Sheltered from socioeconomic preoccupations of the type that infuse the plots of many nineteenth-century novels with great dynamic energy (such as Balzac's *Le père Goriot* or Sand's *Horace*), Meilcour and his worries appear rather frivolous. Indeed, in the opening paragraphs of this memoir novel, Meilcour sums up the concerns of his younger days, saying, "L'idée du plaisir fut, à mon entrée dans le monde, la seule qui m'occupa."[2] [The idea of pleasure was, at the time of my entry into society, the only one that occupied me.] At issue in this novel, then, is the degree to which Meilcour succeeds in distinguishing himself through *le commerce des femmes*, a distinctly nonbourgeois "business," rather than his very acceptance into the closed circle of high society.

Speaking from a position of age and experience, Meilcour reflects back on the social ignorance that characterized his youth. Meilcour's present insights indicate the wisdom and success he gained from his sentimental education. To the green young man, however, the world—and especially the behavior and intentions of women—appeared an indecipherable mystery. Meilcour's timid interactions with Madame de Lursay, his mother's friend who gives him his first taste of seduction, leave him feeling bewildered, because he does not understand the art of conversation. His naive outlook, whereby his evaluations of social behavior based on moral standards of honesty and transparency constantly lead him astray, gives this novel of manners a subtle undercurrent of social critique by highlighting the artificial ground on which this social group interacted.

Despite the fact that Meilcour inherently belongs to this world that appeared so foreign to him in his youth, he is in need of guidance, of an education into the intricacies of the coded behavior that helps keep this elite world closed in on itself. In search of a model, Meilcour chooses Versac, the reigning master of court society. In a key passage of the novel, Versac imparts to Meilcour vital information on the workings of *le monde*, demanding that the young man swear to keep these lessons a secret. Versac enlightens his young protégé about the duplicities involved in social interactions: "[V]ous devez apprendre à déguiser si parfaitement votre caractère, que ce soit en vain qu'on s'étudie à le démêler."[3] [You must learn to disguise so perfectly your personality, that it is in vain that people strive to bring it to light.] The more Meilcour hears from Versac, the more confused and horrified he becomes, for he does not understand the point of disguising his virtues and suggesting that his character contains appealing vices. Versac has a response for every objection, and, in a remark recalling an exchange between Molière's Philinte and Alceste, he maintains, "Il vaut mieux, encore un coup, prendre les erreurs de son siècle, ou du moins s'y plier, que d'y montrer des vertus qui y paraîtraient étrangères, ou ne seraient pas du bon ton."[4] [It is better, once again, to accept the errors of one's century, or at least to bend oneself to them, than to show virtues that appear foreign, or would not be of the right tone.] Versac's use of the term "bon ton" brings their conversation to a close on a note that refers it back to the very reasons why Meilcour needs this instruction in the first place. He is unable to grasp the meaning of the expression, as well as that of Versac's circular definition that follows, and Meilcour's situation reminds us how the circles of high society remain impenetrable to outsiders thanks to a certain *je ne sais quoi*: "Ce que nous appelons le ton de la bonne compagnie, nous, c'est le nôtre, et nous sommes bien déterminés à ne le trouver qu'à ceux qui pensent, parlent, et agissent comme nous. Pour moi, en attendant qu'on le définisse mieux, je le fais consister dans la noblesse, et l'aisance des ridicules."[5] [What we call the tone of good company, we, it is ours, and we are quite determined only to find it in those who think, speak, and act like us. For me, in waiting for a better definition, I think of it as nobility, and the ease of ridicule.] The fact that even the insider Meilcour needs lessons on how to behave in society provides insight into how this behavior—learned rather than innate—could potentially be adopted by outsiders with a knack for seductive appearances and social masquerade.

The seduction plots of *Les égarements du cœur et de l'esprit*—Meilcour's interactions with three older women to whom he owes his education and his lovesick pining for the young Hortense de Théville—are characteristic of aristocratic ancien régime fiction. They reflect a carefree class and era when the noble occupation of "commerce intime," the ritualized game of seduction, was enacted by characters apparently unaffected by pragmatic, socioeconomic concerns. All that separates Meilcour from Versac are age and experience, for they come from the same aristocratic background. However, as the century drew to a revolutionary close, the ideological constructs Crébillon described no longer existed. Instead, the nineteenth century opened onto a time when, despite the monarchy's restoration, nobles could no longer deny their uncertain future and waning influence. The idea that the Revolution swept away the idle world of the upper class is expressly articulated by Stendhal in his Restoration novel *Armance*: "Il faut de l'économie, du travail opiniâtre, de la solidité et l'absence de toute illusion dans une tête, pour tirer partie de la machine à vapeur. Telle est la différence entre le siècle qui finit en 1789 et celui qui commença vers 1815."[6] [Economy, stubborn work, solidity, and the absence of all illusion in one's mind are necessary to profit from the steam engine. Such is the difference between the century that ended in 1789 and the one that began around 1815.] As Stendhal's words make clear, the nobility could no longer take its privileged position for granted; instead, members of the aristocracy would have to work for their success in order to compete with the bourgeoisie.

Marivaux's upstart peasant, Jacob, of *Le paysan parvenu* constitutes a prime example of a seducer whose charming effect on women helps him in quite utilitarian ways, and this pragmatic approach to seduction marks him as a precursor to many nineteenth-century seducers. While the libertine model has received more prominence, Marivaux's text reminds us that the aristocratic mode of seduction actually shared the literary stage with others that undermined the ruling class's ideology. Thanks to Jacob's irresistible seductiveness, he rises in society, shedding his rough peasant ways and donning the manners of the upper class. Jacob's financial motivations are clear from the first pages of the novel when he decides to stay in Paris rather than return to his village in Champagne, declaring: "Le peu de jours que j'y avais passé, m'avait éveillé le coeur, et je me sentis tout d'un coup en appétit de fortune."[7] [The few days that I had spent there had awakened my heart, and all of a sudden I felt in myself an appetite for fortune.] In the course of the novel, Jacob follows a familiar literary path toward wealth and status: that of using his success with women to propel himself up the social ladder.

In many ways, Jacob's methods resemble the seductions of his upper-class libertine contemporaries. Like any seducer, Jacob learns to project an identity designed to appeal to the woman he is trying to captivate, using a mixture of truth and artifice. From his first encounters with a woman of a higher social status, the wife of his lord from Champagne—he meets both husband and wife while working at their Paris residence—Jacob comes to realize that his simple peasant manners can actually constitute an attraction for women. Commenting on a remark he made to Madame, Jacob says, "[I]l me parut que la naïveté de mes façons ne lui déplaisait pas."[8] [It appeared to me that the naïveté of my ways did not displease her.] By the time he meets

Mademoiselle Habert on the Pont Neuf, Jacob knows just how to display his rustic naïveté to his advantage when telling the devout bourgeois woman his story. The version of his past that Jacob tells Mlle Habert, though inspired by true events, does not exactly replicate the facts of his situation. Like any good seducer, Jacob evaluates his performance only according to the success of the results it achieves for him. As Marie-Paule Laden has noted, "Because Mlle Habert believes it, the story becomes true and Jacob becomes what he says he is. The performative value which the sign derives from its place in socio-literary codes of style and behavior has totally supplanted its primary referential content."[9] Thus, Jacob has learned the artifice of creating a self-referential space of seduction. As he moves in with this older woman and then proceeds to marry her, Jacob continues to use his peasant ways to his advantage even as he increasingly integrates himself into bourgeois society. This successful seduction allows Jacob to transform his identity completely; he dons bourgeois clothes and a sword, and assumes a new name, Monsieur de la Vallée.

The significance of Marivaux's social-climbing seducer remains ambiguous, however, in part because of the novel's unfinished nature. Marivaux's pen transforms Jacob into a *monsieur*, gives him a bourgeois wife, and even provides him with contacts in the upper bourgeoisie, most notably the "grande dame" Madame de Ferval. When the Count d'Orsan befriends the young hero and then invites him to the Comédie-Française, Marivaux seems to be making a strong statement in favor of his hero's *arrivisme* by allowing him to climb so high from his peasant origins. But Marivaux breaks off his novel with a scene at the end of part 5, in which Jacob suffers humiliation at the theater precisely because he has not learned quite enough to fit in with the more refined aristocratic crowd he encounters there. Amy Wyngaard has noted that Marivaux's retreat from the radical social ideas he has only just put forward is a trait found in his plays as well, yet she also observes: "If Marivaux leaves his reader with the image of Jacob's ultimate failure to pass as an aristocrat, he also suggests that repairing this failure is simply a question of time."[10] An anonymous author stepped in almost two decades later to complete the circle of Jacob's rise in society. In this author's apocryphal conclusion to the unfinished novel, Mlle Habert dies, allowing Jacob to marry an aristocrat who buys the château of the village where the hero was born. Having left home as a peasant, Jacob returns as a lord.

Marivaux's *paysan parvenu* gives fictional expression to a very real social phenomenon of eighteenth-century society: the increasing numbers of ambitious peasants who moved to the city in order to improve their position in society.[11] Writing in the picaresque tradition, Marivaux presents his hero's successes, mixed with a hearty share of setbacks along the way, in a first-person retrospective narrative recounted by Jacob himself. The narrative structure is thus identical to that of Crébillon's memoir novel, *Les égarements du cœurs et de l'esprit*. Further, in both texts older women play a prominent role in advancing the young heroes' sexual education. But while Marivaux presents the possibility of social climbing and shows a heterogeneous mixture of social rank and class among his characters, the world inhabited by Meilcour and Versac appears impervious to outside influences. One could even attribute Jacob's embarrassing mishaps at the Comédie-Française to his ignorance of *le bon ton*, the social language and mannerisms Versac worked to instill in his pupil Meilcour, and as a validation of Versac's perspective that this social discourse effectively allows aristocrats to recognize one another—and thereby to exclude outsiders. Despite his embarrassing mishap at the theater, the young peasant has come perilously close to the aristocracy's fortified outer wall, and the anonymous author's later conclusion certainly dispels any notion that the aristocracy's attempts to shelter itself at the summit of society actually succeed. Written during the same decade, these two novels thus paint contrasting, even incompatible, portraits of the same contemporary society: one celebrating the possibilities of social climbing, another proclaiming the impenetrability of the aristocracy.

In the nineteenth century, however, authors like Balzac and Sand would interweave elements inherited from both the aristocratic and the comic literary traditions. Libertine fiction offers the most developed exploration of the dynamics of seduction even while, in many ways, the comic and picaresque traditions provide a more direct link to the nineteenth century, one known for its realism. Ernest Simon has noted, "All our comic novelists, from Sorel to Sterne and Diderot, expressed, within their works, their awareness of the reproduction of reality as the main purpose of their novels."[12] The fact that novels of the aristocratic, libertine tradition tend to be more widely read today than comic and picaresque novels gives a skewed picture of the scene of seduction in ancien régime France. To compare Balzac and Sand only with libertine fiction would suggest a more radical break in the post-revolutionary period than was actually the case. Whereas seduction could be considered the main purpose and organizing feature of a libertine novel, in both the comic tradition and in the nineteenth century seduction typically serves a more incidental role and acts as a means to another, more utilitarian, end.

Seduction and the Politics of *Arrivisme* in *Le père Goriot*

As one of Balzac's most-read novels, *Le père Goriot* serves as a key point of reference on the landscape of the nineteenth-century novel. For students who may only read one novel from the early part of the century, this is often the one. This text has thus had a profound impact in shaping readers' notions of what it means to be an ambitious young man in Restoration Paris, and what they discover in the hero Eugène de Rastignac is a prime example of the ways in which seduction can serve as a key accessory in the trajectory of social climbing, that all-important nineteenth-century social phenomenon of *arrivisme*.

From the outset of the novel, Rastignac's family situation and goals link him to both of the two eighteenth-century predecessors we previously examined, Meilcour and Jacob. Rastignac moves to Paris in 1819, motivated by a desire to rise in society and driven by "la soif des distinctions" (*PG*, 75) [thirst for distinction]. Balzac's outsider is only marginal in the geographic sense, however, since this poor provincial does come from a good aristocratic family. Thus, Rastignac resembles Meilcour in important ways, as both young men seek initiation into a society to which they belong by birth. In addition, though, Rastignac must demonstrate resourcefulness in finding enough money to purchase the semblance of an idle, aristocratic lifestyle; for him, therefore, *le commerce des femmes* takes on an economic significance that also likens him to Marivaux's Jacob. The challenges Rastignac faces in this endeavor cause him to confront both the social order and his conscience, and the narrator frequently points to Rastignac's inner struggle as his provincial scruples get tested by the temptations of the "labyrinthe parisien" (*PG*, 74) [Parisian labyrinth]. The narrator casts Rastignac in terms reflecting bourgeois values when he notes that the young man intended to achieve success based on his merit alone. Yet, Rastignac's understanding of merit—a combination of bourgeois and aristocratic notions[13]—does not prevent him from taking advantage of the social clout of his well-established relative, the Vicountess de Beauséant, and using seduction to approach wealth and power through Delphine de Nucingen. Balzac's young hero is thus willing to take a utilitarian and self-serving approach to achieving his goals, and the social flux of Restoration society presents a myriad of possibilities for one willing and able to seize them.

This novel has traditionally been read as the story of the male protagonist's education about Parisian society, and the central thrust of the text certainly focuses on that trajectory, tracing Rastignac's movement between the petit-bourgeois world of the Pension Vauquer and the salons of the wealthy bourgeois Chaussée d'Antin and the aristocratic Faubourg Saint-Germain. But when viewed through the lens of seduction, one recognizes the extent to which Delphine acts as a seductress in her own right, strategically manipulating Rastignac. The dynamics of their seduction are shaped by the complementary nature of each one's underlying social agenda: Rastignac, despite his noble name, lacks the influence and wealth that are prerequisites for gaining power in Restoration Paris, while Delphine, enriched through her marriage to the banker Nucingen, lacks the noble alliance necessary for her to be received in the most exclusive circle of aristocratic society. Thus, each one uses the other as they attempt to accomplish their separate goals. Mixed in with their strategic social calculations, however, are feelings of desire, passion, and even love, and it remains difficult for the reader to determine the specific components motivating Rastignac's and Delphine's actions at any given point in the story. In fact, Balzac's purposeful ambiguity regarding the interweaving of sentiment and strategy in this seduction contributes to the narrative interest.

The early episode of Rastignac's disastrous visit paid to Anastasie de Restaud serves to establish his initial ignorance of worldly matters. His well-meaning attempts at conversation fail precisely because, unbeknownst to him, sincerity is not the correct tool for social discourse—especially for a young man hoping to use women to rise in society. Rather than seductively insinuating himself between Anastasie and her lover, Maxime de Trailles, or even gaining the insights he seeks into her relation with Goriot, he simply receives a prompt ejection from her house. Rastignac's mishap thus illustrates the finer levels of distinction existing within the aristocracy: while his higher birth gains him entry to the Restaud's house, it does not make up for his ignorance of Parisian social codes. In this instance, then, Rastignac fares no better than Marivaux's Jacob did at the Comédie-Française.

However, Rastignac is able to recover from his faux pas thanks to instruction from his relative, Madame de Beauséant, who promises to help him *parvenir*—arrive in high society (*PG*, 115). Her invaluable instructions help Rastignac to shed his outsider status and penetrate even further into this world he wants to make his own, achieving the success and power he so desires. However, it must be underscored that Balzac's arriviste tale is far from radical, since Rastignac is climbing *within* the aristocracy and not from one class to another. In the game of acquiring a reputation and power, the truly crucial factor he must learn is "le bon goût" (*PG*, 112) [good taste]. In this sense, Rastignac's barriers are not so different from Meilcour's, and neither young man faces the kind of insurmountable obstruction posed by class differences that Sand's Horace and Marivaux's Jacob confront.

In this novel, Balzac was interested in depicting the temptations encountered by an innocent provincial in Paris. The author sets up two competing paths of influence for Rastignac's education into society. Madame de Beauséant represents the more traditional model of an older woman initiating a younger man. The initiatory role played by salon women has been described by the historian Joan Landes, who has shown the ways elite women helped non-nobles to acquire land and offices by teaching them the styles and manners of nobles: "[W]omen began to redefine nobility and virtue. Not birth, but commerce, venality of office, and intrigue at court became the new coins of power. Women functioned as adjuncts, then, of a system of advancement for merit."[14] In addition to this well-established route to power, however, Balzac created a more subversive mentor figure in the character Vautrin. Marked most distinctively by the sign of "travaux forcés" [hard labor] with which he was branded in prison rather than by his birth, Vautrin figures an immoral, corrupting influence. Vautrin offers Rastignac his own candid evaluation of the keys to gaining power when he tells his young protégé that honesty will get him nowhere and recommends either genius or corruption as the best methods for achieving acclaim in Paris. Furthermore, when Vautrin presents Rastignac with another— criminal—seduction plot centering on Victorine Taillefer, he is trying to lure his young neighbor into taking a route to wealth and power more certain of success than that of using Delphine. Rastignac's moral dilemma over the two paths to success his mentors have laid out for him constitutes an important undercurrent of the novel. Having abandoned his virtuous ideals of achieving success through his own hard work and efforts, Rastignac prefers to follow Madame de Beauséant's advice over Vautrin's criminal plot, even though it turns out that her strategy, although more genteel, also mires Rastignac in society's duplicities.

In presenting Rastignac's pursuit of Delphine, the narrator subtly creates the picture of a seducer whose achievements are due more to the luck of boyish charm than to self-conscious manipulation, not unlike many of Jacob's early successes in *Le paysan parvenu*. Rastignac benefits from Delphine's single-minded attempts to secure an invitation by a grande dame of the Faubourg Saint-Germain, while Delphine's own calculations regarding Rastignac's usefulness to her grant her a degree of power in the dynamics of their relationship. This unusual seduction, where each one plays an active role in trying to pursue separate agendas, leads them into a false situation where Parisian society assumes Rastignac has "conquered" Madame de Nucingen when in fact he has made no progress in his goal to possess her (*PG*, 183). Thus, neither one has complete mastery of their relationship, and the narrator underscores that the dominant position alternates between Rastignac and Delphine: "En passant d'un salon dans un autre, en traversant les groupes, il entendit vanter son bonheur. Les femmes lui prédisaient toutes des succès. Delphine, craignant de le perdre, lui promit de ne pas lui refuser le soir le baiser qu'elle s'était tant défendu d'accorder l'avant-veille" (*PG*, 177). [In passing from one salon to another, in crossing the groups, he heard bragging of his happiness. All the women predicted his success. Delphine, fearing she would lose him, promised him that tonight she would not refuse him the kiss she had refused to grant the day before yesterday.] In effect, then, Rastignac has made great strides toward his goal of increasing his social standing, even if he remains less than successful as a seducer. This situation underscores how appearances can seductively garner the effective weight of reality, since Delphine's change of heart is based uniquely on others' impression of her situation with Rastignac.

The conjunction of events that provides the culmination of Rastignac's education and seduction highlights the extent to which he has represented little more than a pawn in others' plans, even as it places the lucky hero in precisely the advantageous position he sought. With the apartment from Goriot and Delphine that allows Rastignac to leave the Pension Vauquer, he gains a more prestigious address, which signals he is moving up in the world. Thanks to the position he achieves with his newfound access to money, Rastignac's education is complete, and the narrator signals his transformation into a savvy Parisian: "Néanmoins ses derniers scrupules avaient disparu la veille, quand il s'était vu dans son appartement. En jouissant des avantages matériels de la fortune, comme il jouissait depuis longtemps des avantages moraux que donne la naissance, il avait dépouillé sa peau d'homme de province, et s'était doucement établi dans une position d'où il découvrait un bel avenir" (*PG*, 237). [Nevertheless, his last scruples had disappeared the day before, when he had seen himself in his apartment. In enjoying the material advantages of a fortune, as he had long enjoyed the moral advantages of his birth, he had stripped off his provincial skin, and had established himself in a position from which he was discovering a beautiful future.] The metaphor of "stripping off his provincial skin" is highly appropriate, for the ability to change skins, to present an identity to the world that best allows one to reap the rewards of a given situation, is essential to the success of any seducer.

In this novel, then, Balzac represents the materialistic concerns of Restoration society, showing how social ambitions mix with love, driving the young hero and heroine to use seduction to pointedly political ends. Meditating on the particularities of Parisian love, Balzac's narrator says, "L'amour à Paris ne ressemble en rien aux autres amours. Ni les hommes ni les femmes n'y sont dupes des montres pavoisées de lieux communs que chacun étale par décence sur ses affections soi-disant déintéressées. [...] Là surtout l'amour est essentiellement vantard, effronté, gaspilleur, charlatan et fastueux" (*PG*, 236). [Love in Paris bears no resemblance to other loves. Neither men nor women there are dupes of displays decked out in commonplaces that each exposes by decency over his so-called disinterested affections. . . . Especially there love is essentially bragging, impudent, wasteful, false, and pompous.] Balzac's narrator has suggested that in Paris, love and calculation are not mutually exclusive, and for Delphine and Rastignac emotions have come into play in the midst of their pragmatic calculations. That a loving relationship could develop from this calculated seduction recalls another such story, eminently Parisian, between the Princess de Cadignan and Daniel d'Arthez.

Balzac's political commentary goes much farther than the surface events in which a young man and woman use romance to improve their social standing. In the novel's final section, the extended death sequence of Goriot serves as a kind of metaphor for the values of postrevolutionary France. It is particularly illuminating to consider the issues raised in *Le père Goriot* concerning social mobility and seduction, power and wealth, paternity and society, in the light of Catherine Nesci's insightful book *La femme mode d'emploi*, a study of the feminine in Balzac's works. According to Nesci, "safeguarding the assimilation between power and paternity" constituted the credo of postrevolutionary bourgeois ideology.[15] In this novel of high drama in the private sphere, authority is figured as paternity, and Delphine and Anastasie's relationship with their father parallels the shifting and unreliable allegiances of a people who, having killed their king, also severed any sense of unquestioning loyalty to authority figures. Moreover, in words that could equally apply to *Le père Goriot*, Nesci writes of the *Physiologie du mariage*: "[T]he displacement of the public toward the private effectively establishes a place where questions tied to the revolutionary insurrection can be asked in an oblique way: who holds power? and according to what legitimacy? how, and by what compensatory exchange will the historical loss of the king be repaired?"[16] Nesci underscores that because such questions struck at the core of social organization and the answers threatened to upset the very premises of the Restoration, it was too dangerous to confront these issues directly. Yet, because paternal authority in the family paralleled the king's relation to his subjects, fictions of private life could confront similar issues in a less-threatening way. Goriot's situation is especially pertinent to an analysis of how the Revolution affected traditional lines of power. Not only did he make his fortune as a direct result of revolutionary events, but also his paternal authority dwindled with the subsequent loss of his money. As a response to the question concerning the source of legitimate power in postrevolutionary France, this novel thus presents a bleak picture of the status of the traditional social order.

In essence, Goriot's relationship with his daughters rests on economic ties. By giving them a large dowry, Goriot was able to purchase a higher social position for his daughters. But when his wealth runs out, he effectively becomes irrelevant to his daughters' lives and is left to die alone, lamenting his loss of absolute legitimacy based on the sole condition of his paternity. The circumstances of Goriot's death should be read in the context of Nesci's argument of a displacement of public power issues onto the private realm. Such a framework reveals how Balzac stages this family drama as a way to criticize Restoration society, in which the country was governed by a weak monarchy and unquestioning loyalty to authority figures was increasingly superseded by new and unstable forms of power tied to wealth. Thus, Balzac's melodramatic representation of Goriot's death underscores how the gains in power and social standing won by Rastignac and Delphine do not come without the loss of fundamental values, as the coupling of seduction and *arrivisme* produces a forsaking of father and conscience. Granted, the aristocratic Rastignac does display some sense of respect for paternity, and his scruples drive him to attend

Goriot's funeral. Nevertheless, because Rastignac did not stand up to Delphine when she insisted on attending Madame de Beauséant's ball rather than visiting her dying father, he is complicit in her betrayal of paternal authority. By showing the frailty of paternal authority, then, this text represents the gap between Restoration ideology and social reality.

What had only been a subtle subtext of Crébillon's novel—the critique of society's vacuousness and the representation of a social milieu devoid of paternal authority figures (neither fathers nor the king appear in *Les égarements*, a lack repeated in Laclos's *Les liaisons dangereuses*)—receives a more explicit commentary in Balzac's novel. As is characteristic of Balzac's art throughout *La comédie humaine*, however, the writer paints society in all of its complexity, expressing moral judgments with a range of subtly nuanced shades of gray rather than using sharply judgmental blacks and whites. Thus, while sensing Balzac's desire to evoke disapproval of the children's treatment of the father, the reader simultaneously exults with the triumphant Rastignac as he looks down on Paris from the heights of Père-Lachaise.

Horace: Sand's Version of *Arrivisme*

Sand's novel *Horace* tells a different tale of seduction and *arrivisme*, one that diverges from *Le père Goriot* by its historical setting in the July Monarchy of the 1830s and, most significantly, by the eponymous hero's downward trajectory. Rather than concluding with Horace Dumontet poised for success like Rastignac looking down on Paris, this novel not only shows Horace's failed attempts to "arrive" in high society but also contains a pointed critique of the protagonist's goals and exploitation of others. In her 1852 "Notice" to the novel, Sand remarks, "Je tenais peut-être à montrer que les exploiteurs sont quelquefois dupes de leur égoïsme, que les dévoués ne sont pas toujours privés de bonheur" (*H*, 24). [I perhaps insisted on showing that the exploiters are sometimes dupes of their egotism, that the devoted are not always deprived of happiness.] A further distinction between Horace and Rastignac can be traced to their different births, as Horace comes from the lower bourgeoisie. Indeed, whereas Rastignac was an outsider only to the extent that he was poor and a provincial in Paris (obstacles he overcame), Horace—like Marivaux's Jacob—faces the added, and altogether more significant, barrier of class. Thus, the model of social and sexual initiation that Balzac's novel shared quite closely with Crébillon's finds itself thoroughly transformed in the case of *Horace*. The ensuing analysis will examine this upstart figure's attempts to seduce his way into aristocratic society, concentrating on the narrative techniques Sand employs to shape the reader's reaction to her character.

Horace receives his introduction to society through his friendship with the narrator, Théophile. This exemplary young aristocrat maintains few contacts with the privileged world into which he was born, preferring instead to live on the margins of society with his common-law wife, Eugénie, a woman of popular origins who is committed to Saint-Simonian tenets.[17] Aware of his outsider status, Horace asks Théophile for advice on how to behave in society before accompanying him to the Faubourg Saint-Germain home of the Countess and Vicountess de Chailly. Even as Théophile notes that Horace behaves better than he expected, the effects of Horace's conquest of this noble salon are tempered for the reader by the narrator's censorious attitude toward the aristocracy. Early in the narrative, Théophile comments, "La seule chose clairement absurde et blâmable que j'eusse trouvée dans mon nouvel ami, c'était cette aspiration vers la femme aristocratique, en lui, républicain farouche, mauvais juge, à coup sûr, en fait de belles manières [...]" (*H*, 44). [The only thing clearly absurd and blameworthy that I might find in my new friend was this aspiration towards the aristocratic woman, in him, fierce republican, surely a bad judge when it comes to good manners. . . .] Théophile does not approve of Horace's social aspirations, nor does he appreciate his young friend's pretensions to appear more worldly than he is.

Indeed, the most striking feature of this novel—one that sets it apart from Balzac's—is the way in which the young hero, irresistibly seductive to practically everyone he meets, nonetheless remains unattractive to the reader. Despite Horace's ability to charm everyone from the Vicountess Léonie de Chailly, whom he undertakes to seduce, to Marthe and Théophile, the narrative is structured in such a way as to prevent the reader from falling under the effects of Horace's magnetic personality. The text is designed to align the reader not with the *arriviste* child of the times but instead with characters who reject these mainstream goals. In this way, Sand's text performs an "antiseduction," the exact opposite of the narrative seduction we will see in Balzac's *Les secrets de la princesse de Cadignan*, where a woman painted negatively by other characters nevertheless comes across as a charming seductress for the reader. In seeking to prevent the reader's seduction by Horace, Sand promotes her own socialist-inspired agenda.

One of the means by which the text creates a distance between the protagonist and the reader is by causing the reader to question Horace's reliability and judgment. Returning from their evening at the Chailly's, Horace speaks glowingly of Léonie. However, these comments follow immediately upon the narrator's negative portrait of the vicountess. He says, for example, "La vicomtesse Léonie de Chailly n'avait jamais été belle; mais elle voulait absolument le paraître, et à force d'art elle se faisait passer pour jolie femme" (*H*, 166) [The Vicountess Léonie de Chailly had never been beautiful; but she absolutely wanted to appear so, and with art she made herself pass as a pretty woman] and "La vicomtesse de Chailly n'avait jamais eu d'esprit; mais elle voulait absolument en avoir, et elle faisait croire qu'elle en avait" (*H*, 166) [The Vicountess de Chailly had never been intelligent; but she absolutely wanted to be, and she made people think she was.] By beginning two successive paragraphs with sentences of a parallel construction, the text strongly underscores Léonie's superficiality and helps to fix it in the reader's mind. The narrator's comments appear more formulaic than sincere. Further, that Horace would find such a woman attractive calls his judgment into question and prevents the reader from identifying with him.

If the characterizations of both Horace and Léonie are designed to inspire aversion rather than admiration, they only appear all the more suited to one another because of it—in every domain but one: class difference. Compatible in temperament, Horace and Léonie face an important obstacle about which the old Marquis de Vernes, who serves as amorous adviser to both young people, does not fail to warn them. The marquis's admonitions to Léonie focus on very real class distinctions, demonstrating yet again how coded social behavior excluded outsiders. Vernes believes Horace simply lacks the preparation necessary to seduce a woman of such high rank. Yet, as an illustrious libertine of the previous generation, the marquis does recognize Horace's innate charm and potential for seduction, and he advises the young man to get another dozen seductions under his belt before he attempts the "grande entreprise" of seducing high-society woman (*H*, 245). According to Vernes, the barriers presented by Horace's lowly birth are impossible to overcome, even though the Revolution has done away with some distinctions. The marquis nevertheless assumes the role of mentor to the young seducer, like Versac advising Meilcour in *Les égarements du cœur et de l'esprit*. Perhaps the most significant tenet of Vernes's system of seduction—and one that will prove insurmountable for Horace—is his code of secrecy: a seducer must never disclose the name of his conquests (*H*, 236). In his refusal to "publish" his victims' names (and Léonie herself figures among those ranks), Vernes differs from other libertines, such as Laclos's Valmont and Merteuil, who seem to take more pleasure in speaking of their seductions than in the act itself.[18] Just as Meilcour reacted with horror to his mentor's revelations, so too Horace is disgusted by what he views as Vernes's calculating profanation of love (*H*, 246). This loss of illusions provides no more of a deterrent from seduction for Horace than it did for Meilcour, however. What does deter Horace is the keen functioning of the aristocracy's social code as it performs its exclusionary role in these circumstances.

In a stroke of shrewd narrative construction, Sand times Horace's seduction of the Vicountess Léonie to coincide with a failed popular uprising in Paris on June 5, 1832, thereby diminishing the aura of the seducer's success. We will also witness the powerful effects of this Sandian technique, whereby the writer infuses episodes of her characters' private lives with the political charge of public events, in *Indiana*, in which Raymon's marriage—and submission—to Laure de Nangy take place at the time of the July 1830 Revolution. In the previous section, we also saw how Balzac tended to use dramas of private life to examine political issues that were considered taboo. Sand's approach involves a more direct linking of personal and political events. In the present example, Horace's own seduction ends up much like the Paris revolt—as an "aborted revolution" (*H*, 251)—largely because he does not follow the marquis's advice about using discretion regarding one's conquests and maintaining the woman's good graces. Filled with pride, Horace burns to tell others of his seduction as a way to increase his own reputation; in particular, he wants to impress the upper-class men, by whom he yearns to be accepted. What he fails to take into consideration, however, is that these men would be more apt to listen to Léonie's denunciations than to his boasting, since he is an outsider. Ironically, Horace is caught in a double bind that both forces him to tell and punishes him for telling, as Léonie seeks vengeance and drops him.

This initial taste of high society, which Horace received by association with the vicountess, only makes him more determined to pursue his arriviste plot. Ingratiating himself with the noble Louis de Méran and his friends, he models himself as a dandy (even going so far as to sign his name as Du Montet), a transformation not unlike the one Marivaux's Jacob undergoes upon his marriage to Mademoiselle Habert. Rather than creating a Rastignac-style upstart, though,

Sand is only setting up Horace for his downfall. Looking for an avenue to political power, Horace tries to seduce his way into a marriage with a well-to-do widow. However, Horace simply does not have the social leverage to compete with the vicountess, who continues her vengeance by ruining his chances with the widow. When he persists in trying to establish himself as Léonie's seducer in the eyes of Louis de Méran and his friends, his tactics backfire because they lack chivalry and magnanimity. In effect, Horace's failure can be attributed to his lack of social education and his inability to grasp the intricacies of what Crébillon's Versac termed "le bon ton."

The novel's conclusion further emphasizes the ideological significance of Horace's failure to achieve his goals in Paris not only by showing his return to the provinces but also by holding up two contrasting happy couples in Théophile and Eugénie and Marthe and Paul Arsène. With its two utopian couples, this ending signals a variation of Sand's "erotic quartet," as explained by Naomi Schor: "The erotic quartet is, as is well known, a fundamental component of the Sandian plot . . . ; what is perhaps less well understood is the function it serves, enabling Sand to distinguish two erotic regimes, the realist and the idealist. . . ."[19] Unusual in *Horace* is the fact that the reality figure, whose agenda of social exploitation is unequivocally condemned by the novel, serves as its central character. Sand more typically employs such characters as foils to the heroes and heroines who uphold her political and sexual ideals. For instance, in *Indiana*, the heroine Indiana ends up with an idealist figure in the person of Ralph, while the realist Raymon gets saddled with the harsh reality of his marriage to Laure. Furthermore, Sand gives her novel of arriviste seduction a different tone than Balzac's *Le père Goriot*. Although Balzac's narrator does not fail to underscore for the reader the values Rastignac abandons in order to transform himself into a Parisian, the novel also depicts the hero's reservations about his own behavior, elements that elicit the reader's sympathy. In contrast, Sand creates a more straightforward situation where Horace displays few redeeming qualities, a fact underscored by both Eugénie and Théophile's continual criticism of him.

This difference between Sand's and Balzac's treatment of class politics in postrevolutionary society corresponds to a fundamental divergence on the level of their fictional practice. These two writer friends were well aware of the ideological gulf between them, for in their visits with one another they frequently engaged in spirited discussions. In *Histoire de ma vie* Sand relays one such exchange when she

quotes Balzac as saying to her: "Vous cherchez l'homme tel qu'il devrait être; moi, je le prends tel qu'il est. [...] Mais ces êtres vulgaires m'intéressent plus qu'ils ne vous intéressent. Je les grandis, je les idéalise, en sens inverse, dans leur laideur ou leur bêtise. [...] Idéaliser dans le joli et dans le beau, c'est un ouvrage de femme."[20] [You seek man as he should be; me, I take him as he is. . . . But vulgar beings interest me more than they interest you. I glorify them, I idealize them, in the inverse direction, in their ugliness or their stupidity. . . . To idealize in the pretty and the beautiful, that's a woman's work.] Although Balzac quickly attributes his differences with Sand to those of gender, this opposition deserves more thorough analysis, as it profoundly influences the coloration of each one's fictional world.

Naomi Schor has convincingly shown that this seeming opposition is not necessarily an antithesis. According to her, both Balzac and Sand are idealists, but they idealize in different ways:

> *[I]dealization* is here taken to be synonymous with *hyperbolization*, a form of excess in writing that strains the limits of verisimilitude. . . . The conflation in Sand's writing practice of hyperbolizing and meliorative idealization are what make of her in the eyes of Taine the paradigmatic idealist novelist, whereas Balzac, for all his larger-than-life character types, remains mired in the lower ethical spheres of realism.[21]

If we further draw out Schor's line of reasoning, we see that Balzac was willing to "idealize" according to the sole criteria of whether the material made for interesting fiction, whereas Sand, using her fiction as a vehicle for promoting her personal ideals, idealized only that which corresponded to her ethical views. Therefore, Sand represents her character Horace without "idealizing" him in the Balzacian sense, allowing readers to perceive his mediocrity as such. It is her ethical commitments, then, that lead her to create an antiseduction with *Horace*, whereas Balzac's practice of idealization is well suited to performing narrative seductions that aggrandize talented characters who remain, however, patently unadmirable in the ethical realm.

That Balzac's and Sand's young arriviste characters meet opposite fates is thus not surprising, and both Rastignac's path to success and Horace's outcome of returning disappointed to the provinces would have been experienced by countless young men during the early nineteenth century. The comparison with Marivaux's *paysan parvenu*, Jacob, proves instructive. Depending on whether the comparison is with the Jacob of part 5, humiliated before the aristocracy at the Comédie-Française, or with the Jacob who marries an aristocrat in the apocryphal conclusion, one draws different conclusions. The humiliated Horace closely resembles the first Jacob in his inability to master the aristocracy's social code, whereas the triumphal Jacob's return home could not be further from Horace's condemnation to provincial mediocrity. Like Marivaux, who ended his novel without giving it a proper dénouement, Balzac completed *Le père Goriot* without concluding Rastignac's story. But while Marivaux only alluded to his hero's future success (the structure of the memoir novel means that the reader first encounters the character as a mature and wealthy narrator), Balzac did not hesitate to make Rastignac's arriviste dreams come true in subsequent novels, in which he became a rich count and a minister during the July Monarchy.[22] Of the three examples, Balzac's novel appears the least deferent to aristocratic notions of class hierarchy, although Sand hardly set out to uphold the social order in *Horace*. In condemning Horace to failure in Paris, she does not critique social mobility per se, but rather this character's unscrupulous exploitation of others for the sake of ambition. Indeed, the aristocratic narrator's forsaking of his origins in order to live with Eugénie makes a strong statement in favor of class fluidity.

Revolutionary Ideals: *Le compagnon du tour de France*

Sand's 1840 novel *Le compagnon du tour de France* contains a vivid illustration of the kind of politics and the modes of being and loving that Sand did idealize, while further showing how erotic seduction was at odds with her ethical stance. The writer's negative attitude toward seduction could be said to stem in part from her position of positive idealization and her refusal to reproduce mimetically the patriarchal social order that traditionally configured women either as diabolical seductresses usurping men's "rightful" position of control and initiative or as submissive victims corroborating masculine domination. At issue is the dynamics of asymmetrical power inherent in seduction, which is so inimical to the Sandian ideal of class and gender equality. In espousing the ideal of human equality and demonstrating, through her fictional constructions, that class differences are not indicative of one's worth as a human being, Sand was not inventing a new discourse. Rather, she was advocating ideals that can be found in Enlightenment thought, as well as in the rhetoric of the Revolution. However, whereas the men in power during the Restoration sought to abandon revolutionary notions of social equality in order to reinforce a class and sexual hierarchy that favored them, Sand continued to promote the discourse of equality in her fiction.

In writing *Le compagnon*, Sand conceived of her project as more than a romance narrative plotting the couples Pierre Huguenin and Yseult de Villepreux and Amaury "le Corinthien" and Joséphine des Frenays, for at times the love story gets upstaged by the novel's political subject matter: the story of *compagnonnage*, artisanal workers who traveled around France forming secret associations to advance the cause of their class.[23] In her prologue, Sand signals that her novel represents a meditation on equality, saying, "Tant que la société officielle ne sera pas construite en vue de l'égalité humaine, la société officielle sera caste; et tant que la société officielle sera caste, la société officielle engendrera des sociétés secrètes" (*CTF*, 3). [As long as official society is not constructed in view of human equality, official society will be a caste; and as long as official society is a caste, official society will engender secret societies.] The erotic quartet of *Le compagnon* figures an opposition between idealism (Pierre and Yseult) and reality (Amaury and Joséphine), but the couples also cross class boundaries, with the women coming from upper classes and the men from the working class. Moreover, in representing these relationships, Sand articulates two different types of attachment, with Amaury and Joséphine's distinctly physical passion contrasting to the de-eroticized grounds on which Pierre and Yseult are drawn together. In exploring diverse forms of attraction as well as the nature of both class differences and human similarities, Sand united some of her most fundamental concerns in this novel.

Le compagnon reproduces the Sandian topos of a young man in love who, refusing to seduce the object of his affection, waits patiently until their mutual love is revealed.[24] However, one particular feature of this novel sets it apart from others of this category: in it Sand effects a surprising recuperation of the term "seduction." Vilified when associated with domination, theatricality, or a purely physical passion, seduction functions as a valorized term in this novel when it is figured as a proselytization. In the usual Sandian economy, a character who resorts to seduction constitutes a negative example, while her exemplary heroes and heroines refrain from seduction. Such is the case in *Adriani*, where the eponymous hero honestly reveals his feelings of love for Laure, refusing to pretend they are limited to friendship, and says, "Je vous tromperais; ce serait un plan de séduction, ce serait infâme."[25] [I would be tricking you; it would be a seduction plan, it would be villainous.] This negative deployment of the term is equally present in *Le compagnon*, where it underscores the heroine's distinctly non-coquettish mode of being: "[Yseult] manquait absolument d'éclat. [...] Mais il y avait comme *un parti pris de mépriser le travail de la séduction*" (*CTF*, 198–99; emphasis mine). [Yseult absolutely lacked flash. . . . But there was like *a fixed opinion to disdain the work of seduction.*] Sand's words underscore that it is the "work" involved in seduction—using artifice to create an illusion—that makes it disdainful, thereby reminding us of the importance of authenticity in Sand's fictional universe.

It is paradoxical, then, that Yseult also acts as a type of seductress in this novel. Rather than captivating Pierre with an alluring body or romantic discourse, she attracts him with the political ideals she espouses. Indeed, the two characters are well suited to one another, due to the carpenter's philosophical bent and the heiress's intellectual interests. In the initial description of Pierre, the narrator lays the foundation for their compatibility by giving the *compagnon* both a physical beauty and a nobility that defy his lowly birth. Sand thus promotes a definition of nobility that has nothing to do with class. Pierre's first experience of Yseult occurs when he admires the books and other objects in her study before meeting her; he feels an "ecstasy" in this blatantly desexualized setting that prefigures the nature of their future attraction (*CTF*, 43). Given the two characters' dispositions, it is obvious that this will be no ordinary seduction.

Yseult's act of "seduction" occurs as she speaks passionately to Pierre about her adherence to revolutionary republican politics. The narrator describes not the content of her discourse but the effects of her speaking so as to emphasize its seductiveness:

> [L]a distinction que le goût et la grâce de l'esprit savaient donner aux expressions, la diction élégante et mélodieuse, la voix de la femme émue et pénétrée, le sentiment pur et profond que la jeune fille portait dans cet acte de prosélytisme, mirent tant de charme dans sa déclamation, que Pierre, vaincu et transporté, sentit son visage inondé de larmes. (*CTF*, 337)

> [The distinction that the taste and grace of spirit could give to expressions, the elegant and melodious diction, the voice of the woman moved and penetrated, the pure and profound feeling that the young woman carried in this act of proselytization, placed so much charm in her

declamation, that Pierre, vanquished and transported, felt his face inundated with tears.]

Although Sand's use of language that eroticizes an otherwise nonsexual situation is not unusual in her fiction, her subsequent choice of the term "seduction" strikes the reader as uncommon in Sandian usage: "[Pierre] n'eut pas de résistance contre un tel assaut, pas de méfiance devant une telle conviction, pas de fierté plébienne pour repousser une séduction si touchante" (*CTF*, 338). [Pierre had no resistance to such an assault, no suspicion before such a conviction, no plebeian pride to push back such a touching seduction.] In effect, while Sand attaches a negative value judgment to the work of physical seduction (viewed as self-serving artifice), as in the portrait of Yseult cited above, efforts at political conversion, motivated by a deeply held belief and a desire for the common good, allow for a different kind of seduction that is denounced neither by the narrator nor by any other character. Here, Sand uses the term "seduction" to evoke a passively attractive quality rather than a manipulative act. Furthermore, the fact that this occasion of positivized seduction is also desexualized is not a coincidence, for the first occurrence of this conjunction in the novel happens when Achille Lefort, political activist and friend of the Villepreux family, speaks to Pierre of his own underground political activities: "Ce ton vif et enjoué séduisait Pierre; sa curiosité était excitée de plus en plus [...]" (*CTF*, 165). [This lively and sprightly tone seduced Pierre; his curiosity became more and more excited.] In both of these instances, a form of the word "seduction" evokes the pleasurable feeling resulting when one is pleased by another instead of the physical act of seducing.

This situation suggests that if Sand anathematized seduction in so much of her fiction it was not for its underlying persuasive function of winning over another to one's desire, as that is effectively the result Yseult achieves. But it would be equally misguided to jump to the conclusion that it was the erotic content of certain desires that troubled Sand. Instead, I would argue that it is more the exploitative dimension of sexual seduction—as practiced by Horace, for example—rather than its erotic content, that Sand wished to condemn. Despite the fact that her texts contain countless examples of negative representations of sexual desire, there does exist the compelling counterexample of Consuelo in *La comtesse de Rudolstadt*. That novel, perhaps Sand's greatest, advances a notion of complete love, spiritual and carnal. Perceptively defining how this novel of female initiation differs from the male model that features a spiritual transmutation and rejection of the flesh, Lucienne Frappier-Mazur notes, "*The Countess of Rudolstadt* does not immediately stray from this conception, but it gives an elaboration of the model adapted to a young female figure who learns to recognize the feminine and material part of herself such that, finally, the path of initiation does not end in the rejection, but in the acceptance[,] of the flesh."[26] In the right circumstances, then, physical love can form an integral part of an ideal couple's relationship; it is just that Sand rarely brought these circumstances together in her fiction. In effect, the erotic holds an unstable position in Sand's works, as if the author herself never quite came to terms with her attitude toward it.

An examination of Amaury and Joséphine's relationship and the ways in which Sand structures it in opposition to Pierre and Yseult's exemplary love will help to elucidate precisely what Sand considered to be the ills of sexual seduction. Joséphine, the Count de Villepreux's niece who was born into the bourgeois class but married an old marquis from whom she is separated, conceives a fanciful passion for the sculptor Amaury, who works with Pierre on a carpentry project for the Villepreux. Describing Amaury and Joséphine's relationship, the narrator contrasts it with that of Yseult and Pierre:

> Certes, leur passion n'eut point l'idéal et la chasteté vraiment angélique de celle qu'éprouvaient Yseult et Pierre Huguenin. Tandis que ceux-ci dominaient l'attrait et jusqu'à l'idée de la volupté par l'enthousiasme de l'esprit et l'austérité de la foi, le Corinthien et la marquise, subjugués par l'énergie du désir et par la fougue des sens, s'enivraient de leur mutuelle jeunesse et de leur égale beauté. (*CTF*, 349)

> [To be sure, their passion had nothing of the ideal and the truly angelic chastity of that felt by Yseult and Pierre Huguenin. Whereas the latter dominated their attraction and even the idea of voluptuousness by the enthusiasm of intelligence and the austerity of faith, the Corinthian and the marquise, subjugated by the energy of desire and by the ardor of the senses, intoxicated themselves on their mutual youth and their equal beauty.]

By highlighting the exemplary couple's self-control, Sand admonishes against desire's ability to "subjugate" one's more reasonable faculties. Furthermore, Sand stages this passionate relationship not only as a way to valorize Pierre and Yseult's chaste love by comparison but also to underscore other factors that make people suited to one another despite class differences. Indeed, Sand's interest in creating couples whose compatibility transcends class differences marks a revolutionary aspect of this woman writer's fiction. As Isabelle Naginski observes in reference to Sand's second novel, *Valentine*, "Breaking down the invisible literary codes that routinely restricted the fictional arena to upper-class heroes, Sand here was doing for the category of class what she had done for gender in *Indiana*, refusing to write according to the rules of the male literary order."[27] This analysis holds equally true for *Le compagnon*, for in both these novels Sand highlights unions between couples whose disposition makes them perfectly suited to one another even though class interests would keep them apart.

As the romantic plots reach a climax at the conclusion of the novel, the competing demands of realism and idealism also come to a head, converging around the Count de Villepreux, Yseult's grandfather. A liberal aristocrat who supports Achille Lefort's revolutionary political activities, the count seems to have rejected the prejudices of his class. Upon discovering Amaury and Joséphine's liaison, he displays his adherence to the revolutionary banner of class equality by telling Joséphine that it is no longer excusable to practice morals more befitting the decadent period of Louis XV: "Une femme du monde ne pourrait plus dire, au point du jour, à un manant: «Va-t'en, je n'ai plus besoin de toi!» car il n'y a plus de manants. [...] et aucune femme, fût-elle reine, n'a le pouvoir de persuader à un homme qu'il redevient son inférieur en sortant de ses bras" (*CTF*, 427). [An upper-class woman can no longer say, at daybreak, to an oaf: 'Go away, I no longer need you!' for there are no more peasants. . . . and no woman, be she queen, has the power to persuade a man that he return to being her inferior when leaving her arms.] Underscoring the hypocrisy of aristocrats who insist on their class superiority at the very time they are willing to sleep with their so-called inferiors, Villepreux proclaims his belief in human equality. Furthermore, the old count suggests that Amaury and Joséphine could marry after the death of her husband. At this point, the novel seems to be marching toward a utopian ending of mixed-class marriages, as Yseult—asserting the kind of initiative characteristic of Sand's heroines—asks Pierre to marry her.

However, while the possibility exists for the novel to make a revolutionary statement about equality by effecting an idealistic conclusion, this utopian trajectory remains only at the stage of potentiality.

Indeed, both the realistic couple and the idealistic couple bend to the imperatives of realistic representation, and the novel ends without closure. True to her arriviste nature, the marquise reveals she has no intention of marrying her lover. Moreover, when the situation moves closer to home, the Count de Villepreux proves unwilling to practice the republican ideals he supposedly admired, and he withholds his approval of Yseult's choice for a husband. With the count's wholly credible paternal reaction (he even accuses Pierre of seducing Yseult), Sand achieves a sense of balance as she casts aside the fairy-tale ending. Pierre insists he cannot marry Yseult because he believes that in becoming a parvenu he would no longer be able to pursue his ideals (*CTF*, 454). Instead of closing the door on this marriage outright, though, the text suggests it has only been deferred.

In hesitating before their potential utopia, Sand's characters actually reassert their ethical position rather than abandon it. Yseult states that her filial duty takes precedence over her greater love for Pierre and refuses to cause her grandfather further distress by insisting on her choice in what would have constituted only an act of rebellion. Yseult's willingness to delay her personal satisfaction contrasts markedly with Delphine de Nucingen's neglect of her dying father in favor of her self-serving agenda in *Le père Goriot*. Indeed, Yseult is no common seductress, and her final words to Pierre, in which she tells him that her feelings will not change if he has the patience to wait for her, are characterized by a respect for the other's deeply held beliefs rather than by a desire to persuade. In a gesture toward the prejudices and divisions of contemporary reality, Sand's exemplary characters recognize that their transgressive marriage, like their dream of a society without caste distinctions, is premature.

A defining impetus of Sand's fictional project can be located in her tendency to promote alternatives to the mainstream political scene, a scene driven by economic forces and *arrivisme*. The underground world of *compagnonnage*, as figured by Pierre Huguenin, thrives far from the Parisian social scene, with no dependence on wealth or birth to confer status on the members of its secret societies. It is a world where erotic seduction—with its artifice, theatricality, and manipulation—has no positive role to play. Although utopian in its thrust, *Le compagnon* nevertheless presents a very real social phenomenon, one that Sand researched extensively in writing her novel. In texts such as this one, Sand shows that fiction infused with idealism and high ethical standards could also convey a strong dose of social reality.

BALZAC'S ENTERPRISING SEDUCTIONS: *SPLENDEURS ET MISÈRES DES COURTISANES* AND *BÉATRIX*

In contrast to Sand's works, Balzac's *Comédie humaine* offers myriad examples of that writer's desire to exploit the narrative potential offered by the often unsavory elements of the society around him, regardless of ethical considerations. Indeed, both *Splendeurs et misères des courtisanes* and *Béatrix* feature plots in which seduction figures as an immoral capitalistic exchange, a transaction in which seducers and seductresses act not on their own behalf but to accomplish a third party's master plan. My analysis of these two novels will center on the ways in which the seductions depend on the nascent economy where one's seductive potential can be exchanged for marriage, payment of debts, or social climbing. The marketing of desire in *La comédie humaine* is thus distinctly inscribed in the social flux of early nineteenth-century France, marking a postrevolutionary innovation upon the comic and picaresque novels of previous centuries. In both *Splendeurs et misères* and *Béatrix*, the seduction plots reveal the uneasy mingling of traditional aristocratic social patterns with bourgeois-inspired notions of love and marriage.

The significance of these seductions becomes further illuminated when considered in the light of a fundamental element of Balzac's thinking—namely, what many critics have identified as the writer's equation of sexual expenditure with a detrimental loss of energy. Nowhere is this phenomenon represented more explicitly than in *La peau de chagrin*, where the supernatural animal skin provides a visible reminder to Raphaël de Valentin of the price he pays for satisfying his desires. One also finds texts of *La comédie humaine* where Balzac explores the possibility of recuperating spent energy by directing it toward pragmatic goals. This concern must have influenced Balzac's creation of a distinct breed of dandyism based on strategic performance rather than nonutilitarian expenditure (and embodied in players such as Henri de Marsay or Maxime de Trailles), which we will examine in detail in chapter 4. Likewise, Rastignac and Delphine's seduction in *Le père Goriot* is motivated by socioeconomic considerations as well as by sexual attraction, as they barter money, sex, and an exclusive social invitation. In this section I will address further ways in which Balzac represented the recuperation of sexual energy by having it function, simultaneously, in the market economy. In the case of Collin arranging Lucien's seduction of Clothilde or the Duchess de Grandlieu enlisting Maxime to hire La Palférine to seduce Béatrix away from Calyste, the seductive body constitutes a valuable commodity whose transactions can (potentially, at least) earn material returns, thereby avoiding pure sexual expenditure and loss.

In *Splendeurs et misères des courtisanes*, Jacques Collin acts as a "seduction broker"[28] for Lucien de Rubempré, maintaining operations on several fronts in an attempt to establish his protégé in an aristocratic marriage. Collin succeeds in bringing Lucien under his wing at the conclusion of *Illusions perdues*—devilishly tempting the young man to turn his life over to him, an escaped convict disguised as a priest—whereas he failed to entice Rastignac in *Le père Goriot*. In speeches to each young man, Collin reveals the privileged viewpoint he gains as a marginal figure in society. Exposing his self-serving philosophy to Lucien, Collin claims that in modern society, there actually are no more morals: "Aujourd'hui, [...] le succès est la raison suprême de toutes les actions, quelles qu'elles soient. Le fait n'est donc plus rien en lui-même, il est tout entier dans l'idée que les autres s'en forment" (*IP*, 700). [Today, . . . success is the primary reason for all actions, whatever they may be. Facts are no longer anything in themselves, all that matters is the idea that others form about them.] Collin's approach to life resembles market principles where value is determined by supply and demand, rather than by inherent worth. Having observed from the sidelines how society functions, Collin is able to use this knowledge to take advantage of the system.

A key element in Balzac's plot is the fact that Collin brokers Lucien's seductions rather than undertaking a seduction himself. No doubt attracted to the irresistibly seductive Lucien, Collin is also drawn to the young man because he sees him as "un merveilleux instrument de pouvoir" (*SMC*, 504) [a marvelous instrument of power]. It is as if the illicit nature of Collin's desire makes him a perfect candidate for the recuperation of sexual energy into other goals. Many critics have described Collin as a capitalist, and Charles Bernheimer convincingly demonstrates just how the outsider Collin (also known as Vautrin) operates: "Vautrin is the City personified. His methods and goals are those of capitalism. . . . He sees through the rationalizing deceit of ideology, reading the strategies of that deceit as semiotic codes available for self-interested manipulation."[29] In a society undertaking the long transition from a feudal economy to one ruled by the principles of capitalism, Collin seeks to use his outsider's knowledge to take advantage of those still invested in the traditional ways. He understands the fact that market values have little to do with notions like truth; rather, success requires creating demand or desire for an object based on appearances and perceptions. He is the strategic mind behind Lucien's seductive body.

Collin plots to market Lucien's attractiveness, reinventing the young dandy so that he appeals to an aristocratic family. In order to gain access to this exclusive social arena, Collin calls on the services of Madame de Maufrigneuse, a former victim of Lucien's seductions whom Collin is able to control because of his possession of certain compromising love letters. By holding these letters in reserve with the threat of future public humiliation, he has turned her desire into currency he can exchange on the market of seduction. Collin's possession of these letters thus buys Madame de Maufrigneuse's cooperation, leaving her no choice but to introduce Lucien to Clothilde de Grandlieu, who becomes easily enchanted by him. But her father, the Duke de Grandlieu, looks for qualifications other than the charm and physical appeal that win over the daughter, even refusing to admit the social climber into his home until Lucien has obtained royal permission to use the "de Rubempré" name of his maternal family. More importantly, though, the duke insists that any suitor for his daughter's hand possess not only a name that, in social codes, is considered at least vaguely noble but also the more substantial sign of family land and a château. Despite its waning influence, the aristocracy still exercises a certain amount of control over who enters into its exclusive realm, so Collin attempts to use his renegade ways to make Lucien at least appear to hold the traditional social qualifications.

Collin's manipulations regarding Lucien and the Grandlieu family can thus be said to figure the collision of two worlds in nineteenth-century society. Here the emerging capitalist economy, represented by Collin, trades on its assets of apparent values (disguising otherwise empty signs) in order to mix with the traditionally grounded feudal economy. In a lucid analysis of the function of Lucien's body in Balzac's texts, Peter Brooks remarks on Collin's maneuverings, saying, "His [Lucien's] mentor's concern must be to make the system of sociosexual exchanges yield a more traditional and enduring precapitalist value: land."[30] A master of the new economy, Collin's currency does not function as successfully in the old economy. In a world where lineage is highly prized and scrutinized, the origins of Lucien's new fortune are of keen interest to the social circle of the Faubourg Saint-Germain. A sudden gain in wealth is generally not welcomed in this exclusive social group, where names and land follow a clearly discernible trajectory back in time for generations, and even centuries. Although Lucien appears poised to win the hand to which he aspires, his advantage is just as precarious as the false grounds on which his social pretensions rest. The duke's discovery that Lucien's money comes from an impure source rather than from his sister, as he had previously claimed, immediately and irrevocably closes the door of the Grandlieu mansion to Lucien. In a gesture to traditional, feudal values and Restoration ideology, Balzac plots his novel so that the aristocracy avoids contamination by the parvenu Lucien. The writer's tendency to evoke alternatives to the status quo without, in the end, disrupting the traditional balance of power in society is a phenomenon we will also see in *La fille aux yeux d'or*. Himself an admirer of the aristocracy, Balzac seems to take more interest in constructing novels that simply warn of impending dangers than those that push alternative social forms.

However, at this point Balzac's novel is only halfway to its destination, and Collin and Lucien's failure to infiltrate the aristocracy through marriage are not the novel's last words about social organization and values. With a stroke of the pen in the final section of the novel, Balzac instantly reverses the status of his outlaw character Collin, turning the ultimate rule-breaker into an upholder of the law with his "final incarnation" as chief of police. On the surface of events, it would seem that the narration is exerting control over its freewheeling character, reeling him in by putting him in a position where he must act as an agent of law and order, whereas before Collin took pride in his ability to subvert the system. This narrative act appears conservative in the sense that it converts a menace to authority into an authority figure. However, Balzac's gesture remains profoundly ambiguous. The ambivalence lies in showing how signs that are relative and ungrounded can act in revolutionary ways by overturning conventional practices. Indeed, the very idea that the archcriminal Collin could become a police chief underscores the irrelevance of personal ethics. Even though Balzac writes conservatively by having Collin's plot fail, in the end the satirical message of ethical subversion still comes across. By introducing this complex plot with multiple seduction fronts into his novel, Balzac figures the increasing weakness of the aristocracy, for in representing the mingling of old and new values in postrevolutionary France, he shows the very real potential for infiltration by outsiders.

The Duchess de Grandlieu's seduction plot in *Béatrix* involves a different set of parameters, even as it shares with Collin's scheme the characteristics of a multilayered seduction where the stakes include money and social influence. While the duchess's tactics involve business transactions, her motivation is purely familial: the duchess worries about her daughter Sabine's health, for the young wife is suffering over her husband Calyste's renewed liaison with Béatrix de Rochefide. Not unlike the crisis of the landed aristocracy evoked in *Splendeurs et misères*, the crisis surrounding Calyste and Sabine's marriage figures the conflict between two matrimonial regimes—an older tradition of matching couples based on family alliances and a newer, bourgeois-inspired partnership focused on love and compatibility between two individuals. While their marriage began as a family alliance devoid of love—Sabine even masqueraded as Béatrix to secure the reluctant Calyste's agreement to the marriage contract—the young wife has since substituted true love for the false grounds of their engagement: "Si pour Sabine son mariage était un mariage d'amour, Calyste y voyait un mariage de convenance [...]" (*B*, 859). [If for Sabine her marriage was a marriage of love, Calyste saw it as a marriage of convenience. . . .] And the very fact that the duchess has taken her daughter's lovesickness so seriously suggests the rise of new perceptions concerning love and marriage. Indeed, it is difficult to imagine an aristocratic bride in the eighteenth century falling hopelessly in love with her unfaithful husband rather than simply entering into a liaison of her own.

Calyste and Sabine's situation is further politicized, because Sabine suggests a connection between her husband's absences and the decline of the aristocracy itself. Reacting to Calyste's excuse of staying out late at a club when he had actually spent the night with Béatrix, Sabine chastises her husband and warns him that the "idleness" of young gentlemen like himself, who pass the time smoking cigars and playing whist, hardly constitutes the kind of behavior necessary to combat the rise of parvenus and to regain territory lost by their fathers in the Revolution (*B*, 291). Sabine's comments display an uncharacteristic lucidity regarding the social climate of France, indicating that she speaks as a mouthpiece for higher—authorial—powers. The point Sabine makes recalls Stendhal's analysis of the aristocracy at the time of the Restoration and drives to the heart of the aristocracy's fragile position in society; this social class no longer enjoyed the stable power base from which, during the more carefree days of the ancien régime, it could indulge in an idle lifestyle. Indeed, other Balzac texts show the reverse side of this phenomenon, as when dandies like Rastignac live beyond their means, strategically displaying their idleness in order to acquire positions and power for themselves despite the fact that they do not yet have the wealth necessary to make them true members of the leisure class. By framing Sabine's marital problems in this way, Balzac inscribes these domestic issues in a larger social context, creating an interplay between the public and private spheres, as we saw in *Le père Goriot*.

The duchess devises a clever intrigue designed to return Calyste to his wife, but in order to do so she must also secure Béatrix's rejection of her lover and her husband Rochefide's breakup with the courtesan Madame Schontz. While aristocratic *salonnières* had long been involved in intrigues that mixed the political and the sexual, as Landes's historical study and countless novels inform us, the duchess's scheme is particularly remarkable for the layers of mediation between her and those who actually carry out the seduction. In effect, she needs the aid of a male mediator, a seduction broker with contacts that span the social classes, so as not to compromise herself. Each transaction in this multifaceted seduction plot highlights a different element of postrevolutionary politics. In return for helping the duchess, Maxime requests that she secure the social acceptance of his rich, bourgeois fiancée by welcoming the parvenue into her home. Then Maxime literally hires the Count de La Palférine to seduce Béatrix so that she will abandon Calyste, thereby freeing him to return home to his wife, Sabine. La Palférine displays the qualities of a true mercenary when he agrees to carry out someone else's seduction plot for a compensation that will allow him to pay his debts. Finally, to convince Madame Schontz to relinquish Rochefide, whose reunion with his wife, Béatrix, is viewed as added insurance both that Calyste will be kept away from her and that there will be no duel, Maxime promises Madame Schontz the fulfillment of her own arriviste dream. For her, marriage to a man her social superior means that she can become respectable and no longer live as a kept woman. Through it all, the duchess remains behind the scenes, supplying both her inventiveness in designing these complicated plans and the money necessary to carry them out. Because of the commercial aspects of the duchess's role and her use of a capitalist-oriented seduction broker in Maxime de Trailles, she constitutes a modernized, postrevolutionary version of the salon woman whom Landes described as subversively aiding the rise of parvenus in ancien régime society.

This narrative is thus intimately bound up in the conditions of a mobile society where money acts as a *passe-partout* superseding fixed class boundaries tied to name and birth. Although the noble way of life continued to exert its commanding presence in circles of power throughout the Restoration, the nobility could no longer even pretend to enjoy an unquestioned dominance once the pace at which commoners were gaining access to the upper classes accelerated and money was usurping the social and economic currency of rank. Adapting seduction strategies to the conditions of nineteenth-century society, Balzac represented the climate of shifting power created by a struggle between old aristocratic and new bourgeois forms of social legitimacy. Thus, these seductions are not pure pursuits of the capitulation of the other's desire for the seducer, divorced from all interests save that of affirming the seducer's sense of power and attractiveness, as we think of aristocratic libertine seductions. But while the seductions of Rastignac and Collin/Lucien involve pragmatic strategies of social climbing and La Palférine receives a monetary compensation for his seduction of Béatrix, indicating that these seducers could little afford an idle lifestyle, their relations are no less those of seduction. Indeed, although the aristocratic libertine marked the archetype of the seducer in ancien régime literature, examples like Marivaux's *Paysan parvenu* remind us that utilitarian strategies of seduction are not a postrevolutionary invention. However, the turmoil of the Revolution did turn the libertine figure into a relic, and the nineteenth-century novel inaugurated the dominance of another other type of seducer, the arriviste.

These seductions that mix private sexual politics with the more public issues of social organization, market forces, and class rivalries further reveal Balzac's and Sand's common commitment to creating fictional worlds that explore compelling questions faced by their contemporaries in postrevolutionary France. In weaving these tales of young men and women trying to discover success, love, and happiness, seduction plays an important accessory role without, however, constituting the primary focus of the text, as it often did in libertine novels of the eighteenth century. Characters such as Rastignac, Horace, and Collin are driven by aspirations in the sociopolitical realm (in Collin's case, for Lucien), and they use strategies of seduction as they attempt to achieve their goals. Although very different from both Balzac's and Sand's young arrivistes, Sand's Yseult also draws on the powers of seductive persuasion to achieve political results in a distinctly nineteenth-century social setting. With their deep integration into contemporary reality, Balzac's and Sand's fictions mark a decisive break with seduction novels of the ancien régime, meaning the libertine fiction that focused on seduction to the exclusion—or even distortion—of social reality. Thus, in the nineteenth century, seduction's narrative role evolved along with preferences for different literary styles and forms.

2
Staging Seduction: Theatricality and Masquerade

In inscribing my investigation of how seduction gets staged within the concepts of theatricality and masquerade, I wish to underscore how identities are created and performed within the intersubjective space of interaction between the seducer and the seduced person. An identity, be it one's gender or one's persona as a seducer or seductress, is not something natural or pregiven, nor is it set and unified across time; rather, identities get enacted within particular situations, based on cultural prescriptions and the demands of one's audience. In the case of seduction, the seducer or seductress devises an identity based both on general notions of what women or men want (societal norms) and also according to the specific personality and fantasies of the other person to be seduced. Seducers and seductresses project certain notions of masculinity or femininity that they think will appeal to the other person in order to become the personification of that person's fantasies. The identity performed may differ sharply from who the person is outside the space of seduction, assimilating the artifice and theatricality of seduction to notions of masquerade. Seduction thus highlights the lack of a stable, unified self and the utterly constructed nature of one's identity (identities).

Indeed, in the space of seduction, one's identity is the product of a carefully calculated theatrical performance designed to attract the other's desire. Successful seducers and seductresses manage to impose their will on others by means of persuasion and artifice, overcoming the others' initial resistance. Surface appearances constitute the privileged space of communication, displacing traditional values of being and profundity. In this light, truth has no absolute or objective value, but instead involves strategy and the creation of believable appearances. Consequently, one could say that the scene of seduction is one where theatricality does not stand in opposition to reality, but instead passes for real by creating a credible illusion. The work of a seducer or a seductress, then, consists of performing an identity that the seduced person will accept and believe to be real. This persona is inevitably illusory, a re-presentation of the self that distorts and hides other aspects of one's being that might hinder the creation of a seductive fantasy for the other. Because this intersubjective space of seduction is enacted through performance, divorced from objective truth, it is self-referential; all it takes is the seduced person's belief and acquiescence for this theatricality to be experienced as reality. Thus, for perspicacious seducers and seductresses, a new realm opens up, one in which they have the ability to create a reality whose sole basis lies in convincing appearances.

Despite the great power over the other implicated in the ability to seduce, in the end it is the seduced person who finally holds the keys to success. If one wants to carry off a seduction, the other's complicity must be gained. Consequently, the seducer is master of the game only to the extent that the seduced person grants him or her that status. This qualification of the seducer's power underscores the impossibility of seducing someone who does not wish to be seduced, at least at a certain level, while simultaneously excluding the use of force. The game of seduction thus consists of determining the means to captivate another's desire in spite of that person's resistance. To this end, seducers and seductresses draw on a wide range of tools, rhetorical and corporeal, to present their identity in such a way as to gain the other's consent. In addition to persuasive (and even deceitful) discourse, semiological systems such as clothing and ornamentation are enlisted for their ability to assume a self-referential quality in the seducer's quest to create a convincing identity.

The idea that seduction is grounded in fantasies, the product of theatrical ploys, was perfectly clear to the author of the 1826 seduction manual *L'art de réussir en amour, enseigné en 25 leçons*. The book's tiny format suggests it could have served as a pocket guide for the aspiring seducer, and in it the anonymous author promises to reveal to his male audience "les femmes telles qu'elles sont"[1] [women as they really are]. Yet, in an ironic twist, his system simultaneously involves instructing men on how to appear other than what they are, effecting a split between their inner being and their outer appearance. The author instructs his readers that they must first identify the nature and personality of the woman they wish to seduce. For instance, the strategy one would use with a coquette is different from the strategy one would use in approaching an *innocente*. Further, in a recognition of the theatrical impulses of seduction, the guide describes a whole panoply of techniques one can develop to feign emotions one does not really feel, such as tears or blushing. And in the traditional seduction style associated, for instance, with Valmont of *Les liaisons dangereuses*, the author's rhetoric is overflowing with military vocabulary assimilating "the art of seducing women" to "the art of conquest."[2] This manual thus provides a nonfictional example of many of the strategies and techniques found in the literature of the period, and it underscores the artificial and learned behavior behind the seducer-actor's facade of sincerity.

According to the manual's author, inconstancy and the desire to possess many women—one after another—are natural, such that no amount of role-playing or trickery need be considered excessive when a seducer is being true to his impulses. While the man's overarching desire is to seduce a woman, this text underscores that he must put aside his own distinct personality and appeal to the woman's fantasies in order to attain his ultimate goal. For instance, the author gives the following advice to the man who aims to seduce a capricious woman: "[T]oi, qui dans la lutte que le désir engage avec une femme capricieuse pourras calquer ton humeur sur la sienne, prêter à ton esprit les charmes de la frivolité, et affecter un état constant d'inconstance."[3] [You, who in the struggle that desire engages with a capricious woman can model your mood after hers, give your mind the charms of frivolity, and affect a constant state of inconsistency.] Another of the author's strategies further obliges the seducer to veil himself behind a false identity, for he suggests creating for the intended victim a book of thoughts and fragments of quotations that present the seducer in a positive light—"un portrait de fantaisie qui est censé le vôtre"[4] [a fantastic portrait that is supposed to be yours]. In the realm of seduction, then, theatrical performance comes to represent a necessary tool for happiness rather than a distortion of the truth.

In effect, though, the triumph of seduction often comes at a price—for the seducer, as well as for the victim. It is this price that the manual obscures through its upbeat rhetoric of conquest. Not only does success require a certain amount of self-sacrifice on the part of the seducer, who must delay satisfaction, but also it can involve a kind of doubling and role-playing for the other that distances oneself from one's own desires. The author states: "[N]otre désir sera toujours satisfait, alors que nous manifesterons un désir contraire à celui que nous avons réellement."[5] [Our desire will always be satisfied if we show a desire contrary to the one we truly feel.] For the man who simply seeks to possess as many women as possible, temporarily submitting to a self-alienating identity might seem harmless enough. In the case of a man seducing a woman, the artifice of seduction typically consists of the man feigning to be more virtuous than he really is and to have sincere feelings for the woman when he actually just wants to feel the surge of power and control that comes with the woman's sexual submission. For women the situation is usually more complicated, since a libertine man could enjoy a certain prestige, whereas society prized women primarily based on their virtue. Women simply had more to lose than men. The story of the Princess de Cadignan will provide an example of some of the additional perils faced by seductresses in nineteenth-century France.

Despite the clear advantages men held in this society, the seduction manual presents a picture of sexual relations in which the conquering male effectively submits to the woman's wishes, since her personality and fantasies determine how the seducer should present himself in approaching her. As we are reminded, the power of seduction is not absolute. At issue is a paradox implied in the very nature of seduction: while the seducer or seductress freely chooses an object of seduction, led by his or her desires, the exact nature of one's seductive identity is determined by the other within an intersubjective space. Therefore, seduction must be viewed as a negotiated process rather than a unidimensional enterprise.

In order to reveal further just how theatricality and illusion are used in seduction, this chapter will analyze examples from four texts. Balzac's novella *Les secrets de la princesse de Cadignan* illustrates a seduction performed in the setting of everyday life, and it will be juxtaposed with Sand's story *La marquise*, a text treating a seduction that actually takes place in a theater. Next, the chapter will turn toward two representations of the courtesan as seductress: Sand's eponymous heroine Isidora, and Esther Gobseck in the second part of Balzac's novel *Splendeurs et misères des courtisanes* entitled "À combien l'amour revient aux vieillards." Each of these seductions involves a kind of doubling, but toward different ends, and an important focus of this chapter will be to analyze the varied ways Balzac and Sand represent this experience. Indeed, just as theatricality is fundamental to seduction, so too it proves to be a crucial ideological distinction between the two writers.

The Princess de Cadignan Re-creates Herself

In *Les secrets de la princesse de Cadignan*, Balzac stages his seduction narrative in the drawing rooms of the most exclusive circle of aristocratic society, Paris's Faubourg Saint-Germain. Set in 1833 at the beginning of the July Monarchy, the text—with its richly woven historical details and political commentary—leaves no doubt as to the narrator's disdain for the new bourgeois-influenced monarchy of Louis-Philippe. The opening words of the tale even refer to the July Revolution as a "disaster" (*SPC*, 949), in this case because it destroyed the fortunes of certain aristocrats who had supported the previous king. The change in regime has also been marked by a change in lifestyle for Diane de Maufrigneuse, the Princess de Cadignan. Previously a reigning queen of aristocratic court and salon life who used her power to influence (seduce) many men during the Restoration, Diane's dissolute ways (and not the 1830 Revolution, as she liked to lead people to believe) had considerably diminished her fortune, leaving her financially unable to keep up appearances and forcing her to trade her public position for a quieter, secluded life. Still, this woman has planned one more seduction because, as she reveals to her friend the Marquise d'Espard, she has known many lovers but has yet to experience love. The text thus presents a paradox, since the princess uses the artifice of seduction in order to achieve true love.

When it comes to recounting the tale of Diane's seduction of the writer Daniel d'Arthez, Balzac's text refrains from subtleties, and instead boldly forges a representation striking for its use of theatrical terminology. Multiple references to Diane as an actress (*comédienne*) and to her seduction strategy as a play (*comédie*) include the narrator's comment that she is "la plus grande comédienne de ce temps" (*SPC*, 989) [the greatest actress of this time]. Deftly combining her functions as seductress and actress, the Princess de Cadignan creates an overall artistic effect the reader cannot help but admire. Indeed, Balzac displays his own artistic skill in creating an engaging representation of a woman described in a conversation among some of her former lovers as "la plus monstrueuse Parisienne, la plus habile coquette, la plus enivrante courtisane du monde" (*SPC*, 967) [the most monstrous Parisian, the most skillful coquette, the most intoxicating courtesan in the world]. Balzac effectively "seduces" his readers into rejecting the generally negative opinion the world holds of Diane, not unlike the way her project of seducing the gifted writer Daniel d'Arthez involves nothing less than persuading him to believe in a fictive identity she creates for him.

The princess's choice of Daniel marks a new kind of object for her and reflects her different goals from the past, when her lovers consisted of some of the *Comédie humaine*'s most charming and visible young dandies, including Henri de Marsay, Lucien de Rubempré, and Maxime de Trailles. Daniel holds the double advantage of promising the kind of genius that could inspire true love and leading the quiet life of a serious writer uninterested in participating in the affairs of worldly society, which means that Diane would be unlikely to risk further tarnishing her reputation with this relationship. Whereas aristocratic society had long been exceedingly tolerant of women who engaged in a worldly lifestyle of coquetry, the newly empowered bourgeoisie brought with them a less indulgent attitude toward women's particular form of influence in public affairs. Balzac's representation of Diane's concerns reflects this subtle shift in women's roles away from public life and toward a more secluded domesticity.

The initial scene of the princess's seduction of Daniel takes place during a dinner given by Madame d'Espard. Diane treats this occasion like a theatrical event, and her self-production omits none of the elements of performance: costume, rhetoric, and gestures, she uses them all in order to cast a spell on her victim. So successful is the princess in her art of creating her self as a model of innocence that the narrator comments, "Il était impossible au physionomiste le plus habile d'imaginer des calculs et de la décision sous cette inouïe délicatesse de traits" (*SPC*, 968). [It would be impossible for the most skillful physiognomist to imagine calculations and decision under this unheard-of delicacy of traits.] Diane thus leads a double life, calculating every move she makes, all the while appearing sincere and natural.

One of the princess's strategies for disarming Daniel is her use of highly feminine clothing, and the narrator credits her with being one of the most skillful of all Parisian women in the *art* of "la toilette" (*SPC*, 968). She has carefully chosen her outfit for the occasion of her introduction to Daniel, and the narrator likens it to the dresses seen in Raphael's paintings. This comparison of Diane to a Raphaelesque figure represents a calculation on Balzac's part, designed to evoke a specific type of image in the reader's mind. A reference to Raphael, as Bernard Vannier has shown in his study of Balzacian portraits, is designed to conjure up associations of femininity as divine, angelic, virginal, and pure.[6] A master at manipulating signifiers, the princess thus seems to have all these demure feminine qualities that were actually quite foreign to her. While Diane's appearance captivates Daniel, on another level the narrator's allusion to Raphael's paintings suggests her apparent naïveté to the reader. Even in presenting herself as an angel, however, the princess is not devoid of seductiveness, for the clothes that cover her also manage to suggest what they hide. The narrator comments on her ploy, saying, "Une femme nue serait moins dangereuse que ne l'est une jupe si savamment étalée, qui couvre tout et met tout en lumière à la fois" (*SPC*, 969). [A nude woman would be less dangerous than a skirt so wisely displayed, which at once covers everything and brings everything to light.] The unfailing seductiveness of this manner of dress has become a common reference, as when Roland Barthes underscored in *Le plaisir du texte* the appeal of seemingly innocent skin peeking through gaps in clothing: "[I]t is this twinkling itself that seduces."[7] Barthes's word twinkling could equally well characterize the princess's overall strategy, as she blinds Daniel through a shimmering performance that enables her to appear as she wishes him to see her.

In devising her seduction strategy, the princess is motivated by fears that Daniel would not love her as the Diane de Maufrigneuse known by the rest of Parisian society for having had numerous lovers. Rather, she deploys all of her seductive weapons by engaging in a performance in which she creates for herself the role of a woman appropriate to this great man's love. What is most impressive about Diane's seduction and the masquerade she undertakes is the fact that she plays an illusory role for a man who is in fact fully aware of her tarnished reputation in the eyes of the world. Daniel's friends Rastignac and Blondet have warned him of Diane's long history of coquetry and of squandering not only her own fortune but also those of her admirers. Although unaware of how much Daniel knows, the princess does not try to deny her past when speaking with him during dinner; instead, she suggests that she has been misunderstood by society, thereby preparing the way for Daniel to hear a new interpretation of her story. Her goal is to get him to suspend disbelief and see in her qualities that no one else knows she has.

The princess stages her performance in such a way as to take advantage of the fact that seduction depends not on transparent communication between two people but on an encounter mediated by each one's fantasies. During her dinner conversation with Daniel, Diane punctuates her words with seductive expressions. The narrator remarks, "[U]ne des plus savantes manœuvres de ces comédiennes est de voiler leurs manières quand les mots sont trop expressifs, et de faire parler les yeux quand le discours est restreint. Ces habiles dissonances, glissées dans la musique de leur amour faux ou vrai, produisent d'invincibles séductions" (*SPC*, 972). [One of the wisest maneuvers of these actresses is to veil their manners when their words are too expressive, and to speak with their eyes when their discourse is restrained. These clever dissonances, slipped into the music of their love, true or false, produce invincible seductions]. Here the seductress uses a combination of speech and bodily gestures. Diane's rhetoric and attitude thus complement one another, working together to create an illusion that, in Daniel's mind, replaces objective criteria of true and false.

The princess's method of creating "dissonances" suggests a similarity between her strategy and that of Søren Kierkegaard's character Johannes in *The Seducer's Diary* (1843). An adept rhetoretician, Johannes never misses his mark when he strategically fires his words at his victim Cordelia. He uses a double strategy in his seduction: "I could either use conversation to inflame and letters to cool, or conversely. . . . The contradiction in these movements will evoke and develop, strengthen and consolidate the love in her, in a word, tempt it."[8] Like the princess, this male seducer uses two simultaneous approaches, but in his case both involve speech—verbal or written—and do not make use of physical appearance. Traditionally, male seduction has been most aligned with an intellectually calculating verbal approach (as in the case of Laclos's Valmont), while female seduction has emphasized strategies of the body (as with the legend of Salomé). Significantly, then, Balzac does not hesitate to endow his seductress with both feminine and masculine characteristics. For his character, intellectual calculation and the strategic use of physical appearances constitute inseparable tools of seduction. The Princess de Cadignan thus defies gender stereotypes even as she presents a facade of stereotypical femininity.

Of course, the princess cannot know exactly what fantasies of the ideal woman her intended lover harbors in his mind. As is the case for any seducer or seductress, creating the appropriate identity to present to one's chosen victim involves a certain amount of intuition and guesswork based on the other's personality. This is the tactic advanced by the author of the anonymous 1826 seduction manual, *L'art de réussir en amour, enseigné en 25 leçons* and so many other arts of love written during the Restoration and July Monarchy. Because Daniel is a writer, however, Diane actually can turn to an additional resource in her quest to know her future love's taste. Following their initial meeting, the princess cloisters herself at home in order to read Daniel's works; she can thereby discover the fantasies that haunt his writing and gain material for use in future conversations. In effect, if she wants her identity to ring true and gain the status of reality, she needs Daniel's approving complicity, and studying his writing is one way she hopes to flatter him and gain his approval.

The princess's greatest artistic creation involves telling Daniel a version of her past—which the narrator refers to as her "novel" (*SPC*, 989)—that transforms her from the grande dame of worldly pleasures society knows into a "virgin and martyr" (*SPC*, 996), as she says herself, putting words into the writer's mouth. In lamenting to Daniel during their first encounter, "On ne nous croit pas ce que nous sommes, mais ce que l'on nous fait" (*SPC*, 971) [People do not see us for who we are, but for what others make of us], Diane emphasizes the great power society holds over the individual in fixing notions of one's identity, based on impressions that can often be incomplete or misinterpreted. The princess will continue to build on the idea that there exists within her a noble and innocent woman that no one else has been able to recognize. Clearly, she hopes that in telling her version of things to Daniel, she will persuade him to believe—and love—her. Seen in this light, the identity she presents as Daniel's seductress is less a masquerade than the revealing of long-buried facets of her "true" self. Diane's art lies in her ability constantly to shift the ground between truth and artifice, reality and performance. There is a certain grain of truth in the notion of a buried innocence within her (after all, she had told her friend the Marquise d'Espard that because she had never found love in all of her previous relationships, she was still seeking her first love), but she nonetheless embellishes her self-presentation with misleading interpretations and artifice.

In this second, climatic seduction scene, the princess stages an entire theatrical production, just as she did for her first meeting with Daniel. Rewriting the script of her life history, Diane tells how her mother gave her in marriage to her mother's own lover, the old Duke de Maufrigneuse, so that her daughter's fortune could help him pay his debts. Diane paints her "supposed" affairs as an innocent revenge, a childish attempt to strike out at her mother and her husband, by

whom she felt mistreated. Without denying her behavior, she simply casts it in a more favorable light. In one instance, Diane excuses her scandalous trip to Italy with her third lover by claiming that the minute the young man began speaking to her of love, she left him, thereby implying that there was no amorous relation between them. Not even the fact that she gave birth to a son early in her marriage prevents Diane from serving Daniel an image of herself as a virginal angel. As she presents her situation, she was more nearly an innocent convent schoolgirl playing at being a mother than a woman knowledgeable in matters of sex. Diane's manner of weaving the tale of her past aims to evoke Daniel's sympathy for her.

In order to heighten the effects of her performance, the princess not only uses falsehoods in her discourse but also, for the dénouement, adds the artificial gesture of a sob, manufactured in a way that recalls the seduction manual's instructions on how to provoke signs of sentimental emotions one does not really feel. In contrast, Daniel manifests a real sensitivity; he reacts by putting his head in Diane's lap and crying, thereby showing himself to be her ideal audience. To avert any doubts the reader may have about the princess's true nature, the narrator notes that Daniel's reaction provokes in her "un malicieux sourire de triomphe" (*SPC*, 995) [a mischievous smile of triumph]. Thus, Diane's artifice combines with Daniel's suspension of disbelief, demonstrating the role each partner plays in the creation of a successful seduction.[9] Essential to Diane's art is the blurriness she creates in the category of truth. The narrator describes the accomplishment of her "novel," which could be categorized as a historical fiction, imbued as it is with inventions and distortions, as being delivered with "l'accent inimitable du vrai" (*SPC*, 995) [the inimitable accent of truth]. Indeed, if Diane pulls off her performance, it is not because her utterances correspond to the facts of her past; rather, it is due to the appearance of truth communicated through her mannerisms and illocutionary skill. Her performance is so compelling that she succeeds in moving Daniel; he reacts just as she wishes him to do, despite his knowledge of the facts of her prior existence. The exploit of seducing an informed rather than an innocent victim is a tribute to the strength of the princess's seductive powers as an actress.

The third stage of this seduction, and the one that secures the princess's success, takes place at another dinner given by the Marquise d'Espard. Jealous of her friend's newfound happiness, the marquise invites Daniel alone, along with several of Diane's former lovers. The dandy Maxime de Trailles attacks the absent princess, say-

ing, "Chez Diane la dépravation n'est pas un effet, mais une cause; peut-être doit-elle à cette cause son naturel exquis: elle ne cherche pas, elle n'invente rien; elle vous offre les recherches les plus raffinées comme une inspiration de l'amour le plus naïf, et il vous est impossible de ne pas la croire" (*SPC*, 1002). [With Diane, depravation is not an effect, but a cause; perhaps she owes this cause to her exquisite naturalness: she does not look for anything, she invents nothing; she offers you the most refined efforts as an inspiration of the most naive love, and it is impossible for you not to believe her.] So thoroughly under Diane's spell is Daniel that he continues to act as her ideal audience, despite his knowledge of the truth. Daniel proceeds to grant a reality to the princess's performance when he publicly justifies the woman who seduced him; in other words, he supports the version of the princess she created in her "novel." Daniel's response to Maxime displays both his own genius and the subtle preparation Diane has provided him. He does not try to deny the existence of the princess's adventures, but he does justify her by suggesting that her only mistake was to have adopted behavior normally associated with a masculine role in society. He asks those gathered at the dinner, "Pourquoi ne se trouverait-il pas une femme qui s'amusât des hommes, comme les hommes s'amusent des femmes? Pourquoi le beau sexe ne prendrait-il pas de temps en temps une revanche?" (*SPC*, 1003). [Why wouldn't there be a woman who entertains herself with men the way men entertain themselves with women? Why wouldn't the beautiful sex seek revenge from time to time?] With his questions, Daniel succeeds in turning the tables on his attacker, such that it is no longer Diane but men who are on the defensive. In effect, the act of repetition itself, whereby Daniel redeploys the same justification that Diane had created in her story (her suggestion that she was simply taking a well-deserved revenge) signals that this version of things has gained authority in Daniel's mind. The truth does not matter, only Daniel's feelings.

With this feat, Diane climbs to such dramatic heights that she creates a new reality by means of artifice, and with Daniel's help. Lucienne Frappier-Mazur says of the princess's performance: "Not only is the play performed by Diane de Maufrigneuse more true than nature, as well it should be for an actress of this quality, but also this production creates reality."[10] The idea that a staged seduction could ring truer than nature turns on its head the conventional notion that what is natural is somehow more pure. In fact, Balzac describes the princess's performance as approaching "la vérité pure" (*SPC*, 996) [pure truth], and through his words he underscores that beyond the realm of mere objective facts, there exists another kind of truth, superior because it is a form of art. It is the skill, ingenuity, and creativity with which the princess masterminds her seduction of Daniel that cause him to suspend disbelief when faced with the spell of her artistic representation of herself. In *Les secrets de la princesse de Cadignan*, theatricality works to create an other reality—real in the sense of its effectiveness in inspiring belief—that replaces the traditional criteria of true and false; it rejects transcendental guarantees in favor of the self-referential.

Before examining the implications of the princess's successful seduction as played out in the text's conclusion, I wish first to turn to Sand's *La marquise*, which will provide material for comparison.

The Marquise's Seduction in a Theater

The anonymous heroine of *La marquise*, the elderly Marquise de R... , becomes the internal narrator of this text as she tells the young narrator the story of her past, concentrating on her love for the actor Lélio. An unusual woman who felt out of place in the libertine court of Louis XV where she spent her youth, it is in fact the very qualities that set her apart from the philandering aristocrats of her time that make her very much an idealized Sandian heroine. Until she became captivated by Lélio, the marquise had never experienced passion: her husband of six months left her widowed and disgusted with marriage at the age of sixteen, and all of the men she met subsequently only inspired her contempt. But if her everyday life was lacking in passion, the spectacle of watching the actor Lélio perform on stage provided material for her fantasies. With him she discovered a love that was "un amour passionné, indomptable, dévorant, et pourtant idéal et platonique s'il en fut" (*M*, 58) [passionate, indomitable, devouring and yet platonic and ideal]. This passionately platonic and idealized love is the form of true love so many Sandian heroines yearn to discover, although the marquise is unique for the theatrical setting in which she experiences this love.

By enacting personas and situations, theater creates an imaginary space that bears a resemblance to the self-referential space into which seducers and seductresses lure their victims. Just as actors aim to make their audience forget the real world so as to identify with the illusion on stage, so too the seducer maneuvers in a space where, if he is endowed with enough art, his desires and fantasies—as well as those of the person seduced—can attain a certain reality. However, while the seducer and the actor hold certain characteristics in common, seduction involves more than the collective fascination actors exert over their audience.[11] What differentiates the situation in *La marquise* from a standard theatrical performance is precisely the intimately erotic communication established between the marquise and Lélio, despite the room filled with other spectators.

This text provides a vivid illustration of the way a seducer's performance takes hold in the person seduced, offering an exterior object of desire that corresponds to his or her fantasies. In shifting the male narrator into the position of internal narratee after the text's opening pages so that the marquise can present her own story, Sand privileges the woman's perspective and makes the heroine's experience more immediate to her readers. The marquise uses the word "charme" to describe the actor's effect on her, suggesting that he casts a magical spell over her. She explains her initial reaction to his performance, saying: "Cet homme, qui marchait, qui parlait, qui agissait *sans méthode* et sans prétention, qui sanglotait avec le cœur autant qu'avec la voix, *qui s'oubliait lui-même* pour s'identifier avec la passion; cet homme [...] exerça sur moi une puissance vraiment électrique [...]" (*M*, 62; emphasis mine). [This man, who walked, who spoke, who acted *without method* and without pretensions, who sobbed with his heart as much as with his voice, *who forgot himself* to identify with the passion; this man . . . exercised a truly electric power over me. . . .] The marquise's manner of speaking about Lélio suggests she did not differentiate between his role and his person; in addition, it displays her naïveté regarding his performance, since an actor's ability to give himself up entirely to his role in order to create an illusion of reality actually results from highly methodical work. The phrasing "forgot himself" more nearly reveals what went on in the marquise's mind, suggesting that for her a fictional identity replaced the man Lélio. In fact, when speaking of this phenomenon with the knowledge of hindsight, she says, "Ses émotions feintes, ses malheurs de théâtre, me pénétraient comme des choses réelles. Je ne savais bientôt plus distinguer l'erreur de la vérité. Lélio n'existait plus pour moi: c'était Rodrigue, c'était Bajazet, c'était Hippolyte" (*M*, 68). [His feigned emotions, his theatrical unhappiness, penetrated me as real things. Soon I could no longer distinguish between error and truth. Lélio no longer existed for me: he was Rodrigue, he was Bajazet, he was Hippolyte.] While the marquise now describes Lélio's performance as feigned and theatrical, at the time his role had assumed a certain reality for her: the person on stage *was* the hero he represented. The fact that the marquise both states her present awareness of the performance's artificiality and observes that at the time she viewed this same performance as real serves to remind the reader of this character's double status—as a speaking subject and the subject of her discourse—while simultaneously signaling that she did not remain fooled by the theatrical illusion.

The crucial scene where the marquise encounters Lélio offstage makes it vividly clear that she felt seduced by the identity evoked in the actor's performance, while the man himself held little magic for her. Initially, the marquise is unaware of the key importance of theatrical representation in igniting her feelings for Lélio. When she follows him on the street and then comes face to face with this man in the light of a bar, the marquise believes she has mistaken Lélio for someone else, because the man before her eyes displays none of the charming qualities she found so fascinating in the actor on stage. The marquise's disenchantment can be attributed to the fact that this face-to-face meeting abolished all aesthetic distance by introducing an exterior, bodily referent into a seduction that had previously been based on a self-referential persona evoked in a theatrical space.

Sand's text shows that Lélio's performances captivate the marquise for reasons due both to the heroic roles he portrays and to aspects of himself that he contributes to his personas. Even though the words he speaks on stage were written by others—Corneille, Racine, or Molière—it is Lélio's personalized style that touches the marquise, for she admits that she became easily bored by other actors. Consequently, the marquise's infatuation goes beyond the fictional heroes, despite the fact that in her imagination she believes she is loved not by the actor but by the heroes he plays. When the marquise describes the first time she attended one of Lélio's performances, her admiration focuses on the actor himself and the seductive quality of his voice. Thanks to her regular attendance of Lélio's performances, he even comes to notice her in the crowd. The marquise says she could tell by the way he spoke that his lines were meant especially for her. She even reacted to his performances as an erotic seduction, going so far as to fall back in her box, spent, during intermission. The words she uses to describe her experience reveal a distinctly erotic charge: "Pour moi, je me livrais alors à mon émotion: je criais, je pleurais, je le nommais avec passion, je l'appelais avec folie" (*M*, 68). [For me, I gave myself over to my emotion: I shouted, I cried, I named him with passion, I madly called to him.] Whereas on a certain level the marquise entertains no illusions about Lélio—having seen him in the street, she knows that her version of him exists only so long as he is on stage—it does not prevent her from losing herself in the illusion. She reacted to the performance as if it were real. In this way, her participation in her own seduction by Lélio recalls Daniel d'Arthez in the midst of the princess's spell: he *knew* the truth even as he *believed* his seductress's performance. In both these texts, intelligent and reasonable people become so captivated by the theatrical artifice of seduction that they prefer to suspend disbelief and enter willingly into their fantasy brought to life.

Unlike many traditional representations of seduction that portray the woman as a passive victim of the man's advances, Sand gives the marquise an active role in cultivating her seduction. In this way, the marquise, too, enacts a role, even though Lélio remains the primary performer. For instance, she encourages communication between herself and Lélio by dressing up so as to be noticed. One evening at the theater when the marquise is dressed with particular excessiveness, Lélio decides to find out her name. In this situation, Lélio acts outside his role in order to learn information necessary to write the marquise a love letter, an instrument that serves as a mediator between the theater and everyday life. The marquise even interrupts her story, soliciting her narratee's active involvement when she asks him to read the actual letter. Just as Lélio's letter crosses the distance between himself and the marquise, so too this material object spans the temporal space between the events of the story and the marquise's telling of it. In this way, the marquise treats her storytelling as a seductive performance.

A close analysis of Lélio's letter reveals the marks of a seducer's calculating strategies. He uses rhetorical techniques that underscore the fact that his gift of speech was not limited to lines created by others. Beginning his letter so as to disarm the marquise, he suggests she need not be on her guard with him: "Je suis moralement sûr que cette lettre ne vous inspirera que du mépris, écrit-il; vous ne la trouverez même pas digne de votre colère" (*M*, 77). ["I am morally sure that this letter will only inspire your contempt," he writes; "you will not even find it worthy of your anger."] Next, Lélio uses a technique of seduction that relies on reverse psychology; namely, showing oneself to be already seduced by the other person. Lélio thus paints the marquise as the one who actively seduced him: "Vous n'avez pas pu allumer tous ces feux sans avoir un peu la conscience de ce que vous faisiez" (*M*, 78). [You could not have ignited these flames without being a little bit conscious of what you were doing.] However, no sooner has he evoked the possibility that the marquise has taken an interest in him than he changes course and modestly denies it: "Oh! non: c'est trop de présomption. Non, madame, je ne le crois pas; vous n'y avez jamais songé. Vous êtes sensible aux vers du grand Corneille, vous vous identifiez avec les nobles passions de la tragédie: voilà tout" (*M*, 78). [Oh! no: I'm too presumptuous. No, madam, I do not believe it; you have never dreamed of it. You are reacting to the lines of the great Corneille, you identify with the noble passions of tragedy: that is all.] Skillfully crafting his discourse, Lélio evokes multiple possibilities regarding the marquise's feelings for him, proceeding as if he were a naive bystander even as he strategically prepares the way for asking her to meet him.

The marquise's double reaction to Lélio's letter reveals her inner conflict over the nature of her feelings for Lélio and the space in which her seduction takes place. On the one hand, she consents to meet with him. In so doing, she enters a different self-referential space of seduction, for this time she reacts neither to the heroes of classical antiquity nor to the man Lélio she once saw in a café, but to the identity of the frustrated and confused lover he created in his letter. Thanks to the mobility of the letter—its ability to free itself from referential attachment to the man who wrote it and to exist solely as the identity created on paper—Lélio succeeds in his goal of captivating the marquise. On the other hand, however, she subsequently regrets having agreed to a meeting, precisely because she comes to realize the degree to which her love is tied to its theatrical setting. Once she recognizes that she loves not the man himself but her own phantasmic version of him that he helped to create, she becomes apprehensive about meeting him again on everyday ground.

In crafting the climactic scene of the marquise and Lélio's meeting, Sand foregrounds the issues of theatricality and identity that have been undercurrents of the entire text. When Lélio comes to the meeting directly from the theater and dressed in the elegant costume of none other than Don Juan, this costume not only transports them into a theatrical space but also it triggers a certain set of expectations from anyone familiar with the story of this legendary seducer. Not surprisingly, Sand plays with her readers' expectations and rewrites Don Juan's story. Unlike the famous Spanish hero, Lélio's attitude when he presents himself before the marquise is one of fear and submission. Perhaps because of, rather than in spite of, the timid behavior with which Lélio accompanied his seductive costume, the marquise lets herself be carried away by the passion he inspires in her, thereby granting a certain reality to the seducer's identity signified by Lélio's costume. However, Lélio's ability to elicit an emotional reaction from the marquise works only too well. Overcome by the violence of her emotions, the marquise faints, experiencing a symbolic death and rebirth. When she regains consciousness, she tells Lélio she has been transformed and implores him to help her resist him physically. The would-be "victim" thus thwarts her seducer's wishes and stops short his drive toward the consummation of their relation. Her desire to keep their love on metaphysical terms represents the refusal of a bodily referent, thereby serving to maintain her passion in a self-referential space where she remains in control of her fantasies. Rather than becoming yet another woman who succumbs to Don Juan's advances, she avoids the inevitable abandonment and disappointment associated with the legend by asserting her will and directing the situation according to her personal desires. The marquise's choice, as well as the strong sense of will it represents, inscribes this character with the qualities Sand valued in her heroines, and it also marks a significant distinction between her and Balzac's Princess de Cadignan.

Up to this point, I have analyzed this text for seduction at the level of the plot, but there also exists a case of narrative seduction that functions according to principles similar to those of the erotic seduction. The marquise's act of telling her story creates seductive effects of its own, in relation to her narratee. Several times, the young man seems to forget the temporal distance separating the marquise as a woman in flesh before him and her younger self that she evokes in the space of the narrative. At the beginning of the text, before the marquise starts her story, the narrator notices an attractive portrait of her hanging in her home. Referring to this image of the young woman represented as a nymph on a hunt, he reveals that it responds to his own fantasies. He says, "Sans la dentelle, le satin et la poudre, c'eût été vraiment là une de ces nymphes fières et agiles que les mortels apercevaient au fond des forêts ou sur le flanc des montagnes pour en devenir fou d'amour et de regret" (*M*, 46–47). [Without the lace, the satin and the powder, she really would have been one of those proud and agile nymphs that mortals glimpsed deep in forests or on the side of mountains only to become crazy with love and nostalgia.] Thus, from the text's very outset, the narrator manifests an ability to suspend material reality in order to fall under the sway of representational illusions. Then, at the point where the marquise interrupts her story, wondering if Lélio was consciously employing a strategy of seduction when he came to her dressed as Don Juan, her narratee interjects, "Je ne le crois certainement pas" (*M*, 89). [I certainly do not think so.] His remark evokes his own identification with Lélio and his seduction by the marquise. The young man responds for the actor according to his own understanding of the situation—in other words, with his own phantasmic projections. He even adds a revealing commentary when he remarks, "Elle semblait rajeunir en parlant [...] et dépouiller ses cents ans comme la fée Urgèle" (*M*, 89). [She seemed to get younger as she spoke . . . and to shed her one hundred years like the fairy Urgèle.] With these words, the young man speaks indirectly of his own seduction by the marquise—that is to say, the young marquise whom, in his mind, he substituted for the speaking subject.

By losing sight of the elderly woman—the bodily referent—the narrator undergoes a seduction of a type similar to the one the marquise herself experienced with the actor Lélio when she became infatuated with the classical heroes she saw portrayed before her at the expense of the man presenting them. We thus see that a distinct property of seduction involves an act of substitution performed by the seduced person, who privileges the other's theatrical identity over his or her whole self. Yet, the effects of the seduction last only as long as the performance, and when the young man once again takes up his role as narrator, he comments, "La marquise fit une pause; puis, avec un sourire sombre, et en se décomposant elle-même comme une ruine qui s'écroule, elle reprit [...]" (*M*, 92). [The marquise paused; then, with a somber smile, and seeming to decompose herself like a crumbling ruin, she began again. . . .] To be sure, it is only the seductive illusion that disintegrates, and with it the narrator's fantasies. However, this phenomenon effectively serves to justify the marquise's decision to renounce physical love in the hope of maintaining her fantasies intact. Just as satisfaction extinguishes desire, so too consummation marks the end of seduction. And if Lélio's theatrical identity had merged with reality in the marquise's mind, it could not survive in the real world. Therefore, the marquise's decision to confer her seduction to her imagination can be seen as her way of prolonging it.

Theatricality and Self-Alienation: The Princess and the Marquise

While *Les secrets de la princesse de Cadignan* and *La marquise* resemble one another in that both texts foreground the theatricality of seduction, the two stories' conclusions are remarkably different in their approach to the outcome of the illusory reality and the way the characters experience it. The marquise refuses a physical relationship with a man whom, in a moment of passion, she confusedly calls "Mon cher Lélio, mon grand Rodrigue, mon beau don Juan" (*M*, 88–89) [my dear Lélio, my great Rodrigue, my beautiful Don Juan]. In contrast, the princess not only succeeds in winning over Daniel forever, but she does so without ever leaving her role as actress: "Si elle avait ourdi de si cruels mensonges, elle y avait été poussée par le désir de connaître le véritable amour. Cet amour, elle le sentait poindre dans son cœur, elle aimait d'Arthez; elle était condamné à le tromper, car elle voulait rester pour lui l'actrice sublime qui avait joué la comédie à ses yeux" (*SPC*, 1004). [If she spoke such cruel lies, she had been pushed by the desire to experience true love. This love, she felt it sprouting in her heart, she loved d'Arthez; she was condemned to trick him, for she wanted to remain for him the sublime actress who had performed before his eyes.] In the second sentence, Balzac unites true love and trickery, sincere feelings and social hypocrisy, phenomena which, however, are unequivocally opposed for Sand, a champion of the ideal of true love. Notice that Balzac's sentence manifests a syntactical uneasiness, as if the semicolon hung precariously between two incompatible clauses that have been joined despite the lack of a logical connection between the ideas expressed in each one. Perhaps it is a subtle indication that Balzac himself resists on a certain level. Regardless of potential hesitation on Balzac's part, however, the text conclusively represents the princess's artistic capabilities in a favorable light by transforming her false identity into the couple's founding moment. The juxtaposition of these two texts thus brings out a fundamental difference in perspective between Balzac and Sand, a difference one can situate in their contrasting attitudes toward the doubling and self-alienation involved when one masquerades in an assumed identity for the purpose of seduction.

The Princess de Cadignan, an intellectual and calculating woman, re-creates herself by donning the symbols of naive femininity so as to seduce the man she desires. Thanks to her successful performance, she indeed becomes the angel of Daniel's dreams (*SPC*, 977). Paradoxically, then, in the interest of achieving her ultimate desire for true love, Diane willfully assumes a false identity. Her strategy of feminine *parure* represents a kind of masquerade—a supplement—that carries off a seduction made possible by her "masculine" inventiveness and calculations. The text even refers to her as "un vrai don Juan femelle" (*SPC*, 982) [a real female Don Juan]. As mentioned above, Diane unites techniques that traditional notions of seduction have separated as either masculine or feminine. But even women's efforts to construct a seductive appearance involve a certain amount of intellectual calculation in order to assess the other and determine what would appeal to him. Moreover, since seductive discourse usually proves to be an inseparable companion to the bodily ornamentation of feminine *parure* in both Balzac's and Sand's texts (a characteristic that will become even more apparent as we examine further examples), seductresses rarely use their bodies as their sole weapon. Seduction thus offers a realm where gender divisions are less clear-cut than society wishes to believe.

Even though the princess acts through her own free will and achieves success, the alienating aspects of masquerade nonetheless come into play in Balzac's representation of the outcome of her seduction. The text suggests that this role that Diane chose and invented for herself, performing it to perfection, will no longer result from her free choice. Building on Lucienne Frappier-Mazur's analysis of this text, Allan Pasco remarks, "To keep Daniel, Diane must continue to play the role she has created. . . . By whatever means she must prevent her love from getting out of hand. To keep the man she is beginning to love she must play a lie."[12] The idea that she is "condemned" to fool Daniel suggests that Diane, who is in love, fears he would not find her seductive if she showed herself to him without the veil of an identity that transforms her into an incarnation of ideal femininity. Thus, the Princess de Cadignan's assumption of a theatrical identity represents a limitation imposed on her subjectivity by the process of negotiating with another's desire, since she believes she must reconfigure herself, suppressing certain aspects of her personality, in order to keep the love she wants. One must also ask, however, whether the ideal figure of the angelic woman is truly the one that seduces Daniel. As Pasco reminds us in his reading of the text, Daniel knows that Diane's seductive identity as an angel is but a masquerade, an incomplete version of her self, whereas the woman Daniel loves is her complete self: "He could see beyond the limits of reason and recognize the real Diane de Cadignan—an astonishing combination of wit and elegance, of intelligence and sensitivity, of experience and innocence."[13] Daniel's exact reasons for loving Diane remain ambiguous, for his point of view does not get exposed. Yet, as Pasco's interpretation suggests, we can understand Daniel's love as stemming from his appreciation of the profound complexities within Diane.

This alienating masquerade is not uniquely a feature of female oppression, however, for it would equally be the fate of a man who contrived an identity expressly for the purpose of seduction. The author of *L'art de réussir en amour* certainly advises his readers to adopt an identity suited to the woman's personality rather than to display their true nature, and one need only think of Valmont's self-transformation in order to seduce Madame de Tourvel to know that men are not immune from seduction's self-destructive effects. In practice, however, the male position of dominance in society modifies the significance of a seducer's masquerade. Indeed, self-alienation is more universally the lot of women, particularly in the period when Balzac and Sand lived, since women were most often raised to please men without forming a sense of their own subjective desires. Yet, if the goal of the men dominating patriarchal society was to quash women's sense of self in order to make them docile—and even servile—companions, examples of female self-alienation suggest that this upbringing did not fully succeed in preventing subjectivity, only in damaging it. In his 1863 text *Le peintre de la vie moderne*, Charles Baudelaire formulates his praise of makeup in the form of a masculine prescription: "La femme est bien dans son droit, et même elle accomplit une espèce de devoir en s'appliquant à paraître magique et surnaturelle; il faut qu'elle étonne, qu'elle charme; idole, elle doit se dorer pour être adorée."[14] [A woman is well within her rights, and even accomplishes a kind of duty by working to appear magical and supernatural; she must surprise, charm; an idol, she must adorn herself to be adored.] Baudelaire's commentary provides a means of further distinguishing the feminine masquerade from the masculine one described in *L'art de réussir en amour*, as the author of this seduction manual suggests that most male seducers act from momentary physical lust rather than from a desire to be "adored" in the context of a lasting relationship. Thus, not only one's position in the social hierarchy but also the goals one hopes to achieve through seduction influence the process of negotiating power in seduction and, by extension, the way in which seducers and seductresses experience the potentially alienating effects of their identity.

In Sand's text, the marquise's decision not to enter into a physical relationship with Lélio is presented as a consequence of her increased consciousness of the nature of her own desires. Significantly, her inner transformation, undergone around the time of her final meeting with Lélio, equally manifests itself in the outer sign of her changed appearance. During the period when the marquise attended the theater in order to see Lélio, she took great care in constructing her own seductive costumes. She even had a mirror in her carriage that allowed her to admire her appearance. However, the marquise's self-admiration more nearly manifests her status in relation to Lélio, since she identifies herself as "la femme qui aimait Lélio" (*M*, 66) [the woman who loved Lélio]. Her statement that in loving Lélio she took pleasure in her own beauty reveals the degree to which her sense of self comes from the other whom she loves. Hence the significance of her decision to abandon all adornment for her face-to-face meeting with Lélio. Whereas she dressed up to be noticed at the theater, the space of her seduction, for this meeting she made a conscious decision to discourage Lélio from paying attention to her body. This decision to appear natural not only suggests that she did not expect to encounter the seductive figure she had admired at the theater, but also indicates that her idea of her self has evolved.

In creating the scene of the marquise and Lélio's rendezvous, Sand not only rewrites the Don Juan legend but also she sets their encounter in a boudoir whose decor purposely does not evoke the sumptuous setting of lovers' trysts. Instead, the space exudes a certain purity, due not only to the whiteness of the light reflecting from the walls and furniture but also because of the statue of Isis standing in the middle of the room. The marquise looks in a mirror and glimpses an image of herself and Isis, reflected together as if merged. Different from the image she saw in the mirror of the carriage when she was dressed in enticing clothing, the statue provides her with a new kind of identification. The symbolism of this statue plays into the outcome of the marquise's seduction, and Isabelle Naginski has remarked that Sand uses this Egyptian god to represent not only the search for love and metaphysical initiation but also sublimation.[15] Sand suggests that her heroine's refusal of a physical relationship with Lélio in favor of a metaphysical love results from her newly acquired self-awareness, and hence could mean a renouncement of masquerade. Françoise Massardier-Kenney interprets the marquise's choice in a similar vein: "If Sand admits the masculine role in activating the heroine's desire and pushing her into the world of action, it is on the condition that the heroine's desire remain desire and not extinguish itself by being consummated and inevitably submitted to masculine domination."[16] For desire to "remain desire," it must be kept as a tantalizing possibility rather than being enacted, and it is this interest that often pushes seducers to draw out their conquest—as Valmont does with the Présidente de Tourvel—rather than rushing toward an immediate fulfillment that will usually end the seduction itself. In effect, the marquise, having discovered that she desires not Lélio but his theatrical identity living in her imagination, prefers not to introduce into this space the man who is only a support to her fantasies. Sand's heroine thus avoids the kind of perpetual self-alienation that Balzac makes the Princess de Cadignan's lot.

The different reactions Sand's and Balzac's heroines have to the performance of seduction—the princess's acceptance of a degree of self-alienation in order to have the man she loves, and the marquise's decision not to engage in a negotiation that would require her to give up the noncorporeal mode of her desire—underscore the two authors' diverging attitudes regarding the merits of theatricality versus authenticity. This opposition between Balzac and Sand over theatricality in intersubjective relations likewise comes to the foreground when one compares their representations of the courtesans Esther Gobseck and Isidora (who is not given a family name), for they confront issues of self-alienation similar to those experienced by the princess and the marquise. In placing these female characters in the position of leading a double life, the texts impose on them a division within the self. However, as the following analysis will show, Balzac accentuates Esther's doubling while Sand seeks a way for Isidora to escape hers.

Isidora: A Seductress's Double Identity

Sand's representation of the courtesan figure Isidora focuses on the heroine's attempts to free herself from alienation in disparate identities. In writing this novel, which serves as an interrogation not only of the status of the courtesan in society but also of all women, Sand departs from traditional novelistic forms even as she employs the well-known device of presenting the text as a collection of documents the editor has found and simply published. Part 1, "Journal d'un solitaire à Paris," contains notebooks labeled "work" and "journal" that belong to a young writer with a philosophical bent named

Jacques Laurent. In his journal, Jacques tells of two encounters, first with his angelic neighbor, Julie, and then with the mysterious Isidora. This masked woman whom Jacques encounters at the Opéra ball is described by a dandy as both "la plus belle femme de Paris" [the most beautiful woman in Paris] and "la plus méprisable et la plus méprisée" (*I*, 49) [the most contemptible and the most scorned]. Eventually, she reveals herself to be the same woman he had previously met as Julie. In the second part of the novel, Sand changes narrative techniques and writes in the third person, telling of the relations between Jacques, Isidora (who has since become the widowed Countess de S), and her sister-in-law Alice. Finally, in the third part, two notebooks marked "I" and "A" containing Jacques' reflections on the two women in his life are followed by a series of letters from Isidora to Alice. The physical separation of the two women into different notebooks reflects Jacques' efforts to erect a material division between them, separating the former courtesan from the angelic mother Alice. In this polyphonic novel, Sand treats the difficulties faced by a woman who, uniting the identities of a courtesan and an honest woman, seeks to be loved simultaneously as Isidora and Julie. This novel thus offers a Sandian version of the nineteenth-century vision of femininity as split between the sexual courtesan and the ideal mother.

The name Julie, which readers of French literature associate with Rousseau's most famous heroine, and the space of the greenhouse (*serre*), coupled with the fact that Jacques is reading *The Social Contract* and uses his journal to rewrite his own version of that seminal text of political philosophy, signal that this novel intends to contest preexisting visions of the ideal society. The text opens with Jacques' meditations on the status of women, and he asks the kinds of questions that plagued so many thinkers of early nineteenth-century France. How are women different from men? Are women equal to men? One reason these issues arose in postrevolutionary France is that the Revolution, in turning the king's subjects into citizens, had also raised questions of inclusion and participation in the new nation. The more radical phases of the Revolution had opened a Pandora's box of equality, and not even the restoration of the monarchy could suppress speculation on women's being and their place in society. Geneviève Fraisse has studied these issues in *Muse de la raison: La démocratie exclusive et la différence des sexes*, and she views attempts to designate the female sex as different from men, destined to distinct roles, as a way of preserving the complementary hierarchy of society: "Clearly, women were refused public culture in order to stave off any rivalry between husband and wife, between men and women."[17] Sand's Jacques aims at a more enlightened perspective on women than that advocated by conservative elements in society such as Sylvain Maréchal, who proposed a fictive law outlawing teaching girls how to read.[18] Jacques draws a parallel between women and the poor, for both are kept in inferior positions in society through lack of education. In his quest to decide whether women are by nature inferior to men, he writes, "Or donc, l'induction des pédants, qui concluent de l'inaction sociale apparente de la femme, qu'elle est d'une nature inférieure, est d'un raisonnement [...]" (*I*, 20-21). [Now, the reasoning of pedants, who conclude from the apparent social inactivity of women that they are of an inferior nature, is . . .] With this incomplete thought, Jacques' work notebook breaks off. However, the following section of Jacques' journal begins with the exclamation "Absurde!" This leads the reader to believe that Sand means it as an answer to Jacques' unfinished sentence, despite the different context. As the story develops, Jacques will learn about female nature from experience rather than simply speculating in the abstract.

In the first part of the novel, the split between the heroine's identities as Julie and Isidora is mirrored in the spatial separation between the places where Jacques sees each one: she is Julie in the garden of her home and Isidora at the Opéra ball. When Jacques first meets Julie, he reads her appearance and behavior as signs reflecting his image of the ideal woman. She also appeals to him because her critique of contemporary society resembles his own opinions on the subject. But Jacques' assumptions prove incorrect: however elegant Julie may be, the conclusions he draws as to her illustrious family background in no way correspond to the actual origins of this woman of low birth. Nonetheless, her identity as Julie is not an artificial mask; rather, it is a sincere expression of qualities emanating from her inner self. In effect, it is impossible to determine who, Julie or Isidora, constitutes the "true" identity of this woman. To the extent that Julie's identity is marked by sincerity and credibility, her appearance reflects not the material facts of her existence as a courtesan but her inner reality. Thus, Isidora *is* Julie, as long as Jacques affirms her as such.

In her desire to know true love, Isidora/Julie bears a certain resemblance to the Princess de Cadignan, and both women have maintained a kind of purity and innocence (that of a woman who has never fallen in love) despite their history of sexual promiscuity. However, while both seductresses seek love, their situations manifest a fundamental difference. Diane ends up living with Daniel under an identity that hides part of her self, whereas Isidora, refusing such an arrangement, wants her whole self to be known and loved. Therefore, Isidora undertakes a double seduction. Her initial conquest of Jacques when she meets him as Julie consists strictly of an intellectual admiration. In his journal, Jacques even writes, "Cette femme est un ange. On en deviendrait passionnément épris si l'on pouvait éprouver en sa présence un autre sentiment que la vénération" (*I*, 34). [This woman is an angel. One would fall passionately in love with her if one could feel in her presence a sentiment other than veneration.] Isidora demands more than the adoration of a man who sees her as a divine ideal rather than a woman of this world, however, and Jacques' words inform the reader of the obstacle facing Isidora in her second seduction. She must arouse Jacques' desire and cause him to act on it, since she demands to be loved in the flesh as well as in the spirit. In suggesting that Julie should be placed on a pedestal, Jacques manifests a misguided understanding of Isidora/Julie, an error that stems from a fundamental incompatibility between their fantasies and complicates the process of seduction for Isidora. Whereas Isidora wants Jacques to desire her as Julie, accepting and forgiving her past as a prostitute, Jacques believes he would defile his Julie both in making her an object of desire and in recognizing that she is a desiring subject herself.

While Jacques' feelings for Julie are nothing but virtuous, as Isidora she succeeds in arousing this man's passion for her. Their two encounters at the Opera ball, first by chance and then by rendezvous, place them in a space more befitting Isidora's erotic desire. In these scenes Jacques does not realize he is speaking with "Julie," since Isidora's physique is hidden by her costume. Taking advantage of her anonymity, the mysterious woman talks to Jacques about love, captivating him by her eloquence. In fact, Isidora's words provide a highly effective tool in her efforts at seduction, for Jacques is touched by her incisive and penetrating speech (*I*, 43). Significantly, then, Sand's seductress lures her prey uniquely thanks to her skillful use of discourse: Jacques is charmed without seeing the courtesan's renowned beauty with his own eyes. Thus, by highlighting Isidora's rhetorical virtuosity while radically diminishing the importance of her body, Sand's character counters traditional images of the seductress as one who uses a strategy of physical attraction alone. In this example, Sand goes even further than Balzac did in his representation of the princess's use of calculated speech as a seduction strategy, since Balzac's character reflects a combination of stereotypically masculine and feminine traits while Isidora makes no use at all of the feminine weapon of *parure*.

The novel's first key scene of erotic seduction underscores the heroine's double identity. When Isidora brings Jacques home with her, she unveils herself and reveals the very same woman Jacques has known as the chaste Julie. Seduced separately and differently by each one, Jacques is now forced to confront the angel and the courtesan together. Yet, at the very moment when Isidora strives to unite her two identities, she also admits her inner division, speaking of herself in the third person: "[E]lle vous eût trompé, si elle eût laissé la passion s'allumer en vous dans les circonstances pures et charmantes qui avaient présidé à votre rencontre" (*I*, 51). [She would have deceived you if she had let your passion ignite in the pure and charming circumstances that had presided when you met.] As is so often the case in Sand's works, the heroine strives for authenticity in her relationship with Jacques. Isidora/Julie reveals her past as a courtesan in the hope of attaining her dream of being loved; for, as her words suggest, if Jacques loves only Julie, his love does not reach her as a whole person, but only his fantasies of her. Unlike characters involved in a traditional seduction, where seducers and seductresses consciously use artifice in the hope of luring the other person into believing a false identity, Sand's character tries to behave honestly. On the surface, Isidora seems to obtain her wishes, as Jacques spends the night with her. However, even as he claims to accept her—unsavory past and all—he persists in his underlying agenda of "curing" her, of purifying her by making her renounce a part of her self (*I*, 53). Thus, the situation in which they find themselves is not really the one Isidora had aimed for, as each one remains on the side of his or her own fantasies.

Isidora does not abandon the goal of her seduction, her desire to be loved. Three years after heading to Italy with Count Félix, in the aftermath of her night with Jacques, she returns to Paris a widow and a countess. She married the dying Félix, hoping that her change in status would make her more acceptable in the eyes of society, and to Jacques in particular. But Jacques' situation has changed as well, for he is currently the tutor of Félix's sister's son, and he has fallen in love with his pupil's mother, Alice.

Isidora's continued desire to attract Jacques now takes its inspiration from a different source than her original desire simply to achieve love. Jealousy comes into play as a motivating factor when Isidora seeks to turn Jacques' love from Alice back to herself. She forces him to confront again the divisions of her existence, and when they meet in the garden where their love first bloomed, she expresses her frustrations: "Cette âme pure et généreuse s'agite toujours dans le sein meurtri et souillé d'Isidora; elle s'y agite en vain, personne ne veut lui rendre la vie; elle ne peut ni vivre ni mourir. Vraiment, je suis un tombeau où l'on a enfermé une personne vivante" (*I*, 106). [This pure and generous soul still stirs in the deadly and soiled breast of Isidora; it stirs in vain, no one wants to give it life; it can neither live nor die. Truly, I am a tomb where they have buried a living person.] Isidora elegantly describes her feelings of being boxed in by a society whose prejudices against courtesans do not allow people to see her more complex and, she would argue, true identity beneath the social role of the courtesan that she has felt obliged to play. In presenting herself as misunderstood and misrepresented by society, Isidora resembles Diane de Maufrigneuse when the latter attempts to persuade Daniel d'Arthez to look beyond the image others have of her. Moreover, Isidora's words underscore the fact that it takes two to create a seduction, for her identity as Julie remains little more than a fiction in her mind unless another person believes her and affirms its existence.

This second scene of erotic seduction consists of a double performance leading to a reality that, again, fulfills neither Isidora's nor Jacques' phantasmic desires. For Isidora, saying she is in love represents the equivalent of actually loving someone; her speech acts become the sole measure of her reality. Far from covering herself in an artificial mask in the hope of fooling the man she wishes to seduce, Isidora totally identifies with her performance, "à la manière des grands artistes, avec toutes les nuances de son improvisation brûlante" (*I*, 114) [in the manner of great artists, with all the nuances of her burning improvisation]. She falls under the spell of her own performance and believes it herself. In contrast to the Balzacian seductresses Diane de Maufrigneuse and Esther Gobseck, she does not self-consciously manipulate reality. Sand underscores her heroine's sincerity in her brief 1853 "Notice" in *Isidora* by describing an unnamed woman she met in Paris as the type of seductress on which she did *not* model Isidora: "Je vis parfaitement qu'elle *posait* devant moi et ne pensait pas un mot de ce qu'elle disait la plupart du temps. Elle eût pu être ce qu'elle n'était pas. Aussi, n'est-ce pas elle que j'ai dépeinte dans *Isidora*" (*I*, i; italics in original). [I saw perfectly well that she was *posing* before me and did not believe one word of what she said most of the time. She could have been what she was not. Thus, it is not her I depicted in *Isidora*.] In effect, Isidora is seduced by love, if she does not love Jacques himself. The narrator evaluates Isidora's speech to Jacques, in which she explains her flight to Italy and her marriage to the count in terms favorable to Jacques, by saying that her words are "Sincère, oui; mais véridique, non" (*I*, 112). [Sincere, yes; but truthful, no.] As the manipulative and self-serving courtesan has not totally disappeared in her, she is single-mindedly set on securing a triumph, and she continues to press Jacques until he acquiesces. Isidora succeeds in getting her lover to call her Julie, thereby obliging him to couple sexual desire with divine love. Because Isidora so thoroughly identifies with her performance, Jacques' role more nearly resembles a masquerade than does hers. Their situation represents a Pyrrhic victory, since Jacques only gives himself to Isidora because he has repressed his desire for Alice, the woman he truly loves.

This seduction nevertheless leads to a new reality, since Jacques and Isidora form a couple. Both play their roles to perfection—as does Alice, who, repressing her own love for Jacques and refusing to vie for his affections, becomes their devoted friend. Alice represents a similar type of woman to Isidora's Julie, except that she has no skeletons in the closet. In welcoming her sister-in-law despite her reputation, Alice becomes a role model to her. Sand's version of the tale of the prostitute renewed by love, a theme dear to romanticism, thus uses friendship between two women as a vehicle for rehabilitation, rather than focusing solely on a man as the purifying influence.[19] Alice even calls Isidora by the name "Julie," which had previously been known only to Jacques. To the extent that Sand's story does not uncover a man capable of truly loving Isidora, this heroine is a woman ahead of her time, like so many of Sand's characters. When Isidora discovers that Jacques does not truly love her, she refuses to continue a relationship based on false pretenses and flees to Italy. Largely because of Jacques' inability to love her without judging her past and feeling it taints her with an inferiority that must be cured—a reflection of society's attitude toward prostitution—Isidora does not find the love she so desired. Jacques and Alice seem to fare no better, however, since both are too "pudiques" (*I*, 147) [modest] to act on their feelings. In this way, Sand's novel underscores the fact that the social conventions of the time were as alienating to model women like Alice, who were shunned from a position as a subject of desire, as they were damaging to women denounced for fulfilling society's demand for prostitutes. Instead of foregrounding the seductress's theatrical triumph, then, this novel reveals the high price extracted by social conventions of the period. Isidora's attempt to overcome her past reputation and to start a new life in Paris as a widow fails. Instead, she feels she must escape to a place (Italy) where no one knows her history. In this text, then, Sand uses sympathy and realism to paint the difficulties faced by a former courtesan wanting to improve her life. We will return to analyze more fully the conclusion of this text after taking a look at an example of a Balzacian courtesan.

Esther: Performing Seduction under Duress

Much has been written on Balzac's *Splendeurs et misères des courtisanes* and more generally on prostitution in the nineteenth-century novel.[20] My analysis will focus specifically on the theatrical aspects of Esther Gobseck's seduction of the Baron de Nucingen and its implications for the seductress's identity. Like Sand's Isidora, Esther seeks to rehabilitate her identity, here through a loving relationship with Lucien de Rubempré. Balzac's character differs from Isidora in that Esther seeks to reinvent herself completely and hide her former identity from the man she loves. This desire for dissimulation and secrecy better suits Balzac's narrative interests than does Sand's emphasis on authenticity.

In the first scene, set at the masked ball of the Opéra, Balzac places the issue of Esther's identity on center stage, as a group of dandies tries to uncover the identity of the costumed woman accompanying Lucien. One, the journalist Lousteau, who suspects it is indeed the courtesan known as "the Torpedo" (*la Torpille*), comments on her talents as a seductress: "Elle tient comme une baguette magique avec laquelle elle déchaîne les appétits brutaux si violemment comprimés chez les hommes [...]" (*SMC*, 442). [She seems to have a magic wand with which she unleashes the brutal appetites violently repressed in men. . . .] Lousteau emphasizes Esther's power over men in evoking her ability to submit them to her will. Extremely accomplished in her art, the Torpedo knows how to create an aesthetic distance that allows her to reign over men by seductively arousing their desire without, however, becoming emotionally attached to them. As another of the young men tells the group, "Vous avez tous été plus ou moins ses amants, nul de vous ne peut dire qu'elle a été sa maîtresse" (*SMC*, 442). [You have all been her lovers more or less, none of you can say that she has been your mistress.] This distinction between a lover and a mistress is a key one for Esther's identity, because it indicates that despite the position of an object of exchange to which prostitution has reduced her, her powerful seductiveness has allowed her to maintain a certain degree of control and domination over men.

In her relationship with Lucien, however, its basis in true love encourages Esther to give of herself in such a way that she loses the power she had so successfully retained for herself in her relations as a prostitute. While the seductive courtesan maintains a control that grants her a degree of power, the woman in love gives of herself completely. She, like Lucien, falls victim to control by Carlos Herrera (another incarnation of Jacques Collin), one of the most successfully manipulative and theatrical characters of *La comédie humaine*. Thus, Lucien and Esther are not free to determine their own identities. Once Esther enters into Herrera's scheme for her to seduce Nucingen, the once-again courtesan is forced to lead a double life, for the man she loves and the man she seduces are two different people. Such a division only renders her seduction all the more theatrical and artificial. Further, it underscores the extent to which a successful seduction depends on the masquerade of role-playing rather than an actual interest in the person seduced.

The role Esther plays for Nucingen highlights her strengths as an actress, thereby suggesting a parallel between this courtesan and the Princess de Cadignan. However, because Esther undertakes this seduction for another rather than by her own inspiration, it assumes a markedly different signification than the princess's project. Whereas Diane falls in love with the man she seduces, in *Splendeurs et misères* Esther loves someone else and is horrified at the idea of being unfaithful to him. Compelled to create the illusion of being devoted to Nucingen for the sake of Lucien's fortune, she simultaneously delays the completion of their "contract"—its consummation—until she has received enough money to buy the Rubempré family château for Lucien. Because Esther feels she cannot survive an infidelity to Lucien, beyond her seduction lies death. The goal of this seduction is thus the opposite of a conventional scenario, as Esther, who is not after physical possession, would prefer never to bring the seduction to its culmination. The challenge consists of maintaining Nucingen's interest—and above all his willingness to spend money on her—without allowing him to satisfy his desire for sexual possession.

In Balzac's representation of this seduction, we recognize many indications of its theatrical nature. Under no illusions herself, Esther enacts a performance that will mystify Nucingen and make him believe she loves him. She succeeds in creating an appearance of truth, in spite of a reality that belies it, precisely because her words evoke an image Nucingen wishes to believe. Her rhetorical techniques endow her words with a kind of self-referentiality, as when she appears to tell Nucingen she loves him, but with an all-important nuance: "Tu sais bien que je t'aime" (*SMC*, 685) [You know I love you], she says, so as not to pronounce those three famous words alone. As long as Nucingen believes she has given him a declaration of love, what he "knows" counts more than the exact nature of Esther's feelings for him. His belief in Esther's sincerity is all the seductress needs to create a self-referential space of seduction. Her techniques even resemble those Claude Reichler has identified as constituting the power of Don Juan's seductive discourse. He observes: "[S]eduction is the *counterfeiting* of a right language whose truth, or adherence to things, has been evacuated. Thus Don Juan promises to marry, to pay, to pray: these are *only words*, whose mechanism he reproduces without holding himself obligated to them."[21] Likewise, when Esther tells Nucingen, "Tu me plais maintenant, et je ne sais pas comment cela s'est fait, mais je te préférerais à un jeune homme" (*SMC*, 684–85) [You please me now, and I do not know how it happened, but I would prefer you to a young man], *they are only words* that carry no grain of truth beyond the self-referential space of Esther and Nucingen's interaction. Moreover, Esther uses a conditional verb in saying "I would prefer you" rather than making an actual declaration. This situation illustrates the magic of seduction, for words have the power to create a new space of reality that substitutes itself for the situation existing previously between two people. The theatrical performance of seduction becomes real for the people involved when the victim assents by granting his or her belief.

The text presents Esther as a kind of Robin Hood seeking vengeance and her seduction as a contribution both to social good and to Lucien's future, making her into an admirable figure of revolt against the evils of society. The narrator justifies Esther's behavior by endowing her with qualities that would be deemed acceptable in men (a tactic that recalls Daniel d'Arthez's defense of the Princess de Cadignan). In addition, Herrera assuages Esther's conscience by informing her that Nucingen is a kind of white-collar criminal who has made his fortune by taking advantage of others. But since she herself is an object of exchange between men, she is nonetheless constrained to pass from the purely verbal realm to one of physical relations—a condition that differentiates her from Reichler's Don Juan, as described above. A sexual relationship marks the end of the illusion by which Esther has mystified Nucingen, making him think he is loved, all the while reassuring herself of her basic loyalty to Lucien. It forces her to confront material, bodily reality as the logical consequence of her seduction. By emphasizing her absolute devotion to the man she loves, Balzac's text represents her act of self-sacrifice as one that transforms her into a sublime martyr. Because she and Lucien do not have the freedom to act as two subjects who are masters of themselves, however, Esther's act of devotion—performed in the context of her seductive masquerade—means her death. This seduction constitutes the courtesan's final theatrical performance, as she subsequently commits suicide.

In this novel, the courtesan Esther plays a role determined by criteria that are, above all, narrative. Balzac is less motivated by the social or moral implications of his character's actions than by the demands of his intricate plot, so Esther is returned to prostitution and then sacrificed for the sake of Herrera's complicated seduction scheme. In a perceptive analysis of *Splendeurs et misères*, Charles Bernheimer asserts, "[T]he mobile, transgressive, theatrical prostitute-courtesan seems to figure the creative impulse of Balzacian narrative. . . ."[22] As Bernheimer suggests, the courtesan's role in society gave Balzac material that perfectly suited his approach to storytelling. Balzac's primary focus as a novelist can thus be located in his desire to exploit this seductive figure who is so conducive to interesting plot material. In this regard, the courtesan shares points in common with the Princess de Cadignan, for in both cases a successful seduction (not to mention the masterful narrative describing it) takes precedence over any negative moral implications arising from the seductress's restricted subjectivity. Balzac's primary emphasis on the narrative rather than on the moral sets him apart from Sand, and we will get a better understanding of Balzac's interest in the courtesan figure by juxtaposing *Splendeurs et misères* with *Isidora*.

Seduction and the Appeal of Theatricality

Balzac and Sand manifest strikingly different perspectives regarding seduction and doubling, as represented by the experiences of Isidora and Esther, as well as those of the marquise and the Princess de Cadignan. Esther's seduction of Nucingen orients her in a direction that increases her inner division by dividing her from the identity she had created for herself in her relationship with Lucien. Moreover, Balzac condemns Esther to return to a position as an object of exchange through the transaction between Herrera and Nucingen. As indicated above, the demand for a "narratable" character asserts itself as Balzac's primary consideration, and Bernheimer underscores how Balzac's attitude toward the prostitute differs from that of his contemporary Parent-Duchâtelet, a public hygienist who wrote the 1836 book *De la prostitution dans la ville de Paris*. Bernheimer remarks:

> The same traits of the venal woman's character and behavior that threaten the public hygienist in the discharge of his duties stimulate the novelist's creative invention. The courtesan's refined talent as an actress, her ability to disguise her venality and control the signs of her sexual availability, terrifies Parent, whereas Balzac finds this metamorphic capacity eminently novelistic.[23]

Because Balzac gives predominance to what Bernheimer calls the "novelistic" qualities of the courtesan, the theatricality of Esther's seduction becomes a narrative issue to be adjudicated on aesthetic grounds rather than an issue of the courtesan's subjectivity. Not only does Balzac not feel threatened by the courtesan's sexuality, as does Parent-Duchâtelet, but also he feels free to use Esther as a vehicle for a thrilling plot without paying much regard to the price his character pays, in terms of her person, for her participation in Herrera's scheme with Nucingen. Once Esther's narrative potential has been exhausted through her submission and death, the plot simply discards her and spirals off in another direction in search of more thrills.

In contrast, Sand emphasizes the immorality of the courtesan's position in society; indeed, she sets out to make a social statement in writing *Isidora*. Her heroine moves out of prostitution and into a position as a countess and widow, thereby affording her the freedom to determine her own destiny. This status not only allows her to enter into a relationship with Jacques but it also gives her the possibility of leaving him when she realizes the false grounds of their relationship. Furthermore, an important thrust of Sand's novel resides in her characters' critique of the social order. As discussed above, Sand inscribes her text within the tradition of Rousseau, except that she aims to do women justice by adopting a stance that accords women more respect and equality. Both Jacques and Isidora underscore that society and men impose prostitution on women against their will. Jacques comments on Isidora's double identity, saying, "Dieu a fait la première, la société a fait la seconde" (*I*, 86). [God made the first one, society made the second.] Jacques thereby gives preference to "Julie" while setting up society as responsible for creating the courtesan Isidora. In addition, he suggests that the roots of the problem of prostitution lie in the inequalities among classes, whereby "la société n'a pas donné d'autre issue aux facultés de la femme belle et intelligente, mais née dans la misère, que la corruption et le désespoir" (*I*, 86) [society gave no other possibilities for the faculties of a beautiful and intelligent woman, but born into poverty, than corruption and despair]. One can detect a similarly critical attitude toward the harmful effects of the social order in Balzac's text when the narrator of *Splendeurs et misères* states, "La prostitution et le vol sont deux prostestations vivantes, mâle et femelle, de *l'état naturel* contre l'état social" (*SMC*, 517; italics in the original). [Prostitution and theft are two vivid protests, male and female, of the *natural state* against society.] This comment recalls the Robin Hood theme of Herrera's seduction plot for Esther. Nevertheless, Balzac's text furthers women's object status for the sake of an exhilarating narrative, while Sand's *Isidora* not only contains characters who speak of the need to reform women's role in society but also, in the meantime, finds an alternative for Isidora by having her withdraw to a solitary life in Italy.

Yet one must ask whether this solution, one that recalls in certain ways the marquise's decision to maintain the integrity of her self by refusing a relationship with Lélio, truly is a solution. The "happy" ending Sand creates for the conclusion of *Isidora* depicts the heroine asserting that she feels compensated (*dédommagée*) by witnessing the love between her nephew, Alice's son, and the orphan she has adopted as her daughter in Italy (*I*, 203). But it does not disguise the failure of Isidora's double seduction, her inability to make herself be known and loved by the man of her choice. To be sure, she enters into rewarding relations and knows love through her friendship with Alice and her maternal feelings for Agathe, but the reader is left to wonder how the substitution of filial love for her prior goal of true love between a man and a woman could really represent a satisfactory alternative. Just as in *La marquise*, here Sand articulates a position that suggests a woman is better off alone than in an inauthentic relationship. On the grounds of female subjectivity, such a position makes sense. But if narrative, like seduction, is enacted in the theatrical space of a stage, then the heroine's exit from that stage—here figured in Isidora's retreat to Italy and her voice's resignation, in the text's concluding pages, to a series of letters—signals the inefficacy of Sand's rejection of seduction, at least in narrative terms.

Granted, Balzac's representation of Esther in *Splendeurs et misères* makes her as much a victim of society as Isidora; however, that is not the central issue of the novel. While Sand's text displays a movement away from theatricality, Balzac instead tends to emphasize his characters' theatrical talents. He recognized the limited interest evoked by genuine love, as opposed to the fascinating potential of artifice and theatricality; thus, he entitled a chapter of *Splendeurs et misères* "Chapitre ennuyeux car il explique quatre ans de bonheur" (*SMC*, 115) [Boring Chapter Because It Explains Four Years of Happiness]. In addition, he shows a certain admiration for the courtesan, a figure that he represents as endowed with the same creative faculties as great writers. During the opening scene at the Opéra ball, Lousteau speaks of Esther in the following terms: "[L]a Torpille sait rire et faire rire. Cette science des grands auteurs et des grands acteurs appartient à ceux qui ont pénétré toutes les profondeurs sociales" (*SMC*, 51). [The Torpedo knows how to laugh and make people laugh. This science of great authors and great actors belongs to those who have penetrated all the social profundities.] This comparison of Esther to great writers and actors not only explains Balzac's favorable representation of her but also recalls his equally sympathetic portrait of a high society seductress in *Les secrets de la princesse de Cadignan*. Just as a gift for acting can make a seductress admirable instead of diabolical in the Balzacian world, so too the criminal Jacques Collin is represented favorably in *La comédie humaine*, since, at the core, his talent is also that of the actor. Rather than adopting a critical attitude toward the social hypocrisy of role-playing, as does Sand, Balzac had a perspective on artificial behavior that can more nearly be described as that of fascination. Furthermore, his works are not lacking in great figures—"seducers" in every social domain—who accomplish their design thanks to their ability to play a role successfully.

It is precisely this talent for convincing acting that constitutes the mark of an accomplished seducer or seductress, whatever the particular textual manifestation may be. Regardless of Balzac's and Sand's different perspectives, the texts analyzed in this chapter all endow the instigator of a seduction with the qualities of an actor. However, once the seduction has begun its course, the partners fall prey to fantasies (both their own and the other's), so that neither person remains identical to what he or she was separately. A new dynamic takes over, granting each person an identity that exists solely in the space of seduction. Thus, seduction's unique characteristic could be described as its double status whereby it begins as one person's game of appearances; but once in the intersubjective domain, its artifice is experienced as reality.

3
Seduction's Power Games: Domination and the Social Order

The course a seduction takes is intimately related to the power relations of the players involved, since seduction often serves as a forum for one person to exert his or her will over another. In the popular imagination, a male seducer is the one most likely to be placed in this role, and among the seducers who have acquired mythic status, one of the greatest would have to be Don Juan. His reputation has only increased over the centuries thanks to the various tellings and retellings of his story; he has even been called "the patron saint of seducers."[1] Indeed, the Don Juan-esque seducer has become a type, a model of virility representing the masculine power to overcome any woman's resistance. This seducer "conquers" a woman, only to abandon her as he moves on to the next victim, and his very success—the fact that men strive to imitate him and women find him desirable—creates the impression that masculine domination is a natural and inevitable feature of erotic life. However, the power imbalance inherent to seduction does not necessarily favor the man, for this image that mirrors the distribution of power between men and women in society is not the only face of seduction.

This chapter will explore the contradictory relationship between seduction and domination as represented in Balzac's and Sand's seduction narratives; it will focus on the inner workings of desire and subjectivity for both the seducer and the seduced. How does the will to power get played out in seduction, and how does it affect each partner? How does gender factor into the distribution of power roles? Can seduction exist without some form of domination? Beginning with two texts that present Don Juan-esque tyrants in a seductive light, Balzac's *Un prince de la Bohème* and Sand's *Leone Leoni*, this chapter will next look at Sand's reversal of masculine domination in *Indiana*. Then, we will consider seduction's implication in the dissolution of polar oppositions in *La fille aux yeux d'or*. Seduction, as we will see, depends on an asymmetrical power relationship that, in the end, rarely proves equally satisfying to both partners.

Seduction provides a particularly fertile ground for exploring issues of gender and domination because of the ambiguity involved in its slippery nature. Certain representations of seduction reflect the human craving for clear-cut positions of seducer and seduced, the subject who desires and the other who is won over to that desire, active pursuit and passive capitulation. However, seduction can also problematize these terms as the seducer, falling under the sway of seduction, in turn becomes seduced, or as the two players oscillate between active pursuit and coy distancing. In effect, this second facet of seduction reflects another, contradictory, human fascination: that of experiencing the thrill of uncertainty, at least within controlled circumstances. Therefore, the theoretical principle of seduction reflects a mobile opposition in which the terms are not fixed.

While *masculine* domination does not constitute an inherent component of seduction, the answer to the question of what motivates such representations in Western culture is not difficult to imagine. Patriarchal society was built upon the domination of women by men, and images that glorify the seducer's ability to triumph over the will of his female victim help to perpetuate the appearance that patriarchy is a natural condition. Representations of masculine domination often present such an outcome as an inevitable conclusion, reinforcing the status quo. A prime example of this kind of representation is the legend of Don Juan in its traditional function. James Mandrell, whose study of the Don Juan figure provides an analysis of this seducer's role in Spanish literature from the seventeenth to the twentieth centuries, views the Don Juan story as "patriarchy's seductive attempt to represent its own aims."[2] Furthermore, Mandrell views the myth of Don Juan as "an elaboration of the ways in which the masculine subsumes the feminine."[3] Don Juan's seductions (in all his various guises) are linked to a bipolar configuration of the sexes that orders sexual difference as hierarchical complementarity: the relationship of feminine submission and masculine domination. Indeed, not only seduction but also the social order itself seems to flow naturally from this sexual division of the world. In an article on masculine domination, Pierre Bourdieu explains how the structure of society—a social construction—can appear rooted in natural causes: "[T]he blow that the social world exerts on each of its *subjects* consists in imprinting on its body . . . an actual program of perception, appreciation and action that, in its sexual and sexualizing dimension, as in all the others, functions as nature (cultivated, second), that is to say, with the imperious and (apparently) blind violence of a (socially constructed) impulse or fantasy."[4] Because of the seemingly natural workings of the social order, the way it represents masculine domination as its origin rather than something created by men to favor them, both men and women come to believe in its inevitability. Bourdieu characterizes these mechanisms of inevitability as a *violence symbolique*. While seduction must eschew all physical violence in order to remain true to its art, it is nonetheless embedded in this symbolic violence of the social order.

In examining the various ways Balzac and Sand depict the symbolic violence of domination, this chapter will show how these authors both reproduce and rewrite mythical notions of the seducer. Alongside traditional representations that glorify masculine domination, one also finds a critical vision—in Balzac's works as well as in Sand's—as this domination gets reversed or dissolves into uncertainty and indeterminacy, thereby exposing the contingent nature of the hierarchical relation of male to female. We will see that, paradoxically, although seduction can serve patriarchal ideology, as reflected in traditional representations of Don Juan, it is also a slippery term that can just as well be turned against the social order in ways that expose the phantasmic grounding of masculine domination.

Although none of the texts analyzed in this chapter directly involves a character named Don Juan, elsewhere both Balzac and Sand did represent this figure in ways that reexamine the seducer's mythic status. Because both writers reconsider Don Juan's relation to power and authority, a look at their characterizations of this seducer complements this analysis of sexual domination in their works. We have already seen Sand's rewriting of the Don Juan myth in *La marquise* in the previous chapter, and chapter 5 will address other Sandian demythifications of the Don Juan figure in *Lélia* and *Le Château des Désertes*. In Balzac's case, the sole text containing the character Don Juan is his philosophical study *L'élixir de longue vie*, and it actually sidelines Don Juan's identity as a seducer in order to focus on father-son relations and the desire for power and immortality.

In Balzac's version of the story, Don Juan has the possibility of using his father's longevity potion to bring him back to life once he dies. Instead, he disregards his father's instructions and decides to conserve the magic potion for himself, thereby committing a kind of patricide. Mandrell, in his study of Don Juan, reads the seducer's death at the hands of the Commander statue as providing patriarchy a means to reassert its values through the punishment of the wayward son,[5] but Balzac's version of the story performs the opposite ideological function. In Balzac's text, Don Juan's greed for his father's fortune displaces the preeminence of paternal authority, and this text also paints a negative picture of social institutions such as the church. Rather than representing patriarchal hegemony, then, Balzac's story of Don Juan (written in late 1830 after the July Revolution had further concretized the bourgeoisie's ascendancy over the aristocracy) depicts a society in which traditional lines of power and authority can no longer be taken for granted. In fact, Bernard Guyon, in an analysis of *L'élixir*, proposes a connection between this story and current events: "In the end, the best reading of this text would perhaps be to consider it as a testimony to the *disorder* into which young people of Balzac's generation found themselves plunged. . . ."[6] In *L'élixir*, Balzac does not specifically situate a *disorder* in the sexual arena, but this text does reveal the writer's use of private relations to figure larger social issues, a key feature of *La comédie humaine*.

A common theme in the narratives discussed in this chapter is the assimilation of seduction to a relation of erotic domination. Paradoxically, domination constitutes both a natural expression of the goals of seduction and an impediment to the play of pursuit and resistance that fuels the relation. Thus, when desire for domination forms the impetus of a seduction, it very likely will mark its demise as well. Seduction involves a dynamic energy created between two people when one person resists the other's advances. If the seduced person shared exactly the same feelings as the seducer and surrendered immediately, there would be no tension, and hence no seduction. In the effort to win the seduced person's acquiescence, the seducer may employ methods of manipulation and coercion, and may even try to exert power over the other through domination. The line between seduction and domination can be very fine indeed. The psychoanalysts Roger Dorey and Jessica Benjamin both offer perspectives that help explain how desire becomes entwined with a will to dominate and how power gets distributed in sexual relations, and their theories will help to shed light on Balzac's and Sand's texts.

In his article on relations of *emprise*, Dorey explains this term as a double action of appropriation and domination whereby one person seeks absolute power over the other:

> [I]n a relation of *emprise* it is always and very electively an issue of endangering the other as a desiring subject. . . . *Emprise* thus translates a very fundamental tendency toward the neutralization of the other's desire, that is to say, the reduction of all otherness, of all difference, of the destruction of all specificity; the goal is to return the other to the function and status of an object that can be entirely assimilated.[7]

A subject who seeks *emprise* over another needs to exert his or her agency at the expense of the other's subjectivity. This *emprise*, as Dorey notes, generally takes the form of a seduction, as the conquest is achieved by the use of charm and spells that create an illusion for the other. The seducer's strategy involves displaying a desire and trying to get the other to respond in kind. But unlike the model established in the previous chapter describing how a seducer performs an identity that is designed to elicit the other's desire, in the scenario described by Dorey the seducer aims to destroy the other's specific subjective desires and encourage only desires that correspond to his own.

While the notion of *emprise* explains how the will to power is exercised in the erotic realm, not all seductions take this extreme form. Indeed, Dorey does not describe *emprise* as an all-encompassing model for seduction; instead, it is an erotic perversion that has certain elements in common with seduction. Further, whereas certain myths fueled by masculine fantasies see the seducer as coming from a position of strength, Dorey states the opposite: "The relation of emprise . . . must be interpreted as a true *defensive formation* whose essential function is to hide *lack* as it is revealed in interaction with the other."[8] According to this model, behind the patriarchal model of sexual conquest lies the defensive reaction of an insecure subject, Don Juan's hidden vulnerability. In seduction, then, the motivation for staging an identity that will captivate the other stems from seducers' and seductresses' desire to enact their power and feel the surge of their agency as a compensation for their own insecurities.

Dorey seems implicitly to regard the subject and object of *emprise* as male and female, respectively, thereby reproducing the founding power asymmetry that, as Bourdieu and many feminist scholars have shown, patriarchal society has construed as natural. Dorey, however, never addresses this assumption about domination. Further, he examines only one dimension of the relationship, that of the dominant partner's psyche. In contrast, Benjamin takes an intersubjective approach to the problem of domination in *The Bonds of Love: Psychoanalysis, Feminism, and the Problem of Domination*. According to Benjamin, the value of an intersubjective model over the subject-object perspective traditionally used in psychoanalysis is that "this perspective observes that the other whom the self meets is also a self, a subject in his or her own right. It assumes that we are able and need to recognize that other subject as different and yet alike, as an other who is capable of sharing similar mental experience."[9] Her investigation of what is involved in the dynamics of domination and submission is useful to the study of seduction, because it helps us to understand how the asymmetrical power dynamics can seemingly serve both partners.

Benjamin's insights into domination and sadomasochistic relations reveal how and why certain configurations of desire, power, and subjectivity can cause a seduction to undermine itself. Further, her perspective highlights a significant feature of domination that is often obscured: this erotic problem is intricately related to issues of subjectivity. Recognizing that sadism and masochism are not limited to men and women, respectively, Benjamin explores how these positions have nonetheless become associated with masculinity and femininity, for she believes that psychoanalysis has gone too far in obscuring the role of gender. Benjamin proposes a reconfiguration of gender relations in which the dualistic and polarized vision of complementary differences that characterizes patriarchal society is replaced by one of mutual recognition. Although in the end I will suggest ways that Benjamin's theoretical model should be nuanced, her analysis of the dynamics of sadomasochism nonetheless offers a useful basis from which to consider the role of domination in seduction as well.

As Benjamin describes it, all subjects need to assert the self and to accept their dependency on the other who grants them recognition of their agency, and this fundamental subjective need for recognition involves a paradox: "It [recognition] allows the self to realize its agency and authorship in a tangible way. But such recognition can only come from an other whom we, in turn, recognize as a person in his or her own right. This struggle to be recognized by an other, and thus confirm our selves, was shown by Hegel to form the core of relationships of domination."[10] One of Benjamin's aims in *The Bonds of Love* is to contest Hegel's assertion that the tension of recognition must necessarily evolve into a complementary master-slave dynamic; she maintains that ideally the tension should persist. In this way, all subjects would be able to satisfy the dual needs of asserting agency and receiving recognition by others on whom they are dependent.

However, in sadomasochistic relations, which are modeled on the master-slave dynamic of domination, the subject's needs for both assertion and recognition become polarized; one partner assumes the position of self-assertion while the other serves only as an object on whom the powerful subject acts. The sadist gains self-affirmation as a separate subject by denying all dependency on the other, while the masochist, devoid of subjectivity, receives a sense of identity by his or her association with the master's power. While the polarization characteristic of sadomasochistic relations does serve each partner's subjective needs, albeit in a perverted way, it also leads to the breakdown of mutual tension, such that the relationship finally satisfies neither partner's need for self-recognition.[11] Applying this framework to Dorey's model confirms *emprise* as a perversion that harms not only the person configured as an object whose desires solely serve to confirm the dominant partner, but also the dominating seducer as well. When partners in a seduction become fixed in master-slave positions, the interest dissipates, as with the Don Juan-esque seducer and the victim he leaves behind.

The first two texts for comparison, *Un prince de la Bohème* and *Leone Leoni*, initially do display signs of mutual tension, although they quickly polarize into domination-submission. Because the timing and the emphasis are different, these texts differ from the traditional narrative of a woman seduced and abandoned, as seen in Don Juan's story, in which the seduction passes through the stages of pursuit and resistance, captivation, and then submission as the dénouement. Here Balzac and Sand run quickly through the initial stages of the couple's seduction in order to explore the power dynamics present when the relations are prolonged beyond consummation.

Un prince de la Bohème

Balzac represents the hero of *Un prince de la Bohème*, Count Charles-Édouard de La Palférine, in the tradition of mythical, dominating seducers. As in Dorey's notion of *emprise*, La Palférine's seduction of Claudine du Bruel resembles the work of a predator destroying his prey. In the opening pages of this novella, the portrait of La Palférine highlights his status as "prince de la Bohème," a title that corresponds not to a geographical location, but to a particular stratum of society. Bohemians were young men of talent who found themselves displaced in society after the French Revolution. Whereas Napoleon would have courted them in his time, they had been neglected by the ruling "gérontocratie" (*PB*, 808) of the Restoration. Bohemians were distinguished seducers, which is not surprising, since they made their way in life with bravado, projecting an image belied by their meager circumstances. In order to give a better idea of the kind of lover they represented, the narrator asks his interlocutor to imagine such diverse figures as Richardson's Lovelace, King Henri IV, Rousseau's Saint-Preux, and Chateaubriand's René, among others, all united into one person, forming an amalgam of libertinage and romanticism. Bohemians identified with the noble values of the ancien régime, as evidenced by the fact that La Palférine once refused a duel with a man of a lower social class and would not marry a young bourgeois woman whom he had gotten pregnant. Yet, such aristocratic airs only contributed to the displaced status of young Bohemians in postrevolutionary France.

Like the psychological type Dorey describes as seeking *emprise*, La Palférine's preoccupation with displaying his "superiority" suggests that on a certain level he himself is less than sure of it. His seduction of Claudine, formerly a dancer at the Opera but who has since raised her social status through a bourgeois marriage, provides him with opportunities to display his own powerful desirability. Initially, the impoverished count's aggressiveness is met with Claudine's coldness and efforts to rid herself of this uninvited escort. However, Claudine soon falls completely in love with her masterful seducer. In contrast, for him she remains nothing more than "une délicieuse maîtresse" (*PB*, 809) [a delightful mistress]. From the perspective of Benjamin's model of domination-submission, one sees that each partner does gain something from the relationship: La Palférine receives yet another chance to affirm his domination over women, while Claudine can feel pleased at the idea of being singled out by this man whose aggressiveness suggests a certain power. The text portrays domination as a seductive characteristic by showing Claudine's change of heart from skepticism to submissive love.

La Palférine quickly becomes bored by Claudine's submission, however. He displays a complete lack of respect for the woman who adores him when he tells his friends, "Il n'y a pas de lévrier, de basset, de caniche qui lui soit comparable pour la douceur, la soumission, la tendresse absolue" (*PB*, 819). [There is not a greyhound, a basset hound, or a poodle who compares to her in its sweetness, its submission, its absolute tenderness.] Claudine's submission to the master-seducer has dehumanized her in his eyes, such that he withholds acknowledgment of her subjectivity. And, true to Benjamin's model of the sadomasochistic relationship's lack of long-term viability, as the polarization of their roles becomes more and more absolute, Claudine's submission no longer serves to affirm La Palférine's identity; the esteem of this objectified person holds little value to him. Once the initial seduction expires when La Palférine and Claudine become locked into a master-slave relationship, La Palférine simply tries to amuse himself as best he can by creating situations that display his control over Claudine, such as making dates at odd hours and then canceling them without explanation. Although La Palférine's methods of torturing his victim involve no physical violence, they nevertheless constitute sadistic mental attacks and belong to the structures of *violence symbolique*. Without leaving visible marks, his treatment of Claudine undermines her subjectivity.

Balzac's story provides a prime context in which to explore a male perspective on the psychology of feminine submission. In Claudine's letters to La Palférine, Balzac represents her as a willing victim, someone conscious of the fact that her complete submission leaves her without an identity of her own. She even dehumanizes herself by her description as "cette chose à toi qui se nomme Claudine" (*PB*, 821) [this thing of yours named Claudine]. Claudine's behavior may appear utterly inexplicable, but Benjamin's study provides insights that help us understand it. Benjamin writes of the slave, "[I]t is the master's rational, calculating, even instrumentalizing attitude that excites submission. . . . The pleasure, for both partners, is in his mastery."[12] The masochistic submission that leads Claudine to tell La Palférine, "[A]près t'avoir aimé, on ne peut plus, on ne doit plus aimer personne" (*PB*, 821) [After having loved you, one can no longer, one must no longer, love anyone] reflects a change in her disposition from previous relationships in which she dominated, for she also refers to herself, saying, "moi si impérieuse, si fière ailleurs, moi qui faisais trotter des ducs, des princes, des aides de camp de Charles X" (*PB*, 821). [I so imperious, so proud elsewhere, I who held the leash of dukes, princes, aides to Charles X.] Through its presentation of the submissive position Claudine assumes in relation to La Palférine, the text suggests that she could not help but recognize La Palférine's "superiority" in matters of seductive domination. Because La Palférine's control is so impressively absolute—surpassing even Claudine's own dominating instincts—Claudine actually *wants* to submit to him.

Finally, Balzac finds a way out of this sadomasochistic cycle when he has La Palférine move on to a new victim, and the conclusion of this text goes even further in glorifying the sadistic seducer. Balzac constructed *Un prince* as a *mise en abyme* where the writer Dinah de la Baudraye reads one of her stories, based on "true" events, to another writer-character of the *Comédie humaine*, Raoul Nathan. In the inner frame, Dinah's story depicts Nathan telling the tale of the relations between Claudine and La Palférine to Béatrix de Rochefide. Although Dinah had left the story of the inner frame without a neat conclusion, saying, "Je ne crois pas aux dénouements" (*PB*, 838) [I do not believe in dénouements], Nathan informs her in the outer frame that he has an ending to this tale of domination: "La marquise de Rochefide est folle de Charles-Édouard. Mon récit avait piqué sa curiosité" (*PB*, 838). [The Marquise de Rochefide is crazy about Charles-Édouard. My story piqued her curiosity.] Thus, Nathan's narration planted the seeds for Béatrix's own seduction by La Palférine, a story that forms part of the plot of the novel *Béatrix*.

That this tale of a tyrannically dominating seducer could lead to a second seduction by exciting another woman's interest in this man underscores how Balzac promoted the sadomasochistic dynamic as one desired by women and presented masculine domination as seductive. Elsewhere in *La comédie humaine* Balzac also displays phantasmic ideas about a feminine fascination with forceful men, as when the narrator of *La fille aux yeux d'or* writes of men who have "une sécurité d'action, une certitude de pouvoir, une fierté de regard, une conscience léonine qui réalise pour les femmes le type de force qu'elles rêvent *toutes*" (*FYO*, 1085; emphasis mine) [a security of action, a powerful certainty, a proud gaze, a leonine conscience that realizes for women the type of power they *all* dream of]. In explicitly stating that *all* women desire dominating men, Balzac suggests here that women are masochistic by nature. Further, in *Un prince* he presents Claudine's situation as a progression from willful independence to willing submission. Whether consciously or not, these Balzacian texts reflect the symbolic violence of patriarchal social structures and masculine self-promotion, and the *mise en abyme* structure of *Un prince* highlights with particular acuity the process whereby repetition can make a phenomenon come to seem inevitable and natural.

Leone Leoni

The tenuous status of female subjectivity is at the heart of Sand's representation of a similarly sadomasochistic relationship in *Leone Leoni.* To readers familiar with Sand's polemical stance on feminine submission in her first novel, *Indiana*, this novel could appear surprising for its straightforward and uncritical portrait of the masochistic heroine Juliette. Commenting on *Leone Leoni* nearly twenty years after she had written it, Sand intimated that she had simply undertaken to write a realistic narrative: "Quelle moralité voudrait-on faire ressortir d'une fiction que chacun sait être fort possible dans le monde de la réalité?"[13] [What moral would one like to take from a fiction that everyone knows to be highly possible in the real world?] Although Sand's interests distinguish her depiction of sadomasochistic dynamics from Balzac's *Un prince*, a misogynistic story whose conclusion in a second seduction effectively glorifies masculine domination, Sand does not deny the dominating Leoni's seductive assets in this novel that concludes with Juliette leaving the *honnête homme* Bustamente (who wishes to marry her) in order to return to her renegade seducer. Leoni, like Balzac's Bohemian prince, takes advantage of the women who love him, and he dominates by projecting an air of superiority his actual circumstances do not support. No one he meets suspects the reality of his situation: that his gambling has destroyed his fortune. When he arrives in Brussels, he quickly succeeds in gaining entry to the highest—and wealthiest—social circles by charming everyone he meets: "On l'écoutait avec enthousiasme, on lui obéissait aveuglément; on croyait en lui comme en un prophète [...]" (*LL*, 23). [People listened to him enthusiastically, they blindly obeyed him, they believed in him as a prophet. . . .] Like La Palférine, Leoni has bolstered his image thanks to the aristocracy's social cachet, and the fact that he actually has no money does not change the way others react to his seductive appearance. But whereas Balzac portrays Bohemians in a sympathetic light, presenting them largely as victims of a government whose politics he criticizes, Sand's seducer is only a victim of his own gambling habit.

Sand, like Balzac, uses a framed narrative structure to present her story. During most of the novel, Juliette acts as an interior narrator as she tells Bustamente the story of her relationship with Leoni from the perspective of her position of abandonment. Bustamente himself suggests this activity as a kind of talking cure, a means of helping her to realize that her love is "si misérablement placé" (*LL,* 11) [so miserably placed]. Significantly, Sand includes background information on Juliette's early family relations, providing readers with an invaluable tool for illuminating Juliette's later behavior. In particular, Juliette tells how her mother raised her not as a separate subject but as an extension of herself:

> Quant à ma mère, elle éprouvait comme un double orgeueil à se montrer et à monter sa fille; j'étais un reflet, ou pour mieux dire une partie d'elle-même, de sa beauté, de sa richesse; son bon goût brillait dans ma parure; ma figure, qui ressemblait à la sienne, lui rappelait, ainsi qu'aux autres, la fraîcheur à peine alterée de sa première jeunesse; de sorte qu'en me voyant marcher, toute fluette, à côté d'elle, elle croyait se voir deux fois [...] (*LL*, 14)
>
> [As for my mother, she felt a double pride in showing off herself and in showing off her daughter; I was a reflection, or to put it better, a part of herself, of her beauty, of her richness; her good taste showed in my appearance; my face, which resembled hers, reminded her, as well as others, of the barely altered freshness of her youth; such that, in seeing me walk next to her, all slender, she believed she was seeing herself twice. . . .]

Thus deprived of a sense of her own identity, Juliette seems especially susceptible to masochistic submission. Not only did Juliette's skewed relationship with her mother prevent her from learning to balance separateness with dependency—to borrow Benjamin's terms—but also it gave her no means of developing a sense of herself as a subject of desire. Although Sand represents her heroine in a polarized master-slave relationship, she does not do so without suggesting social reasons, related to her upbringing, as to why Juliette remains so enthralled by Leoni's seductive charms even though he mistreats her. By showing the environmental influences that shaped Juliette's identity, Sand's text represents submission as a socially constructed gender trait, whereas Balzac's text implies that submissiveness is inherently female.

On Leoni's side of the picture, his desire to seduce Juliette appears motivated largely by the kind of *emprise* that, according to Dorey, seeks to stamp out—yet lightly, through charm—any signs of another's will that do not complement the seducer's own desires. Like Claudine with La Palférine, Juliette initially resists Leoni's advances. The daughter of a wealthy jeweler in Brussels, she meets the noble Venetian Leoni at a ball. Sensing Leoni's disdain for the bourgeoisie, Juliette proudly refuses his request to dance, and her coldness inspires Leoni to view her as a challenge worth pursuing. Leoni's highly seductive nature has led him to count on always getting exactly what he wants, and Juliette quickly finds herself unable to resist his seductions.

In a way that recalls the boredom experienced by La Palférine after the tension of the initial seductiveness in his relations with Claudine has dissipated, once Leoni has gained Juliette's submission and spent the money raised from the sale of her father's jewels that they were wearing when he abducted her from a costume ball, the incurable gambler begins pursuing other interests. The reader witnesses Leoni's willingness to use even the most unscrupulous means to further his gambling habit, as when Juliette watches helplessly as Leoni moves to Milan and seduces a rich, aging princess with the aim of inheriting her fortune upon her death. Here and in other instances, Leoni makes no effort to hide his intimate relations with other women. Sand's text also shows quite clearly, however, that the sadistic seducer remains partially dependent on Juliette as a submissive object who affirms his own sense of self. At the slightest mention by Juliette that she would like to leave him, he desperately works to convince her to stay. Thus, despite the intense polarization of their relationship, Juliette has not yet lost all of her leverage. In depicting her dominating seducer, Sand reveals the protagonist's subjective fragility, a weakness that Balzac does not display in his own character, La Palférine.

Sand uses this narrative of masculine domination to launch her own critique of patriarchal society and the lack of affirmative choices it accorded nineteenth-century women. At the conclusion of the text, when Juliette has finished recounting the story of her relations with Leoni, she is faced with both an offer to marry Bustamente and the possibility of returning to her seducer. Neither option, however, constitutes an ideal choice, as both reflect the limitations society imposed on women. Bustamente tries to tempt Juliette with social legitimacy and the title of "doña Bustamente" but he also reveals a darker side when he tells her, "Une femme capable d'aimer et de souffrir comme tu avais fait était la réalisation de tous mes rêves" *(LL*, 124). [A woman capable of loving and suffering like you was the realization of all my dreams.] The seemingly upstanding gentleman is thus not so very different from the dominating seducer, for both seek the woman's submissiveness. Further, Bustamente's comment differentiates him from

Sand's portraits of ideal mates, for her ideal is based on equality, not subservience. In his reading of this novel, Larry Riggs points to the Sadian overtones in Bustamente's attitude, and aspects of this character certainly do resemble the portrait of the dominating sadist as described by Benjamin.[14] In this text, Sand reinforces her critique of the institution of marriage found in so many of her novels.

Though Leoni and his magnetism prove to hold final sway over Juliette, this novel hardly represents the kind of glorification of masculine domination seen in Balzac's text. The fact that the novel closes with Bustamente watching Leoni and Juliette drift off to sea, coupled with Juliette's prior figurative comments to Bustamente about sensing an imminent storm in her life, mitigates the seducer's success and gives the novel a different ideological tone than that created by La Palférine's seduction of Béatrix at the conclusion of *Un prince*. In a letter to Bustamente in which Juliette explains her return to Leoni, she writes, "Je ne suis qu'une malheureuse que la fatalité entraîne et qui ne peut s'arrêter" (*LL*, 128). [I am only an unfortunate wretch led by fate and who cannot stop herself.] Whereas Riggs concludes that Juliette and Leoni's relationship is "more affirmative than any available alternative," I would hesitate to use the word affirmation in this context at all, for it seems that Sand was more nearly depicting an impasse.[15] Elsewhere, Sand does not hesitate to have some of her more strong-willed heroines choose to remain alone rather than in a relationship that does not accord them dignity and equality. The eponymous heroines Isidora, the Marquise de R... , and Lavinia all fit this pattern. In the short story "Lavinia," for instance, the Don Juan-esque seducer Lionel fails in his attempt to reconquer Lavinia, a woman he had seduced and abandoned many years in the past, and, as Sand presents it, Lavinia's refusal is a positive choice based on self-definition:

> [J]e hais le mariage, je hais tous les hommes, je hais les engagements éternels, les promesses, les projets, l'avenir arrangé à l'avance par des contrats et des marchés dont le destin se rit toujours. Je n'aime plus que les voyages, la rêverie, la solitude, le bruit du monde, pour le traverser et en rire, puis la poésie pour supporter le passé, et Dieu pour espérer l'avenir.[16]
>
> [I hate marriage, I hate all men, I hate eternal obligations, promises, plans, the future arranged in advance by contracts and deals at which destiny always laughs. I no longer like anything but trips, reverie,

solitude, the noises of the world, to cross it and laugh at it, then poetry to put up with the past, and God to hope for the future.]

In contrast to Lavinia's affirmation of her own subjective desires, Juliette claims a complete lack of agency, saying that she simply had no will to resist Leoni's magnetism. She explains to Bustamente, "[U]ne main invisible dispose de moi et me jette malgré moi dans les bras de cet homme" (*LL*, 127). [An invisible hand rules me and throws me into this man's arms in spite of myself.] In this text, Sand dispels any sense of glory surrounding the seducer's accomplishment by highlighting its dependency on Juliette's weak sense of self. Significantly, the tale of seduction and passion in *Leone Leoni* has a unique position among Sand's works and does not form part of a pattern.

Both Sand's novel and Balzac's *Un prince de la Bohème* depict the seductiveness of the storytelling situation through narrative frames, but to different ends. In Balzac's text Nathan tells a story to Béatrix, and she gets seduced by the subject of the story, La Palférine, identifying with the submissive female position. In Sand's text, however, the gender roles are reversed. Not only does she allow her character to tell her own story rather than using a third person, but her internal narrator is a woman. Although Juliette's actions toward Leoni demonstrate weakness and submission, Sand places her in a position of power as the one who crafts her own story. Her interlocutor's reaction to the story is similar to that of Béatrix, except that Bustamente experiences a kind of seduction through identification with the male position. His declaration of admiration for Juliette's ability to love even in suffering suggests that he identifies with Leoni's domination and would perhaps even like to play such a role himself. The "talking cure" initially suggested by Bustamente effectively expunges from Juliette any interest she may have had in accepting his marriage proposal. In *Un prince*, the end of one seduction simultaneously serves as the inauguration of a new one, thereby placing the male seducer in a prominent light and signaling a cycle of seduction and abandonment that glorifies the Don Juan-esque seducer. Sand's text, on the other hand, leaves the narrative seduction incomplete, unfulfilled. Bustamente reacts as if seduced by Juliette's story; but he does not succeed in obtaining the object of his affection. He even resorts to violence, plotting to regain Juliette by ending Leoni's life, but fails in this endeavor as well. Sand thereby minimizes the effects of masculine domination in her text. The different ends met by the textual seduction in each case suggest a more fundamental opposition between Balzac's and Sand's attitudes toward power and erotic domination.

In comparing *Un prince de la Bohème* and *Leone Leoni*, we have seen that a seduction's erotic goals—the achievement of the other's sexual submission—are often indistinguishable from the seducer's desire for power, and that sex represents an arena in which to exert power over another. The seducer's need to display his power actually signals a weak, imbalanced subject, suggesting that the power of seduction is perhaps an ironic one. According to Baudrillard, "To seduce is to become fragile. To seduce is to weaken. It is by our fragility that we seduce, never by powers or strong signs. It is our fragility that we put into play in seduction, and it is what gives it this power. We seduce by our death, by our vulnerability, by the emptiness that haunts us."[17] That seduction constitutes the redeployment of fragility and subjective weakness will become even clearer in the ensuing analysis of *Indiana*.

Indiana: Turning the Tables on Masculine Domination

In her first novel, *Indiana*, Sand uses fairly traditional plot elements, finding inspiration in the melancholy *mal du siècle* of romanticism as well as in realism's preoccupation with drawing inspiration from contemporary society. Even as she adopts elements that can be traced to works of such diverse writers as Chateaubriand and Balzac, she shapes them into an original, innovative, and highly personal work of fiction.[18]

While both *Leone Leoni* and *Un prince* concentrate primarily on the sadomasochistic dynamics instituted by the seducer's *emprise* over his victim rather than on the initial seduction itself, in *Indiana* Sand's seducer never actually succeeds in getting the heroine to the point of physical possession. By staging the seducer Raymon's failure, this novel provides an image of seduction other than that of the successful Don Juan. This text's demystification of masculine domination, however, does not promote a simple reversal of power positions. Through the representation of Raymon's continued efforts at seduction, the various ploys he adopts and the transformation of his feelings for Indiana, this narrative highlights the diverse feelings that motivate the desire-to-seduce when it is informed by a struggle for *emprise*.

Further, this story of seduction takes a nontraditional approach by illuminating the effects masculine domination wreaks on male subjectivity as well as on women. In her preface to the 1842 edition of *Indiana*, Sand reflected on this aspect of her first novel: "[L]e malheur de la femme entraîne celui de l'homme, comme celui de l'esclave entraîne celui du maître, et j'ai cherché à le montrer dans *Indiana*" (*Ind*, 46). [The unhappiness of women leads to that of men, as that of the slave leads to that of the master, and I tried to show this in *Indiana*.] Though Sand begins her novel by presenting a highly traditional configuration of relations between the sexes, the course of events shows that she does so only with the intention of overthrowing masculine domination and offering the example of a relation based on respect and reciprocity.

The text introduces Raymon as a successful seducer who has numerous conquests to show for having made seduction his primary occupation in life. Sand shows how Raymon's interest in women arises not only from sparks of physical attraction, as one might assume, but also from the affirmation of his sense of self that he receives through his successes. Raymon's seduction of Indiana's Creole servant Noun has satisfied his vanity and confirmed his reputation as a seducer by giving him "le petit triomphe de l'arracher à vingt rivaux" (*Ind*, 74) [the small triumph of tearing her away from twenty rivals]. Challenge definitely drives Raymon, for once he meets Indiana he loses interest in Noun; he is more excited by the obstacles this new seduction presents. The fact that Raymon continues to pursue his seduction of Indiana even after the initial erotic attraction has dissipated signals that desire for the other is only part of his motivation. Like Isidora, who merges with the role she enacts through performance, Raymon, we are told, is passionate about this seduction like an author for his subject, and when he is in Indiana's presence he loses the ability to distinguish between artifice and reality (*Ind*, 143). His objective strays from an interest in the person Indiana and becomes tied up in his own fantasies and sense of self-worth. Glory, rather than pleasure, motivates his conquest. Therefore, any failure in the domain of seduction signifies a symbolically violent blow to Raymon's identity.

Raymon receives just such a blow when he fails to live up to his self-image as a seducer. In a key scene, he goes to Indiana's room, determined to spend the night with her "afin de ne pas être un sot à mes propres yeux" (*Ind*, 181) [in order not to appear a fool in my own eyes]. The only thing that prevents him from carrying out his seduction is Indiana's intimation that it would be the equivalent of raping her. Although the seducer may use strategies of domination, seduction must be achieved through an artfulness that inspires the other's acquiescence rather than by physical violence. As a consequence of this failure, Raymon's desire-to-seduce becomes even further distorted:

> Alors il jura, dans son dépit, qu'il triompherait d'elle; il ne le jura plus par orgueil, mais par vengeance. Il ne s'agissait plus pour lui de conquérir un bonheur, mais de punir un affront; de posséder une femme, mais de la réduire. Il jura qu'il serait son maître, ne fût-ce qu'un jour, et qu'ensuite il l'abandonnerait pour avoir le plaisir de la voir à ses pieds. (*Ind*, 200)

> [Thus he swore, in his resentment, that he would triumph over her; he no longer swore it by pride, but by vengeance. It was no longer an issue of conquering happiness but of punishing an affront; not of possessing a woman, but of destroying her. He swore that he would be her master, if only for a day, and then he would abandon her for the pleasure of seeing her at his feet.]

Raymon's state of mind here resembles the situation of one who seeks *emprise*, for he does not want to admit that his chosen object of desire could have wishes other than those that conform to his own. And, as Benjamin's model has shown us, Raymon seeks to deny any dependence on the other in order to exert his all-powerful self.

Despite the resistance with which Indiana has met her seducer's advances, a submissive role is not foreign to her, for it is the one she has played in both childhood and marriage. However, rather than represent Indiana's "systématique soumission" (*Ind*, 210) [systematic submission] as natural, Sand's narrator adopts a critical stance and even attaches some of the blame for Delmare's cruelty toward his wife on the too-passive Indiana: "[I]l y avait, nous l'avouerons, beaucoup de sa propre faute" (*Ind*, 207). [Much of it, we admit, was her own fault.] Indiana's relations with both Raymon and Delmare are fueled by the kind of master-slave dynamic described by Benjamin. From the slave's perspective, abandonment constitutes a fate worse than any suffering imposed by the dominating lover, as when Juliette even prefers to die rather than survive the loss of Leoni. In *Indiana*, the heroine and her seducer are oddly bound to one another by a distorted search for recognition.

Subsumed in a dynamics of domination-submission, Indiana and Raymon's seduction creates an unusual combination of pursuit and refusal of one another. When Raymon determines that he will possess Indiana before he loses his opportunity because of her upcoming move to Ile Bourbon with her husband, his impatient desperation causes his artfulness to wane, and Indiana once again stops short his seductive advances. The narrator squarely criticizes Raymon's strategy, or lack thereof, when he says, "S'il eût porté l'art jusqu'à prolonger vingt-quatre heures de plus la situation où Indiana était venue se risquer, elle était à lui peut-être" (*Ind*, 221). [If he had carried art to the point of prolonging for twenty-four hours more the situation where Indiana had come to risk herself, she perhaps would have been his.] However, the fact that Raymon's self-esteem as a seducer is on the line means that he cannot abandon his project even after Indiana moves away. The successful love letters that Raymon sends to Indiana on the Ile Bourbon show that he knows exactly how to get this woman to perform his will, for when she returns to him in France it is as a slave speaking to her master: "Dispose de moi, de mon sang, de ma vie; je suis à toi corps et âme. J'ai fait trois mille lieues pour t'appartenir, pour te dire cela; prends-moi, je suis ton bien, tu es mon maître" (*Ind*, 297). [Dispose of me, of my blood, of my life; I belong to you body and soul. I crossed three thousand leagues to belong to you, to tell you that; take me, I am your property, you are my master.] Indiana's words suggest that she has become the selfless "thing" existing only for the other, as Benjamin describes the sadomasochistic relation. Indiana's change of heart results from her naive belief in Raymon's written declarations of love: as long as she believes Raymon loves her, she is ready to be submissive. It is the only form of love she has known.

However, during the period of Indiana's absence from France, two highly significant events have occurred, one in the public sphere and one in the private. Not only does Raymon's marriage cause him to abandon interest in his project of luring Indiana back to France just at the point when she decides to return, but also the July 1830 Revolution that brought Louis-Philippe to the throne has swept in a new era of bourgeois influence. Throughout the novel, Sand's narrator has not hidden his contempt for Indiana's submission and credulity. Although she never fully succumbs to Raymon, thereby assuring his failure at seduction, she is hardly the model person to teach him a lesson. Instead, Sand reintroduces the character Laure de Nangy in order to bring the seducer to his knees. A scene toward the beginning of the novel in which Laure briefly appears already prefigures her ultimate role. In a conversation at a ball in which several women discuss Raymon's charms, Laure says, "Si c'est un Lovelace, tant pis [...]; je ne peux pas supporter les gens que le monde aime" (*Ind*, 79). [If he is a Lovelace, too bad . . . ; I cannot put up with people the world loves.] An older countess responds with words intended to offer the young woman the fruit of her worldly experience: "Ne parlez pas ainsi [...]; vous ne savez pas ce que c'est, ici, qu'un homme qui veut être aimé" (*Ind*, 79). [Do not speak that way . . . ; you do not know what it means, here, a man who wants to be loved.] Whereas the older woman's remark suggests she believes in the inevitability of masculine domination, Laure lets it be known that she does not share this worldview: "Vous croyez donc qu'il ne s'agit pour eux que de vouloir?" (*Ind*, 79). [You believe, then, that it is only an issue of what they want?] Indirectly declaring that a man's *vouloir* is not synonymous with *pouvoir*, Laure suggests that she plans to be the one in a position of dominance. Laure's words are not just the idle talk of an idealistic young woman, for she does accomplish her will with Raymon once he becomes her husband. Thus, when Indiana finds Raymon in her old bedroom and offers herself to him, he is no longer in a position to accept her. Laure exults in this reversal of the seducer's fortune, "triomphant en secret de la position d'infériorité et de dépendance où cet incident venait de placer son mari vis-à-vis d'elle" (*Ind*, 298) [secretly triumphing from the position of inferiority and dependence that this incident had placed her husband in relation to her]. Although Raymon now knows a relationship of domination-submission, this time he is the one being dominated.

Sand represents Laure's domination over Raymon in such a way as to reverse both traditional gender roles and the distribution of power within the household. By plotting the simultaneous occurrence of the social and domestic revolutions, Sand highlights the political nature of relations between the sexes. Laure's success takes on added significance due to her social status: although she was born into a poor, noble family, as a young orphan she was adopted by a wealthy industrial capitalist, a self-made man who symbolizes the new power structures of the nineteenth century. Laure thus represents the class that benefited the most from the 1830 revolution, and her domination over her husband signals a new era in which nobles were increasingly eclipsed by powerful members of the upper bourgeoisie. Indeed, a nobleman's *vouloir* no longer carried the same force as during the ancien régime. Accordingly, Raymon discovers that while libertinage as a way of life may have succeeded during the eighteenth-century, it does not work in postrevolutionary France. In placing her husband in an inferior position, Laure gains a victory for all female victims of seduction and abandonment, including Indiana's servant, Noun.

While Sand's engineering of her seducer's failure through this domestic revolution does achieve vengeance for women by offering an image to counter those that glorify the dominating seducer, this situation does not alleviate the problem of domination, since vengeance only fuels the cycle of violence. Modern feminists such as Benjamin have warned against any solution that offers no more than a straightforward reversal of existing power structures: "The task is more complex; it is to transcend the opposition of the two spheres by formulating a less polarized relationship between them."[19] In fact, Sand—ahead of her time just like so many of her characters—seemed to realize the pitfalls of such solutions; hence her decision to take her novel beyond the reversal represented by Laure's domination of Raymon. Rather than offering the reversed configuration as the culmination of her story, she continues the text and has Indiana discover how she had underestimated Ralph, the cousin and protector who has loved her all along. With Ralph, Indiana discovers a new vision of love. It is different from the submission she has known in the past, for it is based on mutual respect. Whereas Raymon's identity depended on his ability to dominate others, Ralph "avait appris à se connaître lui-même. Il s'était fait un ami de son propre cœur [...]" (*Ind*, 177) [had learned to know himself. He had made friends with his own heart . . .]. In part 4 of the novel, Sand uses the love between Ralph and Indiana to present a positive vision of relations between the sexes that supersedes those of domination-submission found in the first three parts of the text.

Ralph and Indiana's position on the Ile Bourbon can be viewed as a kind of exile, a word Isabelle Naginski uses in her analysis of the text.[20] Although not completely withdrawn from society, they are very much at its margins in their island paradise, especially since their project of buying freedom for the island's slaves has earned them the distrust and ill will of the other European colonists. Sand's use of withdrawal or distancing from society in order to promote a different social vision is not unique to *Indiana*. In the previous chapter we saw how the Marquise de R... chose to preserve her self and her passion in their integrity by refusing a physical relationship with the actor Lélio, and how Isidora fled Paris to Italy after her failure to redefine her identity free from the social stigma of prostitution. In *Indiana*, Sand's fictional depiction of contemporary society also reveals that the ways of the world are antithetical to the values embodied in her positive characters, such that a self-imposed exile constitutes the most viable arrangement.

Are we to read this utopian ending, with its central focus on the new love forged between Ralph and Indiana and the ethical way of life they have adopted on the Ile Bourbon, as Sand's vision of ideal love? In particular, is this relationship and the love that grounds it platonic or of a sexual nature? The text gives no clear indications that Indiana's fraternal love for Ralph has evolved into something more passionate. Just before Ralph and Indiana take their failed suicidal plunge at Bernica, they kiss, and the narrator notes, "[S]ans doute il y a dans un amour qui part du cœur une puissance plus soudaine que dans les ardeurs d'un désir éphémère" (*Ind*, 330). [There is probably in a love that comes from the heart a more sudden force than the ardors of an ephemeral desire.] Sand effectively posits an opposition between benevolent love and destructive desire. With the punishment of the libertine seducer Raymon through his submission in marriage and the death of the oppressive husband Delmare, this novel serves as a denunciation of men's erotic domination of women.

Sand seems to be saying, in this text and so many others, that the only way to avoid erotic domination, at least in the social circumstances of nineteenth-century France, is to avoid passion. One of her strongest examples of the damaging effects of a blinding desire is Juliette's relationship with Leoni in *Leone Leoni*, and Sand rarely seeks to give her heroines fulfillment in a relationship that combines the ardors of desire with heartfelt love. Given her attitude toward desire, it is not surprising that seduction, in Sand's works, is almost inevitably condemned; devoid of any redeeming value, it is a negative example she can contrast to ideal love. Just as she opposes the artifice of theatricality, as we saw in the previous chapter, so too she allows her moral opposition to domination to guide her as she plots her narrative in *Indiana*. Balzac, on the other hand, has a different perspective on desire and domination.

Polarity Ungrounded in *La fille aux yeux d'or*

In *La fille aux yeux d'or*, Balzac creates a setting for erotic relations that play with masculine and feminine positions. A seemingly straightforward opposition gets contaminated, and subversive ambiguity takes over as the reigning principle. Here domination and submission do not take the path of gender complementarity traditionally imagined for these polar opposites in patriarchal ideology. Instead, the partners Henri de Marsay and Paquita Valdes oscillate between dominant and submissive positions. This phenomenon is even prefigured by the text's opening section on the different spheres of Parisian society, where the narrator carefully differentiates between hierarchical circles only to admit later that these categories are plagued by a seepage from one to the other, as some people rise on the social ladder while others fall. Moreover, the two coveted objects of desire in this society, gold and pleasure, are also assigned a changing relationship in rhetorical terms; first it is "l'or et le plaisir" (*FYO*, 1040) [gold and pleasure], then "le plaisir et l'or" (*FYO*, 1045) [pleasure and gold]. The theoretical principles of the prologue establish a link between it and the seduction narrative that follows, for throughout this text Balzac proceeds by evoking contrasting terms whose opposition proves unstable.

Early in the story, many elements suggest that the reader is presented with a traditional tale of the Don Juan-esque seducer who envisions seduction as a game of conquest and Paquita as "yet another" victim to add to his list (*FYO*, 1064). Success has left de Marsay bored, and, in a situation that recalls Sand's Raymon de Ramière, the obstacles surrounding de Marsay's project to seduce Paquita seem to excite him more than the woman herself. After first meeting her in the Tuileries gardens, he does not immediately follow Paquita's carriage to determine her identity; rather, he lets the enigma surrounding his new erotic interest subsist. When his servant, Laurent, informs him of the tremendous obstacles blocking the path to Paquita, de Marsay is overjoyed by the challenge this project presents him. He thus proceeds in his pursuit of Paquita as if he were cast in "l'éternelle vieille comédie" (*FYO*, 1071) [the eternal old play] of triangular rivalry with another man. And, through the use of military rhetoric, the narrator links this text to mythical representations of masculine seduction.

However, de Marsay's own behavior suggests that he is not quite the dominating seducer the text sometimes represents him to be. Further, the narrator's physical description of him evokes the image of an effeminate man by its notation of such details as "une peau de jeune fille, un air doux et modeste, une taille fine et aristocratique, de fort belles mains" (*FYO*, 1057) [a young girl's skin, a sweet and modest air, a thin and aristocratic waist, very beautiful hands]. In describing his first encounter with Paquita to his friend Paul de Manerville, de Marsay positions himself as her object of desire, a status most often gendered feminine. For instance, he envisions Paquita as the image that inspired the artist who created *La femme caressant sa chimère* and calls her "cette fille dont je suis la chimère" (*FYO*, 1065) [this girl whose chimera I am], further objectifying himself. However, Paquita does not continuously occupy the dominant position in de Marsay's fantasies, for in this same conversation he describes how Paquita's expression seemed to tell him submissively, "Prends-moi, je suis à toi" (*FYO*, 1064). [Take me, I belong to you.] Thus, for this seducer, domination and submission are not mutually exclusive principles.

The series of three meetings de Marsay has with Paquita involves a vacillation between conventional masculine and feminine sexual roles; de Marsay and Paquita alternately adopt the positions of domination and surrender. In effect, their relationship is marked by the kind of mutual tension Daniel Sibony evokes as a feature of seduction when he writes, "[I]n seduction, one cannot say who is the seducer and who is the seduced, who began and who is at the beginning. . . ."[21] The first time de Marsay goes to see Paquita, he does so motivated by a desire to obtain an *emprise* over her. The narrator paints the portrait of a powerfully dominating man: "De Marsay exerçait le pouvoir autocratique du despote oriental. [. . .] Henri pouvait ce qu'il voulait dans l'intérêt de ses plaisirs et de ses vanités" (*FYO*, 1084–85). [De Marsay exercised the autocratic power of the oriental despot. . . . Henri could do whatever he wanted in the interest of his pleasure and his vanity.] However, in their second meeting, the dynamics of control and submission have subtly shifted, a difference signaled at the very moment de Marsay submits to being blindfolded and passively led to Paquita. Rather than a true reversal, though, their roles are marked by a mutual give-and-take. At one moment, de Marsay appears to have regained the master's position, with Paquita as his submissive slave: "Comme un aigle qui fond sur sa proie, il la prit à plein corps, l'assit sur ses genoux, et sentit avec une indicible ivresse la voluptueuse pression de cette fille dont les beautés si grassement développées l'enveloppèrent doucement" (*FYO*, 1089). [Like an eagle that pounces on its prey, he took her in his arms, seated her on his knees, and felt with an inexpressible intoxication the voluptuous pressure of this girl whose generously developed beauty sweetly enveloped him.] But no sooner has he seemingly established his position of dominance than he senses that he is not the reigning master in his lover's boudoir. Paquita reasserts herself by asking him repeatedly, "Veux-tu me plaire?" (*FYO*, 1089, 1091). [Do you want to please me?] Her fancy of dressing de Marsay as a woman adds a gender-bending twist to the tale of erotic domination. In the course of this exchange, de Marsay comes to the realization that Paquita represents a coexistence of contradictory terms: "l'union si bizarre du mystérieux et du réel, de l'ombre et de la lumière, de l'horrible et du beau, du plaisir et du danger, du paradis et de l'enfer" (*FYO*, 1091) [the strange union of mysterious and real, of shadow and light, of the horrible and beauty, of pleasure and danger, of paradise and hell]. If the text emphasizes Paquita's hybrid nature as someone who is virginal without, somehow, being innocent, one cannot forget that de Marsay's masculinity has certainly not been homogeneous itself. Thus, Balzac does not portray a seduction that simply subverts masculine domination, but instead offers a more complicated picture.

Balzac's representation of the third meeting between de Marsay and Paquita reveals a divergence from the traditional eroticism of seduction that serves to bolster the seducer's subjectivity. The intensity of this encounter causes de Marsay to lose the control of his senses he had previously fought so hard to maintain. At this point, eroticism seems to have exerted itself above and beyond the will of the people involved, taking them past a game of rational control to a point where neither one dominates. However, de Marsay receives a startling blow when Paquita, looking at him, cries out "Oh! Mariquita!" (*FYO*, 1102). Due to this symbolically violent attack on de Marsay's sense of masculinity, one would expect his identity as a confident seducer to be completely destroyed. Indeed, the narrator does not hide the crushing significance of this event: "L'exclamation de Paquita fut d'autant plus horrible pour lui qu'il avait été détrôné du plus doux triomphe qui eût jamais agrandi sa vanité d'homme" (*FYO*, 1104). [Paquita's exclamation was all the more horrible for him in that he had been dethroned from the sweetest triumph that had ever increased his male vanity.] Because vanity is such a large part of the seducer's sense of self, as we also saw in the case of Sand's Raymon, de Marsay is struck at the very core of his subjectivity. In this narrative, then, the effects of uncontrolled eroticism are compounded by Paquita's revelation, robbing the seducer of the sweetness of his triumph.

In contrast, the controlled eroticism of seductions that take the form of erotic domination effectively protects against the chaos of a violent eroticism that, according to Georges Bataille, confronts the subject with a breakdown of the limits of the individual self. For Bataille, "Sexual activity is a moment of isolation crisis. This activity is known to us from the outside, but we know that it weakens the sense of self, that it puts it in question."[22] Seducers who aim to dominate their victims are preoccupied by issues of their own subjectivity and use seduction to reinforce their sense of self. They do not seek to experience the weakening of the boundaries of the self that Bataille describes. By taking a controlling approach to erotic relations they are essentially trying to gain recognition of their agency while simultaneously skirting the self-threatening potential of sexual activity. Taking Bataille's work on eroticism as a point of departure, Benjamin describes the protective aspect control assumes in the context of sadomasochistic relations:

> Excitement runs in the *risk* of death, not in death itself. And it is erotic complementarity that offers a way to simultaneously break through and preserve the boundaries: in the opposition between violator and violated, one person maintains his boundary and the other allows her boundary to be broken. One remains rational and in control, while the other loses her self. Put another way, complementarity protects the self.[23]

These same words could be applied to domination in seduction, underscoring the fact that the sexual experience is not the main goal of seduction; instead, a seducer seeks power, control, and domination. The other's submission serves to affirm the seducer's sense of self and feelings of desirability. Motivated by anxiety, the dominating seducer tries to affirm the opposite by performing an identity that displays confident self-assurance. In effect, seduction as domination serves to tame eroticism and disguise the subject's fundamental fragility.

While Balzac created this outbreak of chaotic forces in his text, by the conclusion he has eliminated the subversive elements from his narrative. He evokes a feminine sexuality whose power is threatening to men, but then reduces this force that menaces masculine domination. Following the marquise's murder of Paquita, the text isolates this violent and sexually deviant woman by having her withdraw to a convent. The restoration of masculine power is further signaled by de Marsay's resumption of a normal life: his return to the Tuileries gardens where he can see and be seen by other fashionable people in

Paris, and potentially can find a future object for seduction. The social order gets restored, and traditional power structures reassert themselves; the man's life will continue as usual, whereas the women involved end up murdered or in self-exile. But this return to "normalcy" could only take place by dint of the text's previous revelation of the potential for disorder. De Marsay is not entirely a Don Juan-esque figure, nor is Paquita's identity that of the submissive female promoted by patriarchy; instead, both lie somewhere in between. In her analysis of the text from the perspective of psychoanalysis, Shoshanna Felman reads Balzac's narrative as a dramatization of sexual difference, and she writes, "[F]emininity is uncanny in that it is not the opposite of masculinity but *that which subverts the very opposition of masculinity and femininity.*"[24] In this light, femininity appears as a disruptive force, one that subverts the smooth functioning of the masculine social order. At least in its initial stages, then, Paquita's version of femininity allows this seduction to proceed in such a way that the domination and power asymmetry are not locked into traditionally gendered positions, but instead allow for playful reversibility.

Even the fact that the status quo of masculine domination gets restored in the end does not erase the significance of Balzac's representation of alternative possibilities for the configuration of relations between the sexes. *La fille aux yeux d'or* reveals that masculine domination is not an essential ingredient in sexual relations, thereby exposing the constructed nature of the patriarchal social order. Although Balzac portrays these alternatives as threatening, he also reveals their fascinating appeal. This tendency to expose multiple perspectives, even to evoke possibilities he does not personally espouse, is true for the writer's works on a larger scale as well. Commenting on Balzac's relatively undogmatic approach to representing society, Pierre Barbéris has observed: "*La Comédie humaine*, in effect, is not a peremptory and monocolored work; it does not flow in one direction. If Balzac had been royalist or republican, . . . he would not have written *La Comédie humaine*. He then would only have seen one side of things, and his work would be psychologically and sociologically dead."[25] Indeed, Balzac's works display great diversity in the sexual, political, and social ideas they represent. Balzac seems to delight in exploring the ambiguities of human nature and social interaction. By letting his desire to reproduce society as he observed it drive his narratives rather than being ruled by a fixed moral or social agenda, Balzac expanded the horizons of nineteenth-century narrative.

Domination, Seduction, and Flirtation

In analyzing texts by Balzac and Sand where seduction takes the form of erotic domination, we have seen that despite Western society's coding of domination as "masculine" throughout the social order, the actual sex of domination is reversible: male, female, or an oscillation between the two. While Balzac and Sand depart from traditional representations of the Don Juan-esque seducer, as seen in *Indiana* and *La fille aux yeux d'or*, we find that the two writers differ profoundly in their approaches to representing domination. Although both texts present erotic desire in a destructive light, they diverge in their messages about the harmful effects of domination. In Sand's text, Raymon's search for erotic domination destroys Noun, evokes a submissive slavery in Indiana, and even torments the seducer himself. At the novel's conclusion, Sand "heals" the harmful effects of this domination by creating a new couple, who base their relationship on mutual love and respect. In Balzac's novel, seduction also proves destructive of many lives, notably those of Paquita and the marquise. But while Paquita seriously wounds de Marsay's masculine pride when she shouts her female lover's name in a moment of ecstasy, the concluding scene suggests that de Marsay's relation with Paquita seems to have left no permanent psychological effects. De Marsay resumes his life as normal, and the world need never know about this incident. The male-dominated social order emerges triumphant from Balzac's text, whereas Sand proposes a new kind of society. Her opposition between dominating desire and mutual love almost seems to prefigure Benjamin's theory of mutual recognition as a way to end the subject-object polarization that so often leads to erotic domination. Yet, while such alternatives to domination may provide an irresistible appeal, they also imply limits on human emotional life by excluding certain forms of expression.

For the play of power remains an immutable feature of erotic life, and it is this issue that Benjamin tries to finesse in her depiction of sexual relations free from domination. "In my view," she writes, "the simultaneous desire for loss of self and for wholeness (or oneness) with the other, often described as the ultimate point of erotic union, is really a form of the desire for recognition. In getting pleasure *with* the other and in taking pleasure *in* the other, we engage in mutual recognition."[26] Despite the obvious advantages of mutuality and equality, this vision of erotic relations seems oddly virtuous. Benjamin's argumentation tends to sidestep the very real human need to experience power and mastery, precisely the forces that drive seducers and seductresses. While seduction does constitute a reversible relation, with the potential for both partners alternately to hold the position of control, it will always be an asymmetrical power relation. At every stage of a seduction, one person pushes forward while the other holds back. Eventually, one person gives in to the other's advances, such that a successful seduction always ends in a polarization between dominant and submissive positions. Domination, then, is an essential component of seduction.

Benjamin's notion of sexual relations stands in stark contrast to Bataille's description of eroticism, which underscores the violent nature of sexuality: "Essentially, the domain of eroticism is the domain of violence, the domain of violation."[27] At times, Benjamin does seem to acknowledge this facet of eroticism, as when she writes, "What distinguishes Eros from perversion is not freedom from fantasies of power and surrender, for Eros does not purge sexual fantasy—it plays with it."[28] Or, "If the denial of recognition does not become frozen into immovable relationships, the play of power need not be hardened into domination."[29] When they play with positions of power and submission, both partners realize that in enacting a sexual fantasy their roles are both theatrical and momentary, rather than fixed expressions of their subjectivity. This sexual role-playing evokes a situation where domination and submission exist in a separate realm that contains the dangers of master-slave polarization rather than allowing these positions to become fixed and definitive of one's subjectivity. For all of her useful insights, however, Benjamin tends to lose sight of the all-important notion of *play* with positions of power. Driven by an urgency to denounce the ways that parent-child relations and social institutions foster split subjectivities according to masculine domination and feminine submission, Benjamin devotes most of her attention to exploring ways to find a balanced subjectivity that favors neither gender—through shared parenting, for instance—rather than examining what form a true play with erotic domination might take.

One could say that Benjamin's new model of erotic relations is to domination as flirtation is to seduction. Flirtation and seduction bear many characteristics in common, as both involve creating a captivating image to present to another in the hope of gaining the thrill of feeling desired by that other. But flirtation is more playful than seduction, because the flirt does not use strategies of manipulation to cause another to give in to a desire he or she initially resisted. Flirtation gives pleasure to both players, since both try their hand at charming the other rather than one person pursuing while the other puts up barriers of resistance. Further, whereas seduction delays the ultimate move toward possession in order to savor it all the more, flirtation can take the form of endless play. Adam Phillips writes: "The generosity of flirtation is in its implicit wish to sustain the life of desire; and often by blurring, or putting into question, the boundary between sex and sexualization."[30] Phillip's words underscore the fact that rather than driving ultimately toward a sexual relation, flirtation can add a playful sexual undercurrent to various aspects of everyday interactions. Thus, whereas seduction culminates by one person triumphing in the other's acquiescence and sexual submission, flirtation has the potential to remain more of a mutual, equal relation—the kind of reciprocal relation envisioned by Benjamin. A relation based on mutual flirtation, however, cannot be categorized within the realm of seduction, since its goals and dynamics are fundamentally different. And, while flirtation flourishes in contemporary society, it has not supplanted seduction—evidence that seduction, with all its destructive potential, does respond to a deep human need.

Indeed, as the textual examples analyzed in this chapter suggest, seduction exists partly because of a human need to feel powerful and able to exert control over another person in the sexual arena. Although an individual's place in the social order influences the dynamics of a seduction, two people's relative power based on class and gender does not predetermine their positions in seduction. While the first two examples in this chapter show cases where Balzac and Sand depict traditional, male-dominated power relations, each with his or her own particular angle on the subject, the second two texts grant female characters active, dominating roles in their sexual relations, at least part of the time.[31] If Benjamin's analysis of how traditional gender roles lead to a bipolar hierarchy rather than relations of equal subjects is correct, it is astonishing that in the nineteenth century male-female relations were not even more skewed toward male power. According to Alain Corbin, it was not until the end of the nineteenth century that rituals of flirtation and increased interest in and acceptance of women's pleasure provided couples with a new eroticism: "Between a better-warned girl and a boy more concerned with his partner's pleasure, a new understanding can form, a mutual satisfaction succeed selfish assault."[32] During Balzac's and Sand's era, however, male domination would have been the norm.

Thus, Balzac's more favorable representation of masculine domination and feminine submission, although not the only position found in *La comédie humaine*, does not strike the modern reader as unusual for the time. As for Sand, despite the grimly realistic social portrait found in *Leone Leoni*, she had a different social agenda than Balzac, and her fiction largely promotes an ideal love based on equality between the sexes. Given the difficulty of achieving mutual recognition between men and women when the entire social order was imbued with masculine domination, it is not so surprising that in her writing Sand had trouble reconciling love and equality with passionate eroticism. More often than not, she set love and passion in opposition, as if she felt she had to desexualize love in order to make it compatible with her heroines' ideals. In novels such as *Le compagnon du tour de France* (Pierre Huguenin and Yseult de Villepreux), *Indiana* (Ralph and Indiana), and *Horace* (Paul Arsène and Marthe), Sand represents her ideal couples in loving, yet de-eroticized, relationships. In her own life, Sand took the audacious step of separating from her husband and writing to support herself. While she enjoyed great freedom and a succession of lovers, in her fiction she largely refrained from detailing relationships that made women full and equal participants in the sexual realm. Thus, while both Balzac and Sand sometimes adopt nontraditional approaches to representing gender roles, when it comes to the question of domination the views of each were largely shaped and determined by his or her sex. The male writer favored his male characters, often at the expense of his female ones, while the female writer sought affirmative roles for her female characters.

Seduction, by its very nature, can never enact a relation between equal subjects, because it is based on asymmetrical power. Even if both partners enjoy equal status in other realms of their existence, the intersubjective space of seduction demands that they play oppositional, unequal roles. But the will to dominate another that drives seducers' and seductresses' desire paradoxically carries within it the very reasons for a seduction's end. Once domination has been achieved through the other's surrender in sexual consummation, the energy of seduction has also been consumed. Like desire, which, as Lacan has taught us, is based on a lack, one that can never be fulfilled, seduction requires an unattained—though not completely unattainable—object to pursue.

4
Êtres séduisants: The Seductions of Narcissistic Coquettes and Dandies

The preceding chapters have primarily examined cases of seduction where the seducer or seductress singles out a victim, then purposefully designs an individualized strategy to bring about the other's sexual capitulation. Underlying this form of seduction and the type of strategizing it entails is a fundamental lack of harmony between the desires of the seducer or seductress and the person seduced. Something—be it social pressures, expectations based on gender roles, or personality conflict—prevents the seduced person from finding the other person seductive, at least initially. The dynamics of pursuit and resistance typical of seduction arise as the seducer and seductress attempt to overcome the other's initial resistance and make themselves seductive in the eyes of the seduced person. However, literature also contains many examples of characters who are defined by a seductiveness so pervasive that all those around them fall under the sway of their charms without the seducer or seductress having to invest heavily in creating a seduction plan. In Balzac's and Sand's works, these characters tend to be portrayed as coquettes and dandies, such as Balzac's Foedora (*La peau de chagrin*), Béatrix, and Lucien de Rubempré (*Illusions perdues*) and Sand's Lélia and Célio Floriani (*Le Château des Désertes*). These coquettes and dandies can best be characterized as *êtres séduisants*, since they seduce simply by being seductive, as opposed to the *être séducteur*, who must take a more active role in planning and strategizing a seduction. Further, *êtres séduisants* are marked by a fundamental narcissism that goes well beyond the normal dose found in most people; it becomes one of the defining traits of coquettes and dandies. This chapter will examine how narcissism and gender inform the unique dynamics of the *être séduisant*'s seductions, highlighting the ways in which the sociohistorical context of postrevolutionary France influenced the writers' attitudes toward both coquetry and dandyism.

By cultivating the self as an object of desire, narcissistic coquettes and dandies cause others to desire them as well.[1] This seductiveness goes well beyond simple attractiveness, since it is the narcissist's particular way of operating through double meanings and mixed signals, of begging to be noticed without seeming to pay attention, of speaking a language that says "I want you around" without quite saying "I want *you*" that creates a mysterious aura of desirability. However, while narcissists' outer appearance may evoke infinite desirability, at the same time their seductiveness represents a double-edged sword. It gives rise to a helpless—and often hopeless—passion in others, even as it results from a wounded subject. Heinz Kohut, a psychiatrist who has extensively studied narcissism, underscores that "the ego's anxiety relates primarily to its awareness of the vulnerability of the mature self," and he adds, "The principal source of discomfort is thus the result of the psyche's inability to regulate self-esteem and to maintain it at normal levels."[2] The narcissist's seductive exterior acts as a screen, both displaying a carefully arranged persona and hiding a fragile, divided self. Effecting a chasm between interior reality and exterior image, narcissists try to disguise their lack of unity. Contrary to appearances, then, the narcissist enters the game of seduction not from a position of strength, but because of a driving need for self-affirmation, from the desire to be desired. In order to bolster the ego, narcissists seek to surround themselves with a crowd of admirers. The fact that these coquettes' and dandies' seductions stem from an inner fragility suggests certain psychological links between them and the dominating seducers examined in chapter 3, reinforcing the notion that the display of strength in seduction serves to compensate for weaknesses.

Narcissism alters the dynamics of seduction in significant ways. The narcissistic *être séduisant*'s beauty combines with an aura of inaccessibility to create an irresistibly enigmatic appeal that spontaneously attracts admirers without the narcissist having to develop additional strategies of seduction. Instead of the traditional seducer or seductress's role, where an *être séducteur* takes an active stance by singling out a victim and then purposefully designing a strategy to bring about the other's sexual capitulation, the narcissist takes a more passive approach to seduction. For the *être séduisant*, strategic activity focuses more on the self than on an exterior object of desire. Kohut gives a theoretical account of this phenomenon in "Forms and Transformations of Narcissism" when he identifies exhibitionism as "the principal narcissistic dimension of all drives, an expression of the narcissistic emphasis on the aim of the drive (upon the self as performer) rather than on its object."[3] Someone who is *séducteur* generally has a specific exterior object in mind, while one who is *séduisant* most likely does not.

This opposition between the *être séduisant* and the *être séducteur* has the advantage of distinguishing between active and passive behavior while bypassing the latter term's long-standing assimilation to femininity and masculinity. As examples from the works of Balzac and Sand will show, men and women alike display themselves in the traditionally female position of the object of desire. However, many theorists—including Freud—have actually described narcissism as a feminine characteristic. One of Freud's principal aims in his paper "On Narcissism" was to posit the existence of a sexual difference regarding men's and women's ways of loving or desiring. He argues that men accede to the "higher" realm of the anaclitic object choice, whereas women tend to get stuck in a stage of narcissistic object choice, "probably the purest and truest feminine type" and "the feminine form of erotic life."[4] Freud even relates a woman's seductiveness directly to her narcissism: "Such women have the greatest fascination for men. . . . It seems evident that one person's narcissism has a great attraction for those others who have renounced part of their own narcissism and are seeking after object-love; the charm of a child lies to a great extent in his narcissism, his *self-sufficiency* and *inaccessibility*. . . ."[5] Freud suggests that men are seduced by a narcissistic woman precisely because she represents a nostalgic fantasy of their own "lost" narcissism. However, in her book *L'énigme de la femme*, Sarah Kofman contests Freud's assertion that men have renounced their narcissism. Revealing both Freud's contradictory statements and the instability of his terminology, Kofman identifies a Freudian blind spot when she notes, "[T]he text tends to reduce object love to narcissistic love, since object love is a simple transfer of original narcissism."[6] In revealing these links between narcissistic and object love, Kofman argues that narcissism is not a sex-based trait, as Freud would have liked us to think.

The fact that narcissism and passivity influence the sexual life of both men and women makes the space of conjunction between seduction and narcissism one where sexual stereotypes fall apart and manifest themselves as ungrounded. In this space of oscillation, the opposition active/passive does not necessarily correspond to that of masculine/feminine. Balzac's and Sand's texts show that male seducers are just as apt to operate in a narcissistic mode of seduction as female seductresses are. Therefore, a gender-neutral opposition between *être séducteur* and *être séduisant* better captures the panoply of roles Balzac and Sand created for their characters.

Coquetry and Femininity

An examination of the gender traits of coquettes and dandies reveals these characters to be hybrid creatures bearing a distinctive mixture of masculine and feminine characteristics. In the case of the coquette, her outer appearance exhibits her femininity, and she seemingly places herself in the feminine position of a seductive object. However, she simultaneously holds traditionally masculine powers, such as maintaining control over a relation, and she may even use her power to subvert the man's desire for possession. Georg Simmel's portrait of the flirt (which the French version translates as "coquette") in his essay "Flirtation" highlights the narcissistic game at which the coquette excels, one of attracting others' desire while simultaneously keeping her distance: "[T]he distinctiveness of the flirt lies in the fact that she awakens delight and desire by means of a unique antithesis and synthesis: through the alternation or simultaneity of accommodation and denial. . . ."[7] Simmel's notion of the flirt, or coquette, underscores that she is a figure who skillfully plays on contradictions and double meanings. Men cannot help but find themselves attracted to this *être séduisant*, but the coquette rarely allows any one man access to the object of his desire.

Further, the coquette's use of her femininity as a front for accomplishing other goals likens her game to the masquerade as described by Joan Rivière. Rivière views womanliness in terms of a mask put on by women to disguise their possession of a "masculine" intellectual capacity: "Womanliness therefore could be assumed and worn as a mask, both to hide the possession of masculinity and to avert the reprisals expected if she were to possess it."[8] Likewise, the coquette's feminine seductiveness represents a kind of social posturing, because the man is at once enticed by her beguiling exterior and frustrated by her strategy of withholding. As an *être séduisant* and a narcissist, the coquette wants a crowd of admirers to appreciate her feminine beauty, but she is generally both too narcissistic and too concerned with protecting her reputation to take an interest in actively seducing any one man. The masquerade of coquetry thus provides a way for the threatening, "phallic" woman to disguise her intentions behind an exterior that connotes familiarity and harmlessness to men.

Analyzing the seductions of narcissistic coquettes provides an especially interesting way to compare Balzac's and Sand's works, because in the novels *La peau de chagrin*, *Lélia*, and *Béatrix* the authors appear to engage in a kind of dialogue with each other by "correcting" each other's portrayals of feminine characters. In all three texts, a young man falls desperately in love with a seductive older woman. Beginning with Balzac's Foedora, we will next read Sand's Lélia as her answer to Balzac's "femme sans cœur." While both women appear as narcissistic temptresses from the exterior, Sand portrays Lélia sympathetically, showing her inner constellation to be quite different from Foedora's. But Balzac did not leave Sand with the last word, and his novel *Béatrix* offers two female characters: the eponymous heroine, a narcissistic coquette, and the intellectual and independent Camille Maupin, who shares certain characteristics in common with Lélia. In addition, we will examine the interplay between the seductresses' inner narcissistic drives and the perception of them derived from others' exterior gaze. Like their literary predecessors in the works of Molière and Marivaux, Balzac's coquettes are women who delight in creating public displays of their seductiveness. Both Foedora and Béatrix take pleasure in igniting impossible desires in their admirers, and this practice is especially evident in Foedora's relations with Raphaël de Valentin and Béatrix's relations with Calyste du Guénic. In both cases, the coquette's erotic pleasure lies in making herself feel desired, all the while remaining inaccessible. Conflicting goals arise between the man's desire for possession and the woman's desire to prolong the seduction in a relation that grants her so much power. This form of coquetry thus represents a kind of flirtation with seduction, as opposed to the *être séducteur*'s more straightforward strategizing, since the coquette's goal is infinitely to defer the consummation rather than to build up to a climax of capitulation. In contrast, Sand's "coquette" departs from the traditional psychology of coquetry, and Lélia's narcissistic traits will be shown to result more from male characters' projections than from her inner constellation. In effect, by creating the complex character of Lélia, who may appear cruel to her suitors but who definitely is not without a heart, Sand suggests to Balzac that he misunderstood women's hearts in his characterization of Foedora.

La peau de chagrin and Balzac's "femme sans cœur"

In Balzac's *La peau de chagrin*, the fantastic tale of a young man's engagement with a magical skin that fulfills his every desire while slowly killing him in the process, the character Foedora's very entry into the novel is doubly mediated by masculine efforts to define her. Not only does the heavy-handed chapter title cast this enigmatic and emblematic woman as "La femme sans cœur," but also, during most of this chapter, the text presents Raphaël de Valentin's point of view. This male character acts as a first-person interior narrator, telling some friends the story of his life. Foedora's entire existence in the novel is thus mediated by the masculine gaze, a point emphasized by the fact that Raphaël's initial attraction to the seductive coquette gets ignited not by an encounter with Foedora herself, but by his friend Rastignac's verbal portrait of her. Rastignac offers an object to which Raphaël can attach both his social aspirations and his erotic desires, a scenario that recalls Rastignac's own trajectory in *Le père Goriot*. We are reminded that in Balzac's *Comédie humaine* social climbing represents what Janet Beizer has termed "a sublimated form of erotic conquest."[9] Because Foedora is not even present when Raphaël falls under the sway of her charm, she represents an extreme case of the passive *être séduisant*.

The reception at which Raphaël first meets Foedora offers the perfect setting for him to observe her in the midst of social interactions. He discovers that this woman who has so enchanted him also unleashes her seductiveness on a multitude of other admirers. Thanks to her ability to encourage and discourage her suitors at once, the coquette remains inaccessible to all, thereby capitalizing on one of the seductive traits Freud attributes to his narcissist, and Simmel to his flirt/coquette. True to form, Foedora narcissistically refuses to love anyone, all the while coquettishly placing herself at the center of male attention. As Raphaël observes in a pithy formula so characteristic of Balzac's writing, "[U]ne femme est coquette tant qu'elle n'aime pas" (*PC*, 152). [A woman is a coquette as long as she does not love.] Men find Foedora frustrating because she upsets the usual balance of power in relations between the sexes, as indicated by Rastignac's remark:

"Ne se donner à personne, et permettre à tout le monde de mettre là sa carte! si j'étais libre, je voudrais voir cette femme soumise et pleurant à ma porte" (*PC*, 149). [Not give herself to anyone, and allow everyone to place their cards there! if I were free, I would want to see this woman submissive and crying at my door.] It is precisely the enigma of the narcissistic woman who holds herself beyond the reach of her admirers and who crafts her femininity into an artificially exaggerated display that Raphaël sets out to resolve.

Raphaël's investigation into Foedora's suspected psychological and physical anomalies leads to one of the most memorable scenes of the novel: the moment when the protagonist decides to spend the night hiding in Foedora's room. The protagonist describes his plan, saying it was "[p]our examiner cette femme corporellement comme je l'avais étudiée intellectuellement, pour la connaître enfin tout entière. [...]" (*PC*, 179) [in order to examine this woman corporally as I had studied her intellectually, in order finally to know her entirely . . .]. We recall Raphaël's narrative of how he watches Foedora undress, only to discover no bodily imperfections. What he does find, however, is Foedora's secret talent and pleasure: singing. And he interprets this pleasure in sexual terms when he says, "[E]lle paraissait s'écouter elle-même et ressentir une volupté qui lui fût particulière; elle éprouvait comme une jouissance d'amour" (*PC*, 182). [She seemed to listen to herself and to feel an ecstasy particular to herself; she felt a kind of erotic pleasure.] This coquette has found a form of eroticism that coincides with her narcissistic self-absorption and does not necessitate an exterior object. Balzac thus places Raphaël in a position of gaining knowledge about which Foedora herself remains unaware. Or perhaps she simply refuses to speak, since, earlier in the text, she had refrained from explaining herself when Raphaël commented that she would make a "sujet précieux pour l'observation médicale" (*PC*, 158) [valuable subject for medical observation]. Raphaël's "knowledge," however, is based solely on his limited evaluation of the situation rather than on insights gained from the woman's perspective. Like Freud's reading of femininity, which, as Shoshanna Felman has noted, actually tells only what femininity means to men,[10] Raphaël's analysis is based solely on his own feelings of insecurity and frustration—and here we must underscore that Raphaël serves as the author's autobiographical projection.

The scene in the bedroom constitutes one of the rare times in the novel when Balzac allows Foedora to speak her mind on the subject of men and her aversion to amorous relationships. In a conversation with her servant Justine that Raphaël overhears from his hiding place, Foedora adamantly rejects Justine's suggestions that she marry and have children: "Me marier? non, non. Le mariage est un trafic pour lequel je ne suis pas née" (*PC*, 183). [Get married? No, no. Marriage is a trade for which I was not born.] Whatever narcissistic inability to love another that may hamper Foedora's erotic life, this coquette has squarely attributed her difference to an entirely other set of reasons, and they are social rather than psychological. As an independent coquette, Foedora can enjoy a degree of power over the men seduced by her, and her narcissism does not preclude her from playing at seduction. In fact, seduction actually allows this woman to escape the traditional limitations imposed on her gender, as she refuses a role that would subordinate her to men. Further, she skillfully transforms the vulnerabilities of narcissism into a powerfully seductive weapon. But the coquette's social position is truly precarious, for not only does her reign depend on her not loving any one man but also it requires her continually to produce the effects of seduction that retain her admirers.

In the third and final section of the novel, Balzac stages the public downfall of the seductress who has provoked a tormenting passion in Raphaël, staging it at the opera house. The fact that Foedora's suffering does not go unnoticed by her rivals, the other women of the audience, marks a loss of admiration as significant as that signaled by Raphaël's scorn, for according to Marivaux, coquettes thrive on the satisfaction they gain from staging their superiority over other women. In his "Réflexions sur les coquettes," Marivaux explains, "Les coquettes ne s'aiment pas, et ne sont pourtant bien que lorsqu'elles sont ensemble. Savez-vous ce qu'elles cherchent en se prenant pour compagnes? le plaisir de l'emporter l'une sur l'autre: elles vont pourvoir à la nourriture de leur vanité, et faire assaut de charmes [...]"[11] [Coquettes do not like one another, and yet are not well unless they are together. Do you know what they look for in seeking one another's company? the pleasure of having the upper hand over one another: they supply the food for their vanity, and make an assault of charm. . . .] Thus, Foedora's seemingly extreme reaction is, in fact, quite in line with the circumstances, at least as Marivaux understands coquetry. Narcissism would only amplify the coquette's jealous feelings of rivalry, since the insecurity and vulnerability characteristic of the narcissistic personality would make her all the more susceptible.

Balzac ends his novel on a note of social commentary. In a dialogue with a fictive reader, the author responds to questions about whatever became of Foedora, saying, "Elle était hier aux Bouffons, elle ira ce soir à l'Opéra, elle est partout, c'est, si vous voulez, la Société" (*PC*, 294). [She was at the Bouffons yesterday, she will go to the Opéra tonight, she is all over, she is, if you will, Society.] Thus, in the novel's final lines, Balzac enlarges Foedora's role by making her an allegory of society. This seductress who, due to her narcissism, has been characterized as cold, calculating, and thoroughly lacking a heart subsequently becomes the negative standard in which postrevolutionary France has, according to Balzac, placed its values. Although Balzac could write Foedora into social oblivion by ending her powers of coquetry, he could not stop the course of history, which was increasingly tending toward self-centered narcissism. On another level, we can also read Foedora, representative of Society, and her spectacular public humiliation as Balzac's way of venting the frustrations he felt as a young man trying to woo influential women and make a place for himself in Parisian society. Any impotence the socially ambitious young writer felt in the early stages of his career could be channeled into his writing where, as opposed to real life, he did have the power to enact his will. Balzac's negative portrayal of Foedora as Society thus reveals not only the writer's political dissatisfaction but also his personal feelings of frustration with women.

Lélia: A Misunderstood Seductress

In his novel *La peau de chagrin*, Balzac positions his seductress so that both her seductive strengths and her narcissistic fragility come to the reader largely refracted through others' perceptions of her. On the occasions when Foedora does reveal her own inner perspective, she does not command much sympathy, since the representation of the coquette's inner self largely confirms others' negative judgments of her. This is not the case in Sand's *Lélia*, however. In this novel, a polyphonic structure gives full voice to a number of characters, male and female, thereby allowing for a very different reading of the seductress. While many similarities exist between male perceptions of Lélia and Foedora, the situation changes dramatically as one pierces through the seductress's outer facade to discover her inner self. The chorus of voices speaking both about and for Lélia presents the picture of a woman misunderstood by men, who nevertheless find her seductive. Thus, whereas Balzac focuses his novel on the young hero and offers a portrait of heartless coquette based almost entirely on male projections, Sand sets out to provide a more balanced picture of the heroine's psychology. When read in conjunction with *La peau de chagrin*, Sand's complex characterization of Lélia seems to suggest that just as the novel's male characters misjudge the heroine based on their own limitations and frustrations, so too Balzac perhaps fails to understand the female *être séduisant*'s heart and her reasons for withholding herself from men.

Besides the different vision of the narcissistic seductress it produces, Sand's *Lélia* is also singular in that it involves not one but two versions of the novel, because of the extensive rewriting the author undertook between 1833 and 1839. In her introduction to the modern edition of the 1839 version, Béatrice Didier pinpoints the main differences between the novel's two versions: "G. Sand cut out small errors of style or of taste; but above all, and systematically, all that had excited the curiosity of her readers in 1833; each time a sentence could be interpreted as [indicating] Lélia's frigidity or homosexuality, it was corrected. . . ."[12] In effect, Sand's extensive revisions to her novel—her efforts to diminish the narrow, sexual interpretation of her heroine's coldness in favor of a more idealistic, sublime, and feminist problematic[13]—suggest that the writer felt her readers of 1833 had misunderstood Lélia as well.

The figure of the enigma, which plays a role in Raphael's fascination with Foedora, also serves as a motivating factor in the young poet Sténio's desire for Lélia.[14] In the opening pages of both versions of the novel, Sténio speaks to Lélia in a voice expressing his confused feelings of desire and fear, of horror and fascination. He wishes to know and understand this mysterious woman whose seductiveness has captivated him even as the seeming self-sufficiency of "Cruelle Lélia" (*L II*, 1:67; *L*, 17) frustrates him. Not only does Sténio detect in Lélia a number of qualities associated with the narcissist, but he even suggests later that it is precisely her self-absorbed detachment that makes her so seductive. He speaks of her "mobile indifference" and calls it her "strongest seduction" (*L II*, 1:89; *L*, 46). Sténio's hurt, resentful feelings for Lélia sometimes get redeployed as he makes cruel attacks on her. In this sense, Sténio resembles another frustrated suitor, Raphaël. Like Sténio with Lélia, Raphaël wants to believe that Foedora's ability to resist him must stem from some physical deformity.[16]

Sand shows how Sténio, in his frustration, views himself as "le jouet que vous vous amusiez à tourmenter" (*L II*, 1:97) [the toy that you amuse yourself by tormenting]. In fact, the 1833 version contains a passage where Lélia does paint herself in sadistic terms when speaking of her relationship with a former lover:

> Je me renfermais dans un système d'indifférence et de légèreté qui réveillait tous ses doutes. J'enchaînais l'élan quelquefois involontaire et fougueux de ses sens par une ironie glaciale. [...] Je l'enivrais malignement de caresses douces et chastes. Je jouais de lui comme un vautour avec sa proie. Tantôt je le faisais souffrir et je jouissais de son mal. [...] (*L*, 200)
>
> [I closed myself in a system of indifference and of lightness that awakened all his doubts. I controlled the sometimes involuntary and spirited outburst of his senses by a glacial irony. . . . I maliciously inebriated him with sweet and chaste caresses. I played with him like a vulture with its prey. Sometimes I made him suffer and I took pleasure in his pain. . . .]

Sand's decision to strike this passage from her new version of *Lélia* suggests that she preferred for her heroine to represent herself in a more positive light, thereby underscoring more strongly the difference between outer and inner perceptions of her.

Sténio is only one member, albeit the loudest, of a chorus of men who raise their voices against a seductress they believe to be diabolical. The priest Magnus (suffering from fits of madness and given to hallucinations) speaks of Lélia as possessing a devilish power over him: "Lélia! ma perte, ma séduction, ma ruine! Lélia! qu'il m'était défendu de posséder, de désirer même! Lélia! l'atroce et l'infâme qui est venue me chercher au fond du sanctuaire, qui a violé la sainteté de l'autel pour m'enivrer de ses infernales caresses!" (*L II*, 1:110; *L*, 80). [Lélia, my fall, my seduction, my ruin! Lélia, whom I was forbidden to possess, even to desire! Atrocious and infamous Lélia who came to look for me at the rear of the sanctuary, who violated the holiness of the altar in order to inebriate me with her infernal caresses!] And, although Lélia's friend Trenmor generally respects her, he nonetheless criticizes her behavior toward men:

> Vous êtes vaine, Lélia, ne vous y trompez pas; votre orgueil vous défend de vous soumettre à l'amour, il devrait vous défendre en même temps d'accepter l'amour d'autrui. [...] Ce plaisir que vous vous donnez d'inspirer l'amour et d'en suivre le ravage dans le coeur des hommes, c'est une satisfaction puérile et coupable de votre amour-propre: faites-la cesser, ou vous en serez punie. (*L II*, 2:6)
>
> [You are vain, Lélia, do not fool yourself on this; your pride forbids you from submitting to another's love, it should forbid you at the same

> time from accepting another's love. . . . This pleasure that you take in inspiring love and in following the ravage in men's hearts, it is a childish and guilty satisfaction of your self-esteem: make it cease, or you will be punished for it.]

This analysis of Lélia effectively characterizes her as a coquette who delights in seeing men suffer because she refuses herself to them, and it resembles Balzac's portrayal of Foedora.

However, when hearing Lélia speak about herself, one could hardly think of a less appropriate term for this *être séduisant* than that of the narcissistic coquette. In contrast to the negative perceptions formed about Lélia by men who find her seductive, Lélia presents herself sympathetically. These different perspectives allow the reader to see the heroine from multiple points of view and to observe better the split between her inner and outer identities. Sand shows her heroine's evolution through the course of the novel, particularly in the second version, as Lélia's narcissistic qualities are sometimes displaced by a transcendental outlook. When Lélia first speaks in the third chapter, her initial impulse is to criticize Sténio's efforts to define her in stark oppositional terms, as coming from heaven or hell, representing either an angel or a demon. According to Lélia, no such simple categorizations exist, since "[l]'esprit du mal et l'esprit du bien, c'est un seul esprit, c'est Dieu; c'est la volonté inconnue et mystérieuse qui est au-dessus de nos volontés. Le bien et le mal, ce sont des distinctions que nous avons créées" (*L II*, 1:65; *L*, 15) [the spirit of evil and the spirit of good, they are one single spirit, it is God; it is the unknown and mysterious will that is above our will. Good and evil, they are distinctions we have created]. Lélia thus chastises men for trying to define her according to oppositional categories—ones that men have created but that do not suit her situation. Lélia's exterior traits suggestive of a narcissistic personality give way to a very fertile inner life, such that her apparent lack of desire for others more nearly reflects her dissatisfaction with the outer world. Thus, Lélia's spiritual absorption unequivocally differentiates her from the Balzacian *femme sans cœur*, just as her strong sense of self distinguishes her from more narcissistic seductresses.

Lélia resembles Balzac's Camille Maupin of *Béatrix* in her wish to fulfill her young love's desire even if it means stepping aside to let a surrogate act in her place. She asks the courtesan Pulchérie, her sister and double, to stand in for the physical act of Sténio's seduction. In a scene of substitution in which Pulchérie disguises herself as Lélia and embraces Sténio, he does not even realize he is with another. Once he does learn of the sisters' ruse, Sténio manifests his limited perspective by cursing Lélia for throwing him into the arms of a prostitute. His egotism prevents him from seeing the other's point of view, from realizing that Lélia is jealous and hurt over his inability to distinguish between Pulchérie and herself. Further, Lélia defends herself against what others perceive as her frigidity, explaining that she simply prefers an ideal, sublime love. The narrator blames Sténio for the failure of his seduction to lead to anything more between Lélia and himself, saying that the young man could not understand Lélia's superiority to other women, nor her belief that God meant for men and women to be equal. The text thus foregrounds Lélia's situation as someone remarkably seductive, yet tragically misunderstood.

Not only does Sand's characterization of Lélia reveal the limitations of Balzac's depiction of the *femme sans cœur* but also in this novel she once again demystifies a male-centered legend that has traditionally been unfavorable to women, that of Don Juan. Sand must have been intrigued by Don Juan's bravado and his popularity in certain circles, for she wrote about this figure on several occasions. Her use of Don Juan in *Lélia* is particularly striking for the straightforward way in which Lélia reveals the ridiculousness of Don Juan's seeming glory. In the process, she humiliates Sténio, who had taken to modeling himself after the infamous seducer, in front of those assembled to hear her speak at the Camaldules convent. Lélia declares Don Juan, and by extension Sténio, a fool to believe that "la femme est une chose faite pour le plaisir de l'homme" (*L II*, 2:124) [woman is a thing made for man's pleasure]. By revealing the false assumptions men make when they attribute qualities to women based on their own desires or frustrations, Sand—through Lélia—could be seen as lecturing to Balzac about his own misunderstanding of women.

The fatal combination of misunderstood seductiveness crystallizes in the scene of Sténio's and Lélia's final meeting, after years have gone by, when Sténio sneaks into her room at the Camaldules convent. As told in the 1839 version, he finds himself seduced all over again upon seeing Lélia, serene and "plus belle qu'elle n'avait jamais été" (*L II*, 2:131) [more beautiful than she had ever been]. Lélia speaks freely of her love for Sténio; however, if they are able to converse directly for once, it is only because Sténio is effectively dead to Lélia.[17] Nonetheless, they are finally able to confront their misunderstandings and irremediably different perspectives. Lélia tells Sténio, "Ce cœur, si froid, si altier, si insensible, selon vous, Sténio, est un incendie qui me dévore. [...] J'aime, répondit Lélia en le repoussant avec une fermeté mêlée de douceur; mais je n'aime personne, Sténio; car l'homme que je pourrais aimer n'est pas né, et il ne naîtra peut-être que plusieurs siècles après ma mort" (*L II*, 2:137). ["This heart, so cold, so haughty, so insensitive, according to you, Sténio, is a fire that is devouring me." . . . "I love," responded Lélia, pushing him back with a firmness mixed with sweetness; "but I love no one, Sténio; for the man I could love has not been born, and he will perhaps only be born several centuries after my death."] This scene from a chapter added to the 1839 text thus serves to differentiate all the more starkly the chasm between Lélia and others' perception of her.

Rather than concluding that Lélia suffers from stagnation in a state of narcissistic object-choice, the reader learns that her inability to find exterior objects of desire in which to invest her love results from an utter absence of men able to love her as she insists on being loved: as an equal. The fact that Lélia is deterred by the lack of a worthy love object signals that Sand is representing her heroine in an idealist mode, as these circumstances would not have prevented a realist character from falling in love. When read from Lélia's perspective, the novel offers a resounding critique of patriarchal society and the state of relations between the sexes, a "feminist" discourse Sand consciously amplified for the 1839 version. Lélia's inability to find a man capable of loving her as she needs to be loved also suggests a common bond between her and other remarkable Sandian heroines, such as the eponymous Marquise and Isidora. Further, by creating Lélia as a character who does not turn out to fit the mold of stereotypical coquetry into which the text's male characters would like to place her, Sand provides an important female perspective on gender relations that counterbalances that of male novelists like Balzac.

In a period marked by its faith in the progress of humanity, Lélia remains pessimistic and skeptical, specifically because of the disequilibrium of power between the sexes. Lélia explains her withdrawal into herself as a veritable necessity of self-preservation: "[L]'homme tient à la société; quoi qu'il fasse, il ne peut s'isoler, et la société repousse le lien illégitime. Il faut donc que l'existence de la femme disparaisse, absorbée par celle de l'homme; et moi, je voulais exister" (*L II*, 2:136). [Man is attached to society; whatever he does, he cannot isolate himself, and society pushes off illegitimate ties. It is thus necessary that the existence of woman disappear, absorbed by that of man: and me, I want to exist.] Speaking through Lélia, Sand expresses the idea that women's particular subjectivity is forcibly suppressed by the symbolically violent workings of the social order. However, Lélia's retreat into a convent does not actually signify her passive resignation, for as abbess of the Camaldules she undertakes the mission of educating young women. Her devotion to the cause of helping others indisputably marks Lélia as not narcissistic. In her convent work, though, as in her ideas about love and marriage, Lélia proves to be ahead of her time. The church brings a suit against her, and she is accused, in part, of heresy. In effect, Lélia's independence—both in her relationships and in her ideas—confounds society's notion of the "natural" order of things, thereby resulting in her demonization.

Triangles of Desire in *Béatrix*

With his novel *Béatrix*, Balzac puts into play not only the eponymous heroine, a narcissistic coquette who is another "femme sans cœur," but also an intellectual and independent woman, the writer Camille Maupin, who provides an interesting comparison to Sand's Lélia. Balzac modeled Béatrix after the Countess Marie d'Agoult, whom he obviously was not trying to flatter. Both Béatrix and Foedora can be read in the context of contemporary debates over women's role in society. Like Foedora, who lives outside the bounds of traditional female roles by refusing the norms of marriage and children, Béatrix flamboyantly rejects society's efforts to push women into a domestic role and leaves her husband to travel to Italy with her lover, Conti. These characters' coquetry constitutes a direct opposition to the domesticity increasingly urged upon women in postrevolutionary France, as evidenced by the efforts of both popular novels and prescriptive literature to carve out a domestic sphere for French women. In analyzing this literature for women, the historian Denise Davidson has found that these works posit a strict opposition between the good woman, who is selfless and domestic, and the bad woman, who is egotistical and coquettish.[18] Davidson suggests that the reason why these writers of the Empire and Restoration worked so hard to promote a less public role for women was that in reality many women had not embraced such a role. This hypothesis seems confirmed by Balzac's own vision of society as represented in *La comédie humaine*, which certainly contains many influential, public, and coquettish women.

The reader's perception of Foedora was strongly colored by mediation through the other's gaze, and Balzac uses this strategy again in *Béatrix*. This time, however, it is through another woman's eyes that the seductress is first presented to the young man who will become infatuated with her. Based on Camille Maupin's verbal portrait of the Marquise Béatrix de Rochefide, Calyste du Guénic finds the marquise irresistibly *séduisante* without even meeting her. This portrait sets in motion the forces of female rivalry, which function not only as the primary motivating factor in the narcissist Béatrix's seductions but also as a driving principle of the novel's plot. In an analysis of the coquette's behavior that echoes in many ways the words of Marivaux about the dynamics of rivalry in coquettes' interpersonal relations, Pierre Saint-Amand observes:

> If the coquette can only exist in this imaginary relation (combat) with man, she also needs to exist in relation to other coquettes. At most, she is less attached to attracting the man's attention than to convincing him of her superiority over her companion. Rivalry thus appears as the dynamic element of coquetry.[19]

Béatrix's dependence on rivalry with other women to ignite her own desires inscribes her seductions in the form of a Girardian triangle. As put forth in *Mensonge romantique et vérité romanesque*, Girard's concept of "desire according to the *Other*" maintains that one does not spontaneously start to desire someone; rather, a third person's desire for a particular object serves as a model for another's desire to imitate.[20] The following analysis will examine the triangles of Béatrix's seductions and compare Camille Maupin to Lélia in order to shed further light on both the role of narcissism in coquetry and Balzac and Sand's literary dialogue about strong, independent women.

Rivalry first brought Béatrix and Camille together, and it is also the force that governs the relations between the two women and Calyste. As Camille tells Calyste, her unusual friendship with Béatrix began over the marquise's jealous admiration of Camille's intellectual standing in society, and the reader gathers that Camille's perceived superiority over Béatrix is not solely due to the fact that Camille tells her point of view. When Béatrix arrives for a visit at Camille's country estate in Brittany, Camille—who had previously rejected the ardent Calyste's love for her—sets out to help him win Béatrix. Camille devises a plan whereby she and Calyste pretend to be lovers in order to make Béatrix interested in Calyste. As Girard would say, Camille provides a model for Béatrix's desire to imitate. The narrator comments on the efficacy of Camille's strategy: "Jamais aucune créature de son sexe ne fut soumise à de plus véritables séductions et à un plus pénétrant machiavélisme que ne l'était la marquise [...]" (*B*, 778). [Never had any creature of her sex been submitted to truer seductions and to a more penetrating Machiavelianism than was the marquise. . . .] Reminiscent of the "seduction brokers" examined in the previous chapter, Camille plans for Calyste to gain with Béatrix the success that Raphaël failed to achieve with Foedora.

Balzac's characterization of Béatrix as a coquette is particularly evident once she discovers Camille's plot and decides to toy with her young admirer's affections. The narrator foregrounds the keen pleasure coquetry gives Béatrix because of its ability to assuage some of the insecurities resulting from her narcissism: "Enfin les vanités particulières à la femme française et qui constitutent cette célèbre coquetterie d'où elle tire sa supériorité, se trouvaient caressées et pleinement saitsfaites chez elle: livrée à d'immenses séductions, elle y résistait, et ses vertus lui chantaient à l'oreille un doux concert de louanges" (*B*, 794). [Finally, the vanities particular to French women, and which constitute this celebrated coquetry from which she draws her superiority, found themselves caressed and fully satisfied in her: delivered to immense seductions, she resisted them, and her virtues sang in her ear a sweet concert of praise.] Ironically, Béatrix receives the ultimate gift her narcissistic need for flattery could want when Calyste actually attempts to kill her by pushing her off a seaside cliff. Rather than marking an occasion for Béatrix to let down her guard, however, her brush with death and her feelings of love that result from it only serve to reinforce her will to resist Calyste, and she relies more than ever on flirtation as a way to maintain control and distance. Subsequently, Béatrix allows Calyste to approach her and speak of his overwhelming love for her, all the while holding him at arm's length and restraining his passion. Such coquettish behavior proves well suited to the narcissist, as it allows her to view herself as an object of desire without having to display any feelings of her own; it also keeps Béatrix in the position of control.

In the third part of the novel, however, Balzac sets his coquette up for her downfall—a seemingly inevitable conclusion for this type of woman in *La comédie humaine*. Abandoned by her lover, Conti, Béatrix takes a renewed interest in Calyste, who has moved to Paris and married Sabine de Grandlieu. The coquette's narcissistic insecurity clearly drives her rekindled interest in Calyste, since it is motivated more by female rivalry than by an attachment to Calyste as an object of desire. Whereas a pitifully lovesick and single Calyste had not been able to retain Béatrix's interest, she now wishes to attract this married man. Thus, the *être séduisant* now becomes more of an *être séducteur*. The narrator explains Béatrix's strategy, saying, "Béatrix voulait du moins la gloire que donne la perversité. Le malheur d'une jeune épouse, d'une Grandlieu riche et belle, allait être un piédestal pour elle" (*B*, 881). [Béatrix at least wanted the glory of perversity. The unhappiness of a young wife, of a rich and beautiful Grandlieu, was going to be a pedestal for her.] Béatrix then proceeds to torment the young man who had never lost interest in her. In an effort to protect herself from further abandonment, Béatrix determines to act as a "conservatrice." Speaking about men and women in general terms, she says, "Il ne s'agit pas de vous aimer [...], il faut vous tracasser quand nous vous tenons, là est le secret de celles qui veulent vous conserver" (*B*, 863). [It is not about loving you . . . , it is necessary to trouble you when we have you, there lies the secret of those who want to conserve you.] This comment represents a moment, perhaps unique in the novel, when Béatrix's voice does not speak as a facade, and the woman revealed is cold and calculating, yet basically insecure. Balzac carefully controls the reader's perception of Béatrix, ensuring that she remains largely unsympathetic.

However, the seductress is allowed to wreak havoc in the Balzacian world for only so long before other forces rise up to stop her. Not only does Béatrix get punished at the hands of La Palférine for her "perverse" behavior toward Calyste and Sabine, as we saw in analyzing this seduction plot in the preceding chapter, but also a male-bonding session among Maxime, La Palférine, and Calyste gets inaugurated after Calyste's escape from his seductress's clutches. Maxime consoles Calyste over his loss by giving him a description of Béatrix that paints her as not only narcissistic but downright evil as well: "Ne regrettez pas Béatrix, c'est le modèle de ces natures vaniteuses, sans énergie, coquettes par gloriole [...], la femme sans cœur et sans tête, étourdie dans le mal. Madame de Rochefide n'aime qu'elle [...]" (*B*, 940). [Do not miss Béatrix, she is the model of these vain natures, without energy, coquettish by vainglory . . . , a woman without a heart and without a head, numbed in evil. Madame de Rochefide only loves herself. . . .] In effect, Maxime's portrait of Béatrix—marked by a particularly vicious male perspective—acts as an antidote to Camille Maupin's first seductive portrait and succeeds in ridding Calyste of his passion for Béatrix. Like Foedora, Béatrix is represented as evil, and the text presents the reversal of her power as a return to order and a suitable punishment for the heartless coquette.

In a symbolic conjunction of events, the end of Béatrix's coquetry serves to restore two marriages, as Béatrix goes home to her husband and Calyste returns his attentions to his family. La Palférine comments that Béatrix will make "la plus délicieuse maîtresse de maison de Paris" (*B*, 940) [the most delicious lady of the house in Paris], and in obtaining her submission by his seduction he has expunged her previously hybrid character of the stereotypically masculine attributes that had allowed her to dominate and control Calyste. The novel's closing scene further emphasizes the return to order and domesticity when Sabine's mother arrives for an unannounced visit and finds Calyste bathing and Sabine sewing clothes for their unborn child. Balzac's attitude toward the domestic bliss evoked in the conclusion of this novel could be interpreted as ironic, however, since the couple's apparent happiness was contrived through the duchess's elaborate seduction plot with Maxime and La Palférine. Indeed, this restoration of family life represents something less than the triumph of bourgeois values. Béatrix may have lost her contest with Sabine, but Sabine's artificially contrived position in relation to her husband is no more secure than it was when she originally masqueraded as Béatrix to entice Calyste to marry her.

This novel's opposition between Béatrix and Sabine reflects the one Davidson identified between the bad, coquettish woman and the good, domestic woman. But, whereas authors of conduct books sought to substitute the good for the bad, Balzac gives a more nuanced portrait of these types, revealing the weaknesses of both models. Even as Balzac overthrows the powers of female coquetry by plotting the downfall of Béatrix (and of Foedora), he does not unequivocably advocate that women be relegated to a domestic role. Indeed, in what could be viewed as ancien régime nostalgia, *La comédie humaine* contains many fascinating portrayals of women who adopt a public role and who continue the aristocratic tradition of exerting influence in the world of men. Aristocratic values had tolerated a more public role for women, and the historian Margaret Darrow asserts that during the ancien régime, women—like men—were courtiers who used their influence to achieve offices, prestige, and patronage.[21] Both Darrow and Davidson have found that in the postrevolutionary period society was no longer so accepting of this aristocratic mode of femininity. Darrow writes, "The aristocracy appropriated domesticity as a class ideal in an effort to answer middle-class criticism of the nobility and, consequently, to forestall the political triumph of the bourgeoisie during the Restoration."[22] Despite this backlash against worldly society identified by both Darrow and Davidson, Balzac portrays female characters as influential salon women who provide aid that serves as a necessary counterpart to men's success.[23] At the same time as Balzac grants women such empowering roles, however, he also represents his coquettes as diabolical for their ability to disrupt masculine domination.

Further evidence of Balzac's conflicted approach to representing female characters can be seen in his portrayal of Camille Maupin. As an intellectual and independent woman who, in addition, is a writer, Camille strays even farther from postrevolutionary ideals of femininity than the coquettes. Balzac does not hesitate to grant this sympathetic character a sharp mind and a quick tongue that serve her both in her professional life and in her personal duel with Béatrix. Yet, Balzac also reveals this woman to be dissatisfied with her inability to find love: "Je mourrai donc sans avoir été ni comprise ni aimée" (*B*, 802). [I'll thus die without having been either understood or loved.] Camille resembles Lélia in the sense that both of these thinking women fail to find a mutually satisfying love. It is almost as if Balzac had Lélia in mind when he created Camille Maupin, but instead of following Sand's lead in portraying a woman who furthers a feminist cause from her post as abbess of a convent, Balzac's character withdraws from society with a sense of resignation and defeat. In her letter to Calyste that secures his acquiescence to a marriage with Sabine de Grandlieu, Camille reveals a deflated version of her former self. Whereas Lélia chose the convent as the best position from which to achieve progress for women in society in her desire to move toward equality for women, Camille leaves society under the banner of retreat, repudiating her writings and her previous stance of skeptical doubt. She even speaks to Calyste of "la religion du devoir" (*B*, 841) [the religion of duty], words that sound foreign in the mouth of a woman who, in her previous life, had chosen a path of independence and avoidance of traditional female roles. By removing Camille from an active role in the rest of the novel, Balzac not only silences the voice of his powerful female character but even makes it happen by her own choice. The example of Camille Maupin thus offers a kind of corrective to the boldness of Sand's Lélia in a novel that, in the end, weighs in heavily in favor of traditional gender roles.

The Coquette's Diabolical Nature

Each of these seductresses has been perceived as cruel, perverse, or demonic by other characters—or even by the author's direct representation of them, in the case of Balzac's Foedora and Béatrix. In contrast, Sand subtly draws a line between others' limited and faulty interpretations of Lélia and the heroine's self-representation by the author.[24] The question begging to be explored, then, is why women who assume the position of an *être séduisant* and play at seduction while largely refraining from conventional sexual relations are, in turn, figured as diabolical by the male imaginary. This phenomenon hardly restricts itself to these nineteenth-century works by Balzac and Sand, but instead makes itself felt as an inherent component of the male experience of female coquetry. For instance, Saint-Amand suggests that in the eighteenth-century seduction novels he analyzes, the coquette represents "one of the modern figures of the sorceress."[25] One of his primary examples is Abbé Prévost's Manon Lescaut, another seductress encaged by the male gaze and prevented by Prévost's confessional narrative from offering her contrasting perspective of self-definition, except in a very limited number of letters and dialogues. However, coquetry is not inherently or necessarily diabolical, despite representations that suggest the contrary.

Therefore, an inquiry into the "diabolical" nature of the narcissistic seductress must be approached from the male perspective. And, in trying to unravel the various layers of eager anticipation and frustrated desires men feel before this seductress, I would begin by pointing to the profound split I have identified between exterior and interior manifestations of narcissism. Perhaps because of this split, narcissistic women appear to men as all the more enigmatic, and inexplicable mysteries tend to provoke a certain amount of fear. Jean Delumeau's historical study *La peur en Occident* traces the roots of female *diabolisation*—women's association with Satan and sorcery—to male fear of female physiology, which remained largely misunderstood until the era of early modern medicine. Delumeau writes, "Attracted by woman, the other sex is just as much repelled by his partner's menstrual flux, smells, secretions, amniotic fluid, birthing expulsions."[26] Additionally, Delumeau underscores that men obliged to remain celibate for religious reasons played a key role in casting women as diabolical:

> [T]he culture then found itself, to a very large extent, in the hands of celibate clerics who could only exalt virginity and unleash themselves

against the temptress whose seductions they feared. It is actually fear of woman that dictated to monastic literature these anathemas periodically hurled against the false and demoniacal attractions of Satan's favorite accomplice.[27]

To the extent that the coquette, like the sorceress of medieval times, represents a woman unattainable by men who desire her (albeit for contrary reasons, since the coquette withholds herself), she shares with the sorceress the quality of being perceived as an exasperating and impossible temptress. Thus, within the realm of seduction, the narcissism underlying most displays of female coquetry meets with men's feelings of desperation at their inability to control and achieve their desire, a situation that subverts traditional configurations of gender, since the coquette, refusing to play a submissive role, holds men at her mercy. When the *être séduisant* is gendered female, she represents an obstacle to male desire.

Dandyism and Male Narcissism

In turning to consider the case of the narcissistic seducer, we find that Balzac's and Sand's most vivid representations of this figure are dandies. Indeed, the dandy is characterized by an underlying narcissism, a quality foregrounded by Emilien Carassus in his description of the dandy: "[T]he dandy builds his self like an idol, and does not cease to offer it to the devoted communion of his faithful, but people do not realize that this permanent celebration betrays a worry. Without a constant effort, the self would be at once inconsistent and exposed. Artifice protects the self all the more in that it is vulnerable and fragile."[28] The dandy creates a certain representation of himself that he projects to the outside world; investing much time and effort in his appearance and manners, he represents the quintessential *être séduisant*. However, just as the narcissistic woman's apparent self-sufficiency is motivated by feelings of insecurity, so too a narcissistic fragility is hidden by the dandy's seamless exterior.

One of the dandy's most universally recognized traits is his effeminate appearance; such characters regularly are endowed with androgynous features that borrow much from the feminine. In *Illusions perdues*, Balzac introduces the dandy Henri de Marsay with the following portrait: "Le premier était de Marsay, homme fameux par *les passions qu'il inspirait*, remarquable surtout par une beauté de jeune fille, beauté molle, efféminée, mais corrigée par un regard fixe, calme, fauve et rigide comme celui d'un tigre: *on l'aimait*, et il effrayait" (*IP*, 277; emphasis mine). [The first was de Marsay, a man famous for the *passions that he inspired*, above all remarkable for a young girl's beauty, soft, effeminate beauty, but compensated for by a fixed, calm, wild, and rigid gaze like that of a tiger: *people loved him*, and he scared them.] Without leaving any question as to de Marsay's sexual potency as a subject of desire, Balzac simultaneously manages to cast him as an *être séduisant*, one who more nearly represents someone else's object of desire rather than an active subject of desire. The dandy effectively confounds sexual stereotypes by his combination of masculine and feminine attributes, constructing his identity with an emphasis on originality that does not respect traditional gender oppositions.

Whereas the narcissistic coquette, as a modern sorceress, represents an age-old female type, the dandy marks a new phenomenon of the nineteenth century, first appearing on the scene in France during the period of the Restoration. In analyzing the seducers Lucien de Rubempré in Balzac's *Illusions perdues* and Sand's Célio Floriani of *Le Château des Désertes*, I will both highlight their dandyism as a reflection of postrevolutionary concerns and compare the representation of their narcissism to that of the coquettish seductress.

Illusions perdues

Balzac's tripartite novel *Illusions perdues* follows Lucien de Rubempré's trajectory from the provincial city of Angoulême, to Paris, then back to Angoulême, and at every step along the way, Lucien's seductive narcissism plays a decisive role in the unfolding of events. An aspiring poet and the son of an apothecary and a noblewoman, Lucien desires literary glory but finds his ambitions alternately aided and thwarted by his narcissistic need for grandeur. Like most narcissists, he possesses the strength of natural beauty, which in his case is developed to the extreme point of a regal elegance that Balzac underscores by comparisons to antiquity. Balzac's narrator evokes "la blancheur veloutée des femmes" (*IP*, 145) [the velvety whiteness of women] in his face; his feet, which would make a man think he was a "une jeune fille déguisée" (*IP*, 145) [young girl disguised]; and his hips, "conformées comme celles d'une femme" (*IP*, 145) [shaped like those of a woman]. In this detailed portrait of Lucien, Balzac emphasizes both his classical elegance and his feminine qualities, a combination that produces irresistibly seductive effects without Lucien having to exert any effort. Lucien provides a prime example of ways in which the erotic life of Balzac's dandies differs from that of his coquettes, since Lucien is represented as neither diabolical nor a mere flirt.

Lucien's first "conquest" by seduction is completely devoid of the kind of intellectual schemes and strategizing that one might expect from a seducer. Instead, matters proceed indirectly, as is more typical of the *être séduisant*. Introduced to the aristocracy of Angoulême as an "enfant sublime," the young poet attracts the attention of Louise de Bargeton, the reigning queen of Angoulême's high society (*IP*, 164). The physical beauty that had gained Lucien the blind devotion of his mother and sister and the adoration of his friend David Séchard proves equally able to transport Lucien across class boundaries. The young poet gains a benefactor who not only encourages his dreams of literary success but also invites him to accompany her to Paris; she describes the capital to him as "le théâtre de vos succès" (*IP*, 249) [the theater of your success]. Up to this point in his life, then, Lucien has lived in an atmosphere resembling narcissistic plenitude, for his seductiveness inspires others to fulfill his needs even before he formulates them as demands.

It is in Paris that Lucien transforms himself from a beautiful yet naive young man into a more worldly dandy. When he arrives expecting to be greeted by immediate literary success, the young poet of Angoulême learns that he has been living under delusions, as the natural talent and beauty that had previously protected him from life's difficulties and setbacks no longer produce the same glowing effects when compared to more selective Parisian standards. In an instructive walk through the Tuileries gardens, Lucien observes in others the existence of a whole art about which he had been totally unaware, that of making oneself up through dress, of constructing an identity based on appearances: "Tous faisait ressortir leurs avantages par une espèce de mise-en-scène que les jeunes gens entendent à Paris aussi bien que les femmes. Lucien tenait de sa mère les précieuses distinctions physiques dont les privilèges éclataient à ses yeux; mais cet or était dans sa gangue, et non pas mis en œuvre" (*IP*, 270). [Everyone made their advantages stand out by a kind of staging that the young men of Paris understand as well as the women. Lucien inherited from his mother the valuable physical distinctions whose privileges glittered before his eyes; but this gold was in its shell and not put into action.] For perhaps the first time in his life, Lucien is filled with feelings of lack, an insecurity that bursts his infantile sense of automatic fulfillment. In effect, the observations Lucien makes during his walk in the Tuileries constitute a first lesson in his initiation to dandyism. He learns that in some situations it takes a little active ingenuity to enhance one's desirability. But his first attempt to appear as a dandy at the opera fails miserably. His clothes only reveal his insensitivity to matters of good taste, an essential factor that sets a dandy apart from the crowd. The reigning king of dandies, Henri de Marsay, comments that the provincial Lucien looks like "un mannequin habillé à la porte d'un tailleur" (*IP*, 280) [a mannequin dressed at a tailor's door]. Here Balzac shows dandyism as functioning somewhat like class differences by excluding outsiders from an elite group, although it is a certain elegance not necessarily based on noble birth that distinguishes dandies.

Meanwhile, Lucien's high hopes of instant success are frustrated upon his discovery of the hard work necessary to achieve true greatness as a writer. He abandons his poetic aspirations—and his principles—when he learns of the easy money and power to be gained in journalism. Balzac represents Lucien's seduction by the world of journalism as a kind of prostitution strategically timed to coincide with the beginnings of his relationship with the actress Coralie. In writing his first newspaper article, Lucien not only comments that he is giving up the "la virginité de ma plume" (*IP*, 393) [virginity of my pen], but the event also takes place in an actress's boudoir. Lucien's narcissistic desire for grandeur has caused him to lose patience, displacing his wish to become a renowned poet. And true to the pattern established in his childhood relations, Lucien exerts no effort in seducing Coralie, since his seductive beauty does all of the work for him. Lucien's narcissism expresses itself differently than that of the Balzacian coquettes analyzed previously, for he likes to immerse himself in physical pleasures, as in his relationship with Coralie, whereas coquettes tend to withhold sex from their admirers.

Thanks to his newfound reputation as a powerful journalist and dandy, the moment is ripe for him to capitalize on his seductiveness in order to anchor himself amid the aristocracy. Balzac displays Lucien's penchant for sexual indulgence in a scene where de Marsay, who has assumed the task of educating Lucien in the ways of Parisian society, strongly advises him to abandon his current lover, Coralie, for a high-society conquest. Faced with a choice between "la belle, l'amoureuse, la voluptueuse Coralie" (*IP*, 487) [beautiful, loving, voluptuous Coralie] or "la sèche, la hautaine, la cruelle Louise" (*IP*, 487) [dry, haughty, cruel Louise], Lucien lets himself be guided by the woman's sexual rather than political advantages and loses his chance to rise to success by association with Louise de Bargeton and her influential relative, the Marquise d'Espard. In this instance, Lucien's desire for sexual gratification prevents him from making the calculated decision of a dandy.

It is only when Lucien becomes truly desperate, after he has lost everything—including Coralie—and returned to Angoulême, that he uses the lessons he learned in Paris. Invited into the home of a noble family of Angoulême, Lucien makes his appearance in borrowed clothes. However, his attitude does not reflect his actual situation, for he is able to enact a split between his inner and outer conditions. Indeed, Rubempré manifests an intimate understanding of the theatrical aspects of dandyism; he knows people will evaluate him based on his appearance, regardless of the false impression he has created. He assumes an air of superiority to correspond with his elegant outfit and proceeds to create a sensation among the women in the salon. Just as Lucien had hoped, Louise de Bargeton falls victim to his feigned self-satisfaction, and she wonders, "D'où lui vient cette fierté? Mademoiselle des Touches serait-elle éprise de lui? [...] Il est si beau!" (*IP*, 677). [Where does this pride come from? Could Mademoiselle des Touches be in love with him? . . . He is so beautiful!] Lucien's behavior effectively resembles the kind of strategic narcissism René Girard attributes to the coquette, as when he says in reference to Freud, "If the narcissistic woman excites desire, it is by seeming to desire herself, by proposing to Freud this circular desire that never leaves itself, she presents an irresistible temptation to others' mimesis."[29] Louise reacts to Lucien as Freud to the narcissistic woman, even though this new attempt to seduce her ultimately fails.

Lucien's final "conquest" of the novel is one of special significance, in part because it sets the stage for the sequel novel, *Splendeurs et misères des courtisanes*. Jacques Collin, in his new identity as the Spanish priest Carlos Herrera, encounters a suicidal Lucien on a country road near Angoulême and entices him to abandon those deadly plans and accompany him to Paris. It is Lucien's narcissism that makes him particularly susceptible to Herrera's seductive discourse. Unlike Rastignac with Vautrin, he cannot resist Herrera's promises of a life enveloped in a kind of narcissistic plenitude even better than the pleasures he knew with Coralie. Herrera tempts him, promising an easy life in which he will become the Marquis de Rubempré, marry into a noble family of the Faubourg Saint-Germain, and obtain a position as a *pair* of France. Thus, the novel closes with Lucien believing he will finally achieve the happy combination of satisfying both his worldly ambitions and his sensual desires.

This example of male narcissism in *Illusions perdues* is at once unique and telling of Balzac's vision both of the dandy and of male *êtres séduisants*. Lucien de Rubempré is a highly seductive man who attracts people of both sexes and from all levels of the social spectrum; and, like many dandies, his particular beauty is of an effeminate nature. But he is also unusual in the Balzacian world in that he never really succeeds in turning his significant assets—a talent for writing and a remarkable physical beauty—into lasting tangible rewards. Although his meeting with Carlos Herrera prevents him from committing suicide at the conclusion of *Illusions perdues*, it in fact only delays the event until late in the sequel novel. Most of Balzac's other dandy characters, such as Henri de Marsay, Eugène de Rastignac, and Maxime de Trailles, enjoy much greater success (a point I will return to at the end of this chapter). As opposed to Lucien, they are defined more by the calculations of an *être séducteur* than by the narcissistic indulgence of an *être séduisant*.

Le Château des Désertes

With her novel *Le Château des Désertes*, Sand shifts the focus away from the hero's narcissistic seductions and onto his learning to let go of his fears so that he can actually love someone. Indeed, it is fear that propels the seductive young actor Célio Floriani to engage in lighthearted affairs rather than to form lasting bonds. By exposing Célio's hidden fears and placing this problematic on center stage, Sand reveals both an important dimension of the inner workings of narcissism and a weaker side of the seducer that does not traditionally get portrayed (a perspective we have already witnessed in *La marquise* and *Indiana*). Aside from analyzing this novel as another example of the dynamics of rivalry that motivates most narcissists' seductions, I will emphasize Sand's representation of Célio's inner confrontation with the forces of narcissism and his ensuing efforts to abandon this pattern of seduction.

In the novel's introductory chapters, Sand lays the groundwork for Célio's narcissistic personality. As is so often the case in Sand's novels, *Le Château des Désertes* is structured around a pair of characters—Célio (an actor) and the narrator, Adorno Salentini (a painter)—

who contrast with each other. Adorno's portrait presents Célio the way he first saw his friend as an actor on stage, in a performance where Célio fails to captivate his audience. Adorno, who has not yet met the actor, evaluates the performance for his female companion and paints Célio as a vain narcissist not so different from the young Lucien: "Il s'est nourri toute sa vie, j'en suis sûr, de l'idée qu'il ne pouvait faillir et qu'il avait le don de s'imposer. Probablement, c'est un enfant gâté" (*CD*, 48). [I am sure that he has nourished himself all his life on the idea that he could not fail and that he had the gift to impose himself. Probably, he is a spoiled child.] Sand even uses the word "coquette" in Adorno's description of Célio. Her word choice creates an affinity between Célio's seductiveness and that of other narcissistic dandies and female coquettes. By choosing a term normally reserved for women, the author also strategically signals narcissism's gender blindness.

In this novel, Sand shows how the nature of a child's relationship with his or her parents can make the child more susceptible to developing a narcissistic personality later in life. Both Célio and Adorno find their adult relations with women strongly shaped by their formative maternal experiences, even as their mothers represent a striking study in opposites. Adorno's mother gave birth to him outside of marriage, and she did not even recognize her son. Thus, Adorno's identity is strongly influenced by his unfulfilled need for affection. By withholding himself from love, Adorno essentially tries to protect himself from repeating the experience of disappointment he felt with his mother. He says, "Je brûlais d'un feu mystérieux trop longtemps comprimé pour ne pas m'avouer que j'allais être en proie moi-même à une passion énergique; mais, lorsque je me sentais sur le point d'y céder, j'étais épouvanté de l'idée que j'allais donner tout pour recevoir peu [...] peut-être rien" (*CD*, 40). [I burned with a mysterious fire too long repressed not to admit to myself that I myself was going to be prey to an energetic passion; but, when I felt myself on the point of giving in, I was terrified by the idea that I was giving all to receive little . . . maybe nothing.] Having never known mutual love, Adorno hesitates to love another at all.

Conversely, Célio's mother had continued to nurture him like a small child up to the time of her death when he was twenty-two, thereby confirming Adorno's first impressions of Célio, as quoted above. Once the two young men become friends following Célio's disastrous performance, Célio tells how he felt abandoned and alone upon losing his mother. He explains to Adorno, "[J]e n'aime pas les femmes, je les

déteste, et je suis affreusement méchant avec elles. J'en excepte une seule, la Boccaferri, parce que, seule, elle ressemble par certains côtés à ma mère, à la femme qui est cause de mon aversion pour toutes les autres [...]" (*CD*, 64). [I do not love women, I hate them, and I am terribly mean to them. I make an exception for one, Boccaferri, because, alone, in some ways she resembles my mother, the woman who is the cause of my aversion for all others. . . .] In effect, both men suffer narcissistic disorders, although for opposite reasons. Whereas Célio knew an unusually prolonged experience of satisfaction and oneness with his mother, Adorno never even felt that original bond. However, the results in both cases are the same, since both are afraid of love.

Although Célio may except his childhood friend Cécilia from his generalized critique of women, his narcissism prevents him from spontaneously desiring her. Instead, his desire develops mimetically, following Girard's triangular pattern that I have traced in other texts. Once Célio learns that Adorno finds Cécilia quite beautiful, he contradicts an earlier pronouncement about her lack of beauty. Despite the ease with which Célio changes his stated opinion of Cécilia, however, he refuses to admit—to Adorno or to himself—that he might have romantic feelings for her. Furthermore, he tells Adorno that he respects Cécilia too much even to think of seducing her. By highlighting the pleasure and glory his identity as a seducer affords him, Célio projects an air of confidence and satisfaction, thereby casting his situation in a positive light. But one begins to realize that his activity of seduction represents more nearly a fleeing from himself than a pursuit of others, a defensive shield rather than a wholehearted choice. In other words, Célio suffers from a split between his inner and outer selves, due to his narcissism.

When Célio's and Cécilia's families move to the Château des Désertes and spend their evenings studying the art of theater by performing their own improvisations of plays, Célio finds that while learning to perfect his art, he is additionally able to lift his veil and face his fear of love. Significantly, the seducer's self-confrontation takes place within the context of their production of *Don Juan*, with Célio playing the role of the legendary seducer. Like Sténio of *Lélia*, Célio has forged an identity as a Don Juan-esque seducer, a facade that allows him to enjoy the self-affirmation of a woman's desire for him without his having to form an attachment to her. Consequently, he shudders when his self-protective edifice begins to crumble as he recognizes his feelings of jealousy over Cécilia. His stage role as Don Juan leaves

him increasingly troubled: "Je ne suis pas Don Juan [...] et c'est pourtant dans ma voie et dans ma destinée de l'être sur les planches. [...] Non! non! [...] je ne suis pas fait pour aimer! Cécilia n'est pas ma mère. Il peut lui arriver d'aimer demain quelqu'un plus que moi, toi, par exemple!" (*CD*, 138). [I am not Don Juan . . . and yet it is in my path and in my destiny to be him on stage. . . . No! no! . . . I am not made to love! Cécilia is not my mother. She could happen to love someone more than me tomorrow, you, for example!] Amid Célio's confused emotions, one element emerges with clarity. The fear that restrains Célio's love stems from his terror at the possibility that the woman he might love would not feel the same kind of unconditional love his mother gave him. Like Don Juan, Célio has preferred to satisfy himself with the momentary thrill of a seduction—"je ne cherche que l'ivresse" (*CD*, 72) [I only look to feel ecstasy], he says of his relations with women—rather than to place himself in a position where he risks incurring the narcissistic wound of rejection and abandonment by someone he loves.

Each time Sand uses the Don Juan legend in her fiction, she emphasizes a different aspect of this infamous seducer. Whereas the mythic Don Juan has historically been represented as continually searching for an ideal woman he can never find, in *Le Château des Désertes* Sand stops short the search precisely by locating Célio's ideal. Rather than viewing Don Juan as someone turned toward conquests to come, Sand situates the ideal woman haunting the seducer in the past: as the mother who provided for all her child's needs, creating for him the plenitude of primary narcissism. Jean Laplanche describes primary narcissism as a stage preceding the child's development of a sense of self. As Laplanche writes, "[P]rimary narcissism, as a psychic reality, can only be the primordial myth of return to the maternal breast."[30] Furthermore, in representing the figure of Don Juan as someone troubled by a narcissistic fantasy, Sand creates yet another demystification of the great seducer. Instead of reflecting a glorious figure of male dominance, Célio as Don Juan reveals the seducer's insecurities.[31]

When Célio emerges successfully from his crisis, the novel can conclude on a happy note with the marriages of Stella and Adorno, Cécilia and Célio. In effect, it was Célio's coquettish projection of a seductive yet highly artificial identity that hampered both his talent for acting and his ability to love. Even before he accepted his passion for Cécilia, Célio did recognize the self-transformative power of his art, for he tells Cécilia's father (who instructs them all in the elements of theater): "[T]u m'as appris à me connaître. Tu m'as rendu l'orgueil en me guérissant de la vanité. Il me semble que chaque jour, ta fille et toi faites de moi un autre homme" (*CD*, 132). [You taught me to know myself. You have returned my pride in curing me of vanity. It seems that each day, your daughter and you make me into another man.] By staging Célio's simultaneous acquisition of true art and true love, Sand promotes love while making the artifices of seduction a synonym for weakness and vanity. Sand thus upholds authenticity as an aesthetic value as well as a superior form of human relations.

Narcissism constitutes a defining character trait for Célio and Lucien, strongly shaping these young men's mode of seduction. Célio's portrayal as a narcissistic coquette underscores the affinity between his mental attitude and that of the dandy Lucien. While Célio's character lacks the dandy's specific historical grounding, one can nevertheless recognize him in Carassus's description of the dandy, since he, too, tries to hide his vulnerability behind the projection of his identity as a confidant seducer. It is in a novel analyzed in chapter 1, *Horace*, that Sand created a narcissistic dandy whose situation is closely linked to the nineteenth-century social setting. Horace's lack of success raises a parallel with the Balzacian coquette who, like Sand's dandy, meets her downfall in the conclusion. The contours of their situations resemble one another, even if the particular reasons for their relegation to a kind of outcast status differ. Foedora and Béatrix are made to suffer because they do not submit to the social order that demands female submission to men's desires and the confinement of female sexuality to marriage relations, while Horace's failure stems from his inability to function within the rules of this—ideal, republican—society, where respect and equality in love form the foundation of a strong society.[32]

The Dandy-Seducer: A Postrevolutionary Figure

When dandyism first made its way onto the Continent in the early nineteenth century as a British import, the term "dandy" had pejorative connotations. Balzac wrote in his 1830 *Traité de la vie élégante*: "Le *Dandysme* est une hérésie de la vie élégante" (*TVE*, 225). [*Dandyism* is a heresy of elegant life.] Defined in contrast to the dandy, Balzac's *élégant* is a man best characterized by his idleness in society.

He is "l'homme qui ne fait rien" (*TVE*, 211) [the man who does nothing] as opposed to "l'homme qui travaille" [the man who works] (*TVE*, 211), or "l'homme qui pense" (*TVE*, 211) [the man who thinks]. So as to establish the *élégant*'s class status as something like an aristocrat, Balzac declares, "Un homme devient riche, il naît élégant" (*TVE*, 225). [A man becomes rich, he is born elegant.] However, the dandy eventually overcame his initially low status, and in *Le dandysme de Baudelaire à Mallarmé* Michel Lemaire notes that the dandy's reputation improved following 1830. According to Lemaire, "He progressively became, under Louis-Philippe, the obligatory model of all elegants."[33] The dandy's rising status during the July Monarchy helps to explain Balzac's subsequent use of the term to qualify some of his most engaging characters. Nonetheless, Balzac seems to have retained a certain sense of his initial opposition between the *élégant* and the dandy, as the aristocratic value of idleness that constitutes a defining trait of the *élégant* does not necessarily characterize Balzacian dandies. The following section will explore the difference between a notion of dandyism as idle *élégance* and the more strategic imitation of dandyism enacted by most dandies of *La comédie humaine*.

The appearance of dandyism in France during the postrevolutionary turmoil of the Restoration and July Monarchy is far from coincidental. The dandy's narcissistic sense of vulnerability and his keen awareness of the fragility of his self appear related to his specific historical position in society. In *Le peintre de la vie moderne*, Baudelaire described dandyism as "une espèce de nouvelle aristocratie, d'autant plus difficile à rompre qu'elle sera basée sur les facultés les plus précieuses, les plus indestructibles, et sur les dons célestes que le travail et l'argent ne peuvent conférer"[34] [a kind of new aristocracy, all the more difficult to break in that it will be based on the most valuable, the most indestructible faculties, and on celestial gifts that work and money cannot bestow]. In this perspective, dandyism represents an attempt by members of the nobility (and by others like artists who enjoyed the direct protection of the nobility during the ancien régime) to counteract the loss of power and influence they suffered as a result of the revolutions of 1789 and 1830. Rather than trying to compete with the bourgeoisie on this rising class's terms, the dandy offers himself as the model of an entirely different set of values. Emilien Carassus observed in *Le mythe du dandy*: "[W]hen, in the 19th century, the reign of money, of bourgeois, commercial, political, or industrial activity is inaugurated, the dandy opposes his scorn to all social insertion submitted to ordinary criteria of success."[35] Maintaining aristocratic traditions of idleness in the face of the bourgeoisie's productivity, dandies invest only in the production of the self, a luxurious expenditure on seductiveness. The dandy's creation of a seductive exterior marks a point of conjunction where the narcissistic exhibitionism of his personal relations joins with his larger yearning for self-affirmation in a changing society.

Unlike the aristocratic or artistic dandy associated, for example, with Baudelaire, the characters Balzac terms dandies do not fully set themselves apart from society, nor do they necessarily define themselves against bourgeois values. Carassus makes a significant observation about Balzac's unique vision of dandyism when he writes of Maxime de Trailles, Henri de Marsay, and Eugène de Rastignac: "Balzac's characters play at dandyism, they use it as one of the accessory means for social elevation, they adopt attitudes that make them considered as dandies, but in fact their ethic admits singular deviations in relation to that to which the dandy subcribes."[36] Rather than making dandyism an end in itself, Balzac's dandies use it as a means to achieve an ulterior goal: positions and power in society. By throwing themselves into the conflict for power and by jockeying for favor in the new regime, these shrewd characters profit from dandyism's elite status, turning it into a strategy of seduction. Whereas later writers' dandies make their marginal social status a point of pride, displaying their difference, Balzac's elegant young men strive to reach the center of power.

Viewed in this light, Balzac's version of the *élégant* turns out to be neither a dandy nor an *être séduisant*, but an *être séducteur* who poses as a seductive dandy to anchor himself as a member of the elite upper class. With the exception of Lucien de Rubempré, Balzac reconciles his dandies' erotic and public lives in ways that are mutually reinforcing and help them to achieve both their sexual and their social goals. Characters like Henri de Marsay and Eugène de Rastignac combine the aristocratic exterior signs of idle elegance with practical bourgeois ingenuity, and their seductiveness only enhances their means of acquiring and holding power.

Whether the person who establishes his identity as a dandy represents an aristocrat who has lost his secure and privileged status in society or someone of bourgeois origins who identifies with the aristocracy in an effort to climb the social ladder, it is a scenario that would have been largely inconceivable without the social upheavals of the French Revolution. Therefore, the literary examples of narcissistic seducers studied in this chapter reflect a historical evolution in modes of seduction.

In *La comédie humaine*, both the coquette and the dandy are conceived as figures who display an aristocratic mode of behavior, and the social causes of their identity intertwine with the psychological foundation of narcissism. Whereas the particular brand of "la vie élégante" led by dandies allowed them to combine bourgeois and aristocratic models, the coquette's aristocratic femininity could not be reconciled with bourgeois domesticity. While Balzac redefines dandyism to provide for his male characters' success, his coquettes do not receive such sympathetic treatment, as witnessed by the coquette's spectacular fall from her position as society's *femme à la mode*. Aside from the social dimensions of the coquette's status and on a more personal and psychological level, Balzac displays a bitter antagonism toward these female *êtres séduisants* by emphasizing the cruel and diabolical nature of their dealings with the men who adore them. Amid the postrevolutionary turmoil in society that created a flux in power on the levels of both class and sex, Balzac strikes out at the most vulnerable target and performs a reactionary gesture by punishing his coquettes for their insubordination while integrating his male dandies into the power structure.

Unlike Balzac, Sand does not decide the success or failure of her coquettes and dandies in such stark, gendered terms. Instead, her abhorrence of all artifice and inauthenticity causes her to condemn the coquettish behavior of narcissistic *êtres séduisants*, both male and female. Horace's failure and Célio's success are defined by whether or not they are able to abandon narcissistic behavior in favor of mutual love. That Lélia, perceived by men as a narcissistic coquette, fails to find love only reflects Sand's conviction that the men of her generation did not know how to love an extraordinary woman who broke the mold of traditional femininity. Like Lélia, Balzac's coquettes suffer in a male-dominated world for their refusal to submit to the bourgeois-inspired model of domesticity. While Balzac's representations of female coquetry highlight women's disempowered status in patriarchal society, his female characters' jealous rivalry reflects the fact that patriarchal society condemns women to seek affirmation of their worth through recognition by men. In contrast, Sand represents Lélia sympathetically—no doubt because of her personal experiences as a nontraditional woman—and she dares to imagine a world in which women would be loved as equals, enjoying power and authority in society.

The narcissistic *êtres séduisants* studied in this chapter represent a conglomerate of beings both passive and active, masculine and feminine. In their relations of seduction, they are clearly marked by the sociohistorical conditions of nineteenth-century males and females. They face the new order of society created by the Revolution and seek self-affirmation from socially designated (male) sources of validation. Yet in some circumstances they display behavior that strays from traditional notions of masculinity and femininity, as when an effeminate dandy resists casting himself as a subject of desire, or when a coquette refuses to take up a submissive position in erotic relations. Moreover, the fragile sense of self that characterizes these narcissists contributes to their unstable, multiple identities, thereby obliging readers, in turn, to view subjectivity as a divided and mobile production rather than a unified entity. Narcissists' seductiveness thus provides an illustration of fluid configurations of gender and desire that, although bipolar, do not always reflect conventional notions of relations between the sexes.

Conclusion: Seduction, a View of the World

Seduction provides an especially revelatory site for illuminating an author's attitude toward society and the artifice accompanying much of social interaction. It is a thoroughly worldly activity, as Baudrillard asserts: "Seduction is always that of evil. Or that of the world. It is the artifice of the world."[1] Moreover, seduction touches upon broader issues of gender roles, class relations, and the distribution of power, both between individuals and in the social order. Seduction politicizes desire, for it is rarely *just* about sexual attraction. Other powerful forces come into play as well, infusing spontaneous lust with calculated design. The strategies employed by seducers and seductresses, the ulterior motives driving them to act and the dynamic positioning of self and other that creates new identities and conditions of reality, constitute some of the key characteristics that set seduction apart from other erotic relations.

In seduction, the persuasion designed to win another over to one's desire often devolves into exploitation and manipulation. Indeed, because success is based purely on the efficacy of one's performance rather than on the degree to which a seducer or seductress genuinely presents the self, in this arena artifice displaces authenticity as the ruling value. As we have seen, Balzac and Sand, contemporaries and friends who addressed certain common issues in their fiction, nonetheless have very different ideological motivations; a different sense of purpose drives each author's writing project. Bernard Guyon has used the term "social aestheticism" to describe Balzac's approach to writing, and he explains, "We mean by that a movement of his sensibility, an orientation of his intelligence, that leads him only to see the world through the eyes of the artist, only to judge men and things according to their aesthetic value without taking any account of their moral value, individual or social."[2] Based on insights gained from analyzing the place seduction occupies in each writer's works, I would oppose a Sandian *social moralism* to what Guyon termed Balzac's *social aestheticism*.

Balzac's narratives can be said to figure his own "seduction" by society, as they reveal his fascination with the powers of artifice and theatricality. His *social aestheticism* allowed him to exploit the narrative potential of all manners of social—and asocial—behavior, such that his personal worldview and the vision of society produced in *La comédie humaine* are not equivalent. In representing a scoundrel like Vautrin, Balzac does not condemn outright this character's immorality. Instead, the writer steps outside ideology to underscore the "talents" that allow this figure to thrive in society. Even Balzac's larger-than-life figures, such as Vautrin and Rastignac, are certainly not paragons of human perfection, yet neither does the exceedingly virtuous Madame de Mortsauf of *Le lys dans la vallée* approach the ideal of an exemplary Sandian character such as Yseult de Villepreux. However, to say that Balzac adopts a largely aesthetic viewpoint is not to imply that *La comédie humaine* presents an amoral world. Balzac's readers do confront the duplicity, artificiality, greed, and self-interest that tend to overtake more virtuous human qualities. Yet, one of Balzac's great strengths as a writer, and a characteristic that generally prevents his personal social and political agenda from weighing down his fictional world, is his ability to adopt multiple perspectives and to reveal that even the most unethical positions contain both strengths and weaknesses.

Sand's relation to seduction is quite the opposite of Balzac's, just as her sense of purpose in writing differs from his approach. In reading Sand, one is quite conscious both of the author's ethical stance and that her texts tend to serve as a vehicle for transmitting a moral message. The numerous representations of seduction and the skillfully crafted, engaging scenes treating theatricality in Sand's works attest to her preoccupation with these themes, as when she brilliantly represents Noun's and Indiana's seductive masquerades in *Indiana* or reveals the workings of seduction's performativity in *La marquise*. But for Sand, the enthralling artifice of seduction inevitably goes from being a purely aesthetic reaction to being a matter of ethics, whereby it is rejected or demoted in favor of some higher ideal of being or loving. Thus, Sand's representations of seduction tend to play a recurring role, serving as a negative example to which she can compare her ideal couples. Furthermore, because of Sand's penchant for narratives structured around pairs of opposites, her plots manifest an almost formulaic quality despite her stylistic variety and formal inventiveness. In her preface to *Le meunier d'Angibault*, Béatrice Didier remarks on the pitfalls a writer can easily fall into when giving voice to social ideas in a novel, arguing that Sand avoids that path:

> There is nothing more boring than the conversations of intellectuals who expose ideas in a novel; the dramatic interest languishes and the reader tells himself that he is not there to read a treatise, but a story. . . . But precisely because she simultaneously has the sense of the real and of the fictional plot, George Sand prevents herself from isolating, as two incommunicable worlds, the utopian couple and the reality couple.[3]

Yet, even with this interaction between reality and utopia on the level of a single text, Sand's repeated use of a technique whereby one couple represents all that is good and the other couple is their negative mirror showing few, if any, redeeming qualities creates a somewhat predictable effect when her works are compared to one another. Granted, Balzac's oeuvre, with its own character types, does not completely escape the formulaic quality I attribute to Sand's writings, as attested by the aforementioned *Le lys dans la vallée*. His narrative style even makes his texts more identifiable than Sand's. It is simply that Sand's moral discourse is more pervasive, and Balzac's more ambiguous.

The different social practices articulated by Balzac and Sand through their writing could also explain the varied types of response their fiction elicits from readers—professional and nonprofessional alike. Just as erotic seduction is a two-way process requiring the victim's assent in order to succeed, so readers are captivated by a text only when it appeals to their sensibility. A text may enthrall its readers by presenting characters with which one can identify or find desirable, obviously, but we also respond to the ideas expressed in fiction, to crafty narrative techniques, or to a pleasing style. With his flair for readerly seduction, Balzac plays upon our fascination with the immoral, continuing to astonish us with the schemes he invents for his characters. His innovative technique of recurring characters makes his fiction come alive for the reader, beyond the pages of the book in hand. Moreover, Balzac delights us with his character portraits and his ability to identify the inner forces driving a character or to make manifest the unspoken dynamics of interpersonal relations. Like Balzac, Sand represents social reality, but with a utopian thrust. She focuses her fictional efforts more on what could be than on what is. Her works satisfy a yearning for the ideal, for a moral universe in which good and right are rewarded—or at least valorized, even when they do not manage to prevail. Thus, the extent to which her fiction "seduces" her readers would depend, in part, on whether or not the readers are sympathetic to the causes she champions. In Sand's ideal world, exceptional women do succeed, sometimes, in finding a man to love them as an equal, and individuals are judged for their inner worth rather than by their position on the social ladder. Furthermore, Sand's remarkable heroines, her upstanding males, and her "noble" peasants offer important models of identification to the disempowered in society and counterexamples to the standard fictional fare of the time; she calls upon readers (those receptive to this call) to question assumptions, prejudices, and stereotypes. Ironically, then, it is Sand's social moralism that constitutes one of her greatest assets as a novelist and her biggest turn-off for readers who remain unseduced either by the content or the aesthetic value of her idealism. In effect, Sand's fiction valorizes respectable qualities, while Balzac's often thrills us with intricate plots that depict humanity's less wholesome side.

Tracing seduction from ancien régime examples in texts by Laclos, Crébillon fils, and Marivaux to the works of Balzac and Sand, I have tried to identify certain timeless principles amid the changing face of postrevolutionary society. The chapters of this book, each exploring a different facet of seduction, together describe a site where individuals enjoy a relatively high degree of freedom. Unconstricted by conventional standards of behavior or even by personal history, as the situations of Isidora or the Princess de Cadignan demonstrate, the seducer or seductress redefines him- or herself to fit the conditions of the moment. And because these conditions are partly determined by the person seduced, whose assent is essential to success, he or she also enjoys a measure of input. Indeed, viewing seduction in terms of performativity has revealed the extent to which seduction is a two-way process negotiated between seducer and seduced rather than the unidimensional conquest one might otherwise envision it to be. Furthermore, creating a seductive new identity can actually work to transform the seducer or seductress's present situation, as when Eugène de Rastignac's apparent intimacy with Delphine de Nucingen creates a favorable impression of him in Parisian salons that eventually does translate into a successful seduction and social influence for the young dandy. Paradoxically, then, the performance of seduction entails substituting compelling appearances for prior reality, thereby creating a new space of reality that encompasses seducer, seduced, and all those who believe it to be real.

For Balzac and Sand, the liberty of seduction offered a means to explore varied—and sometimes conflicting—visions of sexual difference and gender divisions, for their fictional characters do not necessarily mirror the prevailing contemporary attitudes toward masculinity and femininity. During the nineteenth century even more so than today, the sexual activity implicit in seduction was viewed differently for men and women. Balzac's *Physiologie du mariage*, although nominally a guide to assuring marital fidelity, actually asserts the inevitability of male seduction, due to the large number of young single men with natural sexual appetites prowling around: "Quel mari maintenant dormira tranquille à côté de sa jeune et jolie femme, en apprenant que trois célibataires, au moins, sont à l'affût [...] il est impossible qu'ils ne soient pas, un jour, victorieux dans cette lutte."[4] [What husband will now sleep soundly next to his young and pretty wife, upon learning that three bachelors, at least, are lying in wait to seize the opportunity . . . it is impossible that they not one day be victorious in this struggle.] Balzac's text indicates that an attitude of "boys will be boys" prevailed at the time, whereas the risks of pregnancy for women made the consequences of seduction entirely more serious for them. In fact, seduction was even a legal issue, as evidenced by M. Fournel's 1781 *Traité de la séduction*, a text that describes the rights of seduced women and their seducers regarding the issue of paternity. The posture of blame this text displays toward women reinforces the notion that a double standard existed: "Or, quand une fille a le malheur de sentir sa vertu chanceler, il n'est point contraire aux bonnes mœurs d'exiger de son séducteur qu'il se hâtera de lui donner le titre d'épouse légitime, et de réparer par le Sacrement, les suites affligeantes attachées à sa faiblesse."[5] [Thus, when a young woman has the misfortune to feel her virtue wavering, it is not at all contrary to good morals to insist that her seducer rush to give her the title of legitimate wife, and to repair by the sacrament the sorrowful results attached to her weakness.] Balzac's and Sand's fictional treatments of seduction rarely address these material consequences, although Sand's representation in *Indiana* of a pregnant Noun drowning herself following her abandonment by Raymon constitutes a striking exception.

Instead, Balzac and Sand used seduction as an arena for exploring other issues. In many instances, they depicted their seducers and seductresses in defiance of gender stereotypes. The women in their works may exploit the seductive appeal of their bodies, yet they also manifest a shrewd sense of calculation in designing their appearance. By using both corporeal and intellectual attributes, these writers' seductresses—in particular Isidora, the Princess de Cadignan, or Béatrix—form a hybrid of gender types. Furthermore, male dandies were represented with certain feminine qualities, and Balzac specially adapted a mode of dandyism that could be deployed as a strategy of seduction. Sand's interest in male narcissists took a different form, as she explored the divisions and frailties of the masculine subject hidden behind the seductive exterior of a Don Juan in novels like *Horace* and *Le Château des Désertes*.

Power asymmetry constitutes another defining characteristic of seduction, for part of the thrill resides in the display of agency the seducer or seductress enacts by captivating another person's desire. The notion of a power differential offers an additional means to examine representations of gender differences in the social order, as both Balzac and Sand alternately reinforce and subvert the conventional ordering of masculine and feminine roles. While nineteenth-century society instituted mechanisms for excluding women from power in the public sphere, these writers' narratives remind readers that sexual domination knows no gender limitations, as female characters are sometimes shown to appropriate sexual agency. Indeed, the dominating Césarine Dietrich operates by many of the same cruel instincts as the Count de La Palférine or Leone Leoni, while Henri de Marsay and Paquita are represented in a situation of reversible power dynamics. While the instinct toward domination may exist in both women and men, this behavior was perceived differently depending on the gender of the dominant partner. Balzac and Sand seemed to have sensed the transgressive nature of certain representations of feminine seduction, as indicated by Césarine's conversion to domestic femininity and the marquise's withdrawal to a convent following Paquita's murder—conclusions that counterbalance the subversive elements contained within the narrative. In contrast to these female characters, dominant seducers garner esteem, and even desirability, for their exploits. In effect, we are reminded that in a patriarchal society the sexual freedom of seduction extends farther for men than for women.

During the period when Balzac and Sand wrote, class structures as well as political and economic power were in a state of mutation, as French society of the Restoration and July Monarchy witnessed changing relations between the aristocracy and the bourgeoisie. The idle aristocratic art and the utilitarian bourgeois strategies of seduction—two distinct veins of fiction during the ancien régime—became less distinguishable along class lines in the postrevolutionary era. In the fiction of this period, seduction scenarios and plots of *arrivisme* knew a harmonious coexistence due to the waning influence of an aristocratic ideology based on birth. Indeed, the social climbers in search of influence and positions in Balzac's and Sand's fiction come from varied backgrounds, as evidenced by Horace, Lucien de Rubempré, and Rastignac. For all these young men, seduction represents a means of double conquest, sexual and social.

The diverse representations of seduction in the works of Balzac and Sand complement one another in revealing that sexual freedom does not come without a price. Despite the liberty to create oneself anew, to hide fragility behind a seductive exterior, to dominate another person or allow oneself to surrender, to cast aside socially ordained behaviors and simply give oneself to the passion offered by seduction, this relation invokes its own set of restrictions. The self-affirmation gained is often balanced by feelings of self-alienation or by disappointment when the energy that drives seduction dissipates. Furthermore, even as the players eschew standards of behavior prescribed by society, they never actually escape evaluation based on their gender and position in the social hierarchy. Not only are their own sense of identity and other characters' reactions to them socially informed, but this kind of scrutiny operates at the extradiegetic level as well, influencing how an author decides to represent the seduction and how readers interpret it.

Comparing Balzac and Sand, we have seen that while they situate seduction in similar contexts and both writers subvert gender stereotypes, important distinctions exist regarding the attitude each one adopted toward his or her material. Quite likely, sexual difference does shape their contrasting perspectives; however, other factors are also influential. Fascinated by theatricality, Balzac appreciated the aesthetic aspects of seduction's performance and rarely addressed its morality. This approach reflects his overall conception of *La comédie humaine*, where contemporary society is represented in all its facets and moral ambiguity reigns. Sand, however, tended to evoke seduction precisely because she sought a negative example to give texture to the ideal moral landscape represented in a narrative. Her severe censuring of seduction for its frequent motivation in a will to dominate and its negative effects on exploited victims exemplifies her larger concern for all the disempowered in society. For example, her elevation of the "noble" peasant Pierre in *Le compagnon du tour de France*, where she contrasts him to Isidore Lerebours (a man of a higher class but who displays no redeeming character traits) demonstrates that her interest in combating prejudices was not limited to the sexual arena. Furthermore, the significant number of narratives in which the heroine rejects her seducer, even though that choice implies solitude, attests to the great value Sand placed on freedom and equality. Thus, the sexual politics of seduction is an outgrowth of these authors' larger agendas, of how they envisioned their writing.

Regardless of politics, seduction continues to enthrall us—in both literature and life—and it remains a powerful force configuring interactions between the sexes. Balzac's and Sand's contemporaries might have read the seduction manuals analyzed in the introduction, such as *L'art de réussir en amour*, *L'art de connaître les femmes*, and *L'art de faire la cour aux femmes et de s'en faire aimer*. At the beginning of the twenty-first century, we are still trying to discover how best to appeal to the opposite sex. In the past decade in France, for example, those browsing through titles at the local FNAC bookstore could discover the following pop psychology and self-help titles: *Le complexe de Casanova: Les séducteurs impénitents et les femmes qui leur succombent*, *Séduction: Mode d'emploi,* and *Draguer et séduire aujourd'hui*.[6] Another book, a testimony to the French interest in astrology, is simply entitled *Séductions* and offers an astrological approach to attracting another person, including a chapter on "the influence of astrological cycles on your seduction in function of your sign."[7] Surprisingly, the subtitle of Leroy's introduction to *Draguer et séduire aujourd'hui*—"Conquering a Woman"—suggests that the language of seduction has not evolved much over the centuries. While the power disparity between men and women in both the public and private spheres has greatly decreased since the periods about which Balzac and Sand wrote, distinctions between self and other always remain, on one level or another. Whatever the particular social context may be, seduction relentlessly locates the power asymmetry that configures self and other in an oppositional dynamics, providing a forum for seducers and seductresses to display their agency and affirm their desirability by captivating another's desire.

Notes

Introduction

1. George Sand, *Correspondance* (Paris: Editions Garnier Frères, 1964), 1:858, 2:291–92.

2. Even though it falls outside my main time period, I have included Sand's 1851 *Le Château des Désertes* because it addresses thematic issues pertinent to the study of seduction.

3. Rose Fortassier, "Echos des 'Liaisons dangereuses' dans 'La comédie humaine,'" *L'Année balzacienne* (Paris: Garnier Frères, 1976), 277–81.

4. Choderlos de Laclos, *Les liaisons dangereuses*, Coll. Folio (Paris: Gallimard, 1972), 39–40.

5. Ibid., 306.

6. Roy Roussel, *The Conversation of the Sexes: Seduction and Equality in Selected Seventeenth- and Eighteenth-Century Texts* (New York: Oxford University Press, 1986), 113.

7. The traditional model of seduction is epitomized in Jean Baudrillard's *De la séduction*, where the author reproduces society's familiar opposition between the mind and the body to attribute the seducer with a strategy of intellectual *calcul* and the seductress with a strategy based on physical *parure. De la séduction* (Paris: Editions Galillée, 1979), 22.

8. For an analysis of this phenomenon, see, for example, Nancy Armstrong, *Desire and Domestic Fiction: A Political History of the Novel* (New York: Oxford University Press, 1987); Geneviève Fraisse, *Muse de la raison: La démocratie exclusive et la différence des sexes* (Aix-en-Provence: Editions Alinéa, 1989); and Joan Landes, *Women and the Public Sphere in the Age of the French Revolution* (Ithaca, NY: Cornell University Press, 1988).

9. Louis de Saint-Ange, *Le secret de triompher des femmes et de les fixer* (Bruxelles: De la société typographique, 1825), 34.

10. LAMI, *L'art de rendre les femmes fidèles* (Paris: Chez l'éditeur à la librairie française et étrangère, 1828), 21–22.

11. Un ami de Cythère, *L'art de faire la cour aux femmes et de s'en faire aimer* (Paris: Terry, 1837), 21.

12. Ibid., 76.

13. Ibid., 85.

14. Ibid., 77.

15. Ibid., 67.

16. Jules Janin, introduction to *Les Français peints par eux-mêmes, encyclopédie morale du dix-neuvième siècle* (Paris: L. Curmer, 1841), 1:viii.

17. Ibid., xii.

18. Honoré de Balzac, "La femme comme il faut," in *Les Français peints par eux-mêmes* (see note 16), 1:29.

19. "La grande dame de 1830," in *Les Français peints par eux-mêmes* (see note 16), 1:162.
20. P.C. and A. L. R., *L'art de briller en société; ou, Manuel de l'homme du monde*, 3rd edition (Paris: Terry , 1829), 16.
21. L'auteur de la "Biographie dramatique," *L'art de réussir en amour, enseigné en 25 leçons; ou, Nouveaux secrets de triompher des femmes, et de les fixer.* 2nd ed. (Paris: À la librairie française et étrangère, 1826), 154.
22. Ibid., 157.
23. Un ami de Cythère, *L'art de faire la cour*, 205.
24. Ibid., 206.

Chapter 1. Seduction and Society

1. Priscilla P. Clark, *The Battle of the Bourgeois: The Novel in France, 1789–1848* (Paris: Didier, 1973), 138.
2. Crébillon fils, *Les égarements du cœur et de l'esprit* (Paris: Gallimard, Coll. Folio, 1977), 48.
3. Ibid., 245.
4. Ibid., 254.
5. Ibid.
6. Stendhal, *Armance; ou, Quelques scènes d'un salon de Paris en 1827* (Paris: Garnier Frères, 1950), 2.
7. Pierre Carlet de Marivaux, *Le paysan parvenu* (Paris: Editions Gallimard, Collection Folio, 1981), 45.
8. Ibid., 48.
9. Marie-Paule Laden, "The Pitfalls of Success: Jacob's Evolution in Marivaux's *Le paysan parvenu*," *Romanic Review* 74 (1983): 174.
10. Amy Wyngaard, "Switching Codes: Class, Clothing, and Cultural Change in the Works of Marivaux and Watteau," *Eighteenth Century Studies* 33 (2000): 531–32.
11. Ibid., 524–25.
12. Ernest Simon, "A Tradition of the Comic Novel: Sorel, Scarron, Furetière, Sterne, Diderot" (diss., Columbia University, 1963), 4.
13. According to Guy Chaussinand-Nogaret, the notion of merit as an amalgam of bourgeois and noble values can be traced back to the mid-eighteenth century: "After 1760 the notions of worth and honor that had defined the specificity of the nobility up to that point are relayed by a new notion: that of merit, a bourgeois value, typical of the third order, that the nobility integrates, makes its own, that it accepts and recognizes officially as a criteria of nobility." *La noblesse au XVIIIe siècle: De la féodalité aux Lumières* (Paris: Librairie Hachette, 1976), 53–54. All translations in the notes are my own.
14. Landes, *Women and the Public Sphere*, 24.
15. Catherine Nesci, *La femme mode d'emploi: Balzac, de la "Physiologie du mariage" à "La comédie humaine"* (Lexington, KY: French Forum Publishers, 1992), 31.
16. Ibid., 136.
17. The doctrine of Saint-Simonianism, a socialist movement founded by adherents to the ideas of the Count de Saint-Simon (1760–1825), espoused notions such as fraternal love and equality of the sexes. At one point, Eugénie lectures Horace, "Vous savez que je suis de la religion saint-simonienne à certains égards [...] et que je ne vois dans le mariage qu'un engagement volontaire et libre, auquel le maire, les témoins et le sacristain ne donnent pas un caractère plus sacré que ne le font l'amour et la conscience" (*H*, 134). [You know that I follow the Saint-Simonian religion in certain respects . . . and that I see marriage as a voluntary and free engagement, to which the mayor, witnesses, and the sexton do not give any more sacred character than love and conscience.]
18. In *The Conversation of the Sexes*, Roy Roussel describes the type of seduction scenario most associated with Valmont in the following terms: "[The man] mimics a feminine susceptibility to feeling, emotion, and surrender to pleasure, only to lure her to do

the same. Then he tells his friends. He recuperates his surrender as triumph. He has conquered her and added to his reputation, while for her surrender marks inescapable ruin. This is the 'work' of seducing and ruining women which has grown so tedious to Valmont in *Les liaisons dangereuses.*" Roussel, *Conversation of the Sexes*, 21.

19. Naomi Schor, *George Sand and Idealism* (New York: Columbia University Press, 1993), 95.

20. George Sand, *Œuvres autobiographiques*, ed. Georges Lubin (Paris: Pléiade, 1970–71), 2:161–62.

21. Schor, *George Sand and Idealism,* 41.

22. See *Contrat de marriage*, *Ténébreuse affaire*, and *Député d'Arcis.*

23. These artisans formed secret societies to promote progressive treatment of workers, and their origins can be traced back to fraternities of workers who built medieval cathedrals. As part of their training, they traveled for three to five years, performing a "tour de France." James Chastain, *Encyclopedia of 1848 Revolutions* (June 6, 1997), http:/ /www.ohiou.edu/~Chastain/index.htm (accessed August 5, 2003).

24. See also the novels *Adriani*, *Horace*, *Indiana*, and *Tamaris.*

25. George Sand, *Adriani* (Paris: Editions France-Empire, 1980), 95.

26. Lucienne Frappier-Mazur, "Code romantique et résurgences du féminin dans *La comtesse de Rudolstadt* (*Consuelo*)," in *Le récit amoureux*, ed. Didier Coste (Seyssel: Editions du Champ Vallon, 1984), 54.

27. Isabelle Naginski, *George Sand: Writing for Her Life* (New Brunswick, NJ: Rutgers University Press, 1991), 94.

28. Inspired by Christopher Prendergast's use of the commercial term "broker" to describe Vautrin's role toward Lucien, I use the term "seduction broker" to apply to an intermediary figure who advocates seduction strategies that combine the age-old art of captivation with market-inspired economic exchanges. See Christopher Prendergast,*The Order of Mimesis: Balzac, Stendhal, Nerval, Flaubert* (Cambridge: Cambridge University Press, 1986, 97.

29. Charles Bernheimer, *Figures of Ill Repute: Representing Prostitution in Nineteenth-Century France* (Cambridge, MA: Harvard University Press, 1989), 55.

30. Peter Brooks, *Body Work: Objects of Desire in Modern Narrative* (Cambridge, MA: Harvard University Press, 1993), 70.

Chapter 2. Staging Seduction

1. L'auteur de la "Biographie dramatique," *L'art de réussir en amour*, 12.

2. Ibid., 109, 12.

3. Ibid., 39.

4. Ibid., 192.

5. Ibid., 44.

6. Vannier evokes the following qualifications in reference to Raphael: "sublime, celestial, divine, angelic, virginal, purety, grace, innocence, placidity, tranquil joy, modesty." Bernard Vannier, *L'inscription du corps: Pour une sémiotique du portrait balzacien* (Paris: Klincksieck, 1972), 52.

7. Roland Barthes, *Le plaisir du texte*, Coll. "Tel Quel" (Paris: Seuil, 1973), 19.

8. Søren Kierkegaard, "The Seducer's Diary," in *Either/Or: A Fragment of Life*, trans. Alastair Hannay (London: Penguin Books, 1992), 322–23.

9. Shoshanna Felman underscores the importance of belief for a seduction to work when she analyzes Don Juan's use of performative language: "He knows very well that belief is only the effect of reflection. . . . If for Don Juan, saying is doing, doing is above all making believe [faire, c'est avant tout faire croire]. The act of seduction is above all a performance of belief." Shoshanna Felman, *Le scandale du corps parlant* (Paris: Editions du Seuil, 1980), 42.

10. Lucienne Frappier-Mazur, *L'expression métaphorique dans la "Comédie humaine": Domaine social et physiologique* (Paris: Klincksieck, 1976), 126.

11. For an analysis of the distinctions between seduction and the art of acting, see Pierre Sansot, "Une question ontologique: La séduction; Séducteurs, séduisants et amants," *Traverses* 17 (1980): 123.

12. Allan Pasco, *Balzacian Montage: Configuring "La Comédie humaine"* (Toronto: University of Toronto Press, 1991), 40–41.

13. Ibid., 43.

14. Charles Baudelaire, *Œuvres complètes* (Paris: Editions Robert Laffont, 1980), 811.

15. In her preface to *La marquise*, Naginski explains this reference, describing Isis as an "Egyptian incarnation of the search for love and of metaphysical initiation, but to which George will enjoy attributing an image of sublimation." Isabelle Naginski, preface to *Nouvelles*, by George Sand (Paris: Des femmes, 1986), 37.

16. Françoise Massardier-Kenney, "L'espace du féminin dans *La marquise*," *George Sand Studies* 10 (1990–91): 33.

17. Fraisse, *Muse de la raison*, 23.

18. Ibid., 14.

19. In part because of the key role women play in Isidora's "rebirth," Annabelle M. Rea has called *Isidora* "a strongly feminist text." "The Mid-Life Rebirth Journey in *Isidora*," in *The Traveler in the Life and Works of George Sand*, ed. Tamara Alvarez-Detrell and Michael G. Paulson (Troy, NY: Whitson Publishing Co., 1994), 147.

20. See, for example, Bernheimer, *Figures of Ill Repute:* ; and Jann Matlock, *Scenes of Seduction: Prostitution, Hysteria and Reading Difference in Nineteenth-Century France* (New York: Columbia University Press, 1994).

21. Claude Reichler, *La diabolie: La séduction, la renardie, l'écriture* (Paris: Editions de Minuit, 1979), 14; italics added.

22. Bernheimer, *Figures of Ill Repute,* 35.

23. Ibid., 34.

Chapter 3. Seduction's Power Games

1. Daniel Sibony, *Le féminin et la séduction* (Paris: Editions Grasset et Fasquelle, 1986), 9.

2. James Mandrell, *Don Juan and the Point of Honor: Seduction, Patriarchal Society, and Literary Tradition* (University Park: Pennsylvania State University Press, 1992), 262.

3. Ibid., 262.

4. Pierre Bourdieu, "La domination masculine," *Actes de la recherche en sciences sociales* 84 (1990): 12.

5. Mandrell, *Don Juan and the Point of Honor*, 231.

6. Bernard Guyon, "Le 'Don Juan' de Balzac," *L'Année balzacienne* (Paris: Garnier Frères, 1977), 27.

7. Roger Dorey, "La relation d'emprise," *Nouvelle Revue de Psychanalyse* 24 (1981): 118.

8. Ibid., 130 (emphasis mine).

9. Jessica Benjamin, *The Bonds of Love: Psychoanalysis, Feminism, and the Problem of Domination* (New York: Pantheon Books, 1988), 20.

10. Ibid., 12.

11. Benjamin explains: "The master's denial of the other's subjectivity leaves him faced with isolation as the only alternative to being engulfed by the dehumanized other. In either case, the master is actually alone, because the person he is with is no person at all. And likewise, for her part, the slave fears that the master will abandon her to aloneness when he tires of being with someone who is not a person." Ibid., 65.

12. Ibid., 64.

13. George Sand, "Notice," in *Œuvres de George Sand: "Teverino," "Leone Leoni"* (Paris: Michel Lévy Frères, 1861), 182.

14. Larry Riggs, "Class, Gender and Performance in George Sand's *Leone Leoni*," *George Sand Studies* 10 (1990–91): 55.

15. Ibid., 57. Riggs's reading of this novel resembles that of Kathryn Crecelius, who writes in *Family Romances* that *Leone Leoni* ends on a "triumphant note." *Family Romances: George Sand's Early Novels* (Bloomington: Indiana University Press, 1987), 124. While both critics are correct to underscore that Juliette has avoided a confining bourgeois marriage to Bustamente, their insistence on the heroine's freedom, implied by the fact that Sand has set her up to enter into a new series of adventures with Leoni, seems overly idealistic.

16. George Sand, "Lavinia," in *"Leone Leoni" et autres grandes histoires d'amour* (Paris: J'ai Lu, n.d.), 214.

17. Baudrillard, *De la séduction*, 115.

18. For an analysis of Sand's début on the Parisian literary scene in the early 1830s, see Naginski, *George Sand,* 53–56.

19. Benjamin, *Bonds of Love*, 91–92.

20. Naginski, *George Sand,* 75.

21. Sibony, *Le féminin et la séduction*, 9.

22. Georges Bataille, *L'érotisme* (Paris: Editions de Minuit, 1967), 110.

23. Benjamin, *Bonds of Love*, 64.

24. Shoshanna Felman, "Textuality and the Riddle of Bisexuality (Balzac, 'The Girl with the Golden Eyes')," in *What Does a Woman Want?* (Baltimore: Johns Hopkins University Press, 1993), 65; italics in the original.

25. Pierre Barbéris, *Mythes balzaciens* (Paris: Librairie Armand Colin, 1972), 245.

26. Benjamin, *Bonds of Love*, 126.

27. Bataille, *L'érotisme*, 23.

28. Benjamin, *Bonds of Love*, 73–74.

29. Ibid., 223.

30. Adam Phillips, *On Flirtation* (Cambridge, MA: Harvard University Press, 1994), xvii–xviii.

31. For more examples of female domination, see Sand's *Césarine Dietrich* (1870) and Balzac's *La cousine Bette* (1846).

32. Alain Corbin, "Coulisses," in *Histoire de la vie privée: De la Révolution à la Grande Guerre*, ed. Michelle Perrot (Paris: Editions du Seuil, 1985), 547.

Chapter 4. *Êtres séduisants*

1. Freud begins his article "On Narcissism: An Introduction" by stating: "The word narcissism is taken from clinical terminology and was chosen by P. Näcke in 1899 to denote the attitude of a person who treats his own body in the same way as otherwise the body of a sexual object is treated." Sigmund Freud, *General Psychological Theory* (New York: Macmillan, 1963), 56.

2. Heinz Kohut, *The Analysis of the Self* (New York: International Universities Press, 1971), 20.

3. Heinz Kohut, *The Search for the Self: Selected Writings of Heinz Kohut: 1950–1978*. Vol. 1 (New York: International Universities Press, 1978), 438.

4. Freud, *General Psychological Theory*, 69–70.

5. Ibid., 70; emphasis mine.

6. Sarah Kofman, *L'énigme de la femme: La femme dans les textes de Freud* (Paris: Editions Galilée, 1980), 67.

7. Georg Simmel, *On Women, Sexuality, and Love*, trans. Guy Oakes (New Haven, CT: Yale University Press, 1984), 134.

8. Joan Rivière, "Womanliness as a Masquerade," *International Journal of Psychoanalysis* 10 (1929): 306.

9. Janet Beizer, *Family Plots: Balzac's Narrative Generations* (New Haven, CT: Yale University Press, 1986), 118.

10. Shoshanna Felman, "Rereading Femininity," *Yale French Studies* 62 (1981): 19–44.

11. Pierre Carlet de Marivaux, "Le cabinet du philosophe," *Journaux et œuvres divers* (Paris: Bordas, 1988), 372.

12. Béatrice Didier, introduction to *Lélia*, by George Sand (Meylan: Editions de l'Aurore, 1987), 40.

13. See Isabelle Naginski, "Les Deux *Lélia*: Une réécriture exemplaire," *Revue des Sciences humaines* 226 (1992): 83.

14. For an analysis of how the secret functions in *Lélia*, see Pratima Prasad, "Uncovering Narrative Convention in Sand's *Lélia*," *George Sand Studies* 20 (2001): 7–20.

15. Whenever material cited can be found in both versions of the novel, I will give page numbers for each.

16. For a systematic comparison of Foedora and Lélia, one can consult Pierre Reboul's notes to the Garnier edition of *Lélia*, as well as Nadine Lemoine-Guéry's article, "La femme froide chez Honoré de Balzac et George Sand," *Présence de George Sand* 14 (1982): 46–52.

17. Sand substantially changed the novel's final chapters, for in the 1833 version Sténio has already died and Lélia speaks only to his corpse.

18. Davidson writes, "Good women were selfless, domestic creatures who avoided the public eye. Bad women enjoyed being at the center of attention and were egotistical, selfish 'coquettes.'" Denise Zara Davidson, "Constructing Order in Post-Revolutionary France: Women's Identities and Cultural Practices, 1800–1830" (diss., University of Pennsylvania, 1997), 61.

19. Pierre Saint-Amand, *Séduire ou la passion des lumières* (Paris: Méridiens Klincksieck, 1987), 35.

20. René Girard, *Mensonge romantique et vérité romanesque* (Paris: Bernard Grasset, Coll. Pluriel, 1961), 18.

21. Margaret Darrow, "French Noblewomen and the New Domesticity, 1750–1850," *Feminist Studies* 5 (1979): 41.

22. Ibid., 42.

23. See Rose Fortassier, *Les mondains de "La comédie humaine": Etude historique et psychologique* (Paris: Klincksieck, 1974), 328.

24. However, Sand did not always take a stance so different from Balzac's. She also created the narcissistic seductress Césarine Dietrich (in the 1870 novel of the same name), who lacks Lélia's distinctive inner qualities.

25. Saint-Amand, *Séduire*, 12.

26. Jean Delumeau, *La peur en Occident* (Paris: Fayard, 1978), 306–7.

27. Ibid., 313.

28. Emilien Carassus, *Le mythe du dandy* (Paris: Librairie Armand Colin, 1971), 62.

29. René Girard, *Des choses cachées depuis la fondation du monde*, Coll. Le Livre de poche biblio essais (Paris: Editions Grasset & Fasquelle, 1978), 514.

30. Jean Laplanche, *Vie et mort en psychanalyse* (Paris: Flammarion, 1970), 123.

31. For an analysis of Sand's various treatments of the Don Juan myth, see Françoise Genevray, "Le personnage de Don Juan dans *Lélia* et *Le Château des Désertes*," *Présence de George Sand* 10 (1981): 26–31; and Pierre Salomon, "George Sand et Don Juan," *Présence de George Sand* 11 (1981): 47–48.

32. For more on *Horace* as the elaboration of a republican society, see Whitney Walton, *Eve's Proud Descendants: Four Women Writers and Republican Politics in Nineteenth-Century France* (Stanford, CA: Stanford University Press, 2000), 186–87.

33. Michel Lemaire, *Le dandysme de Baudelaire à Mallarmé* (Montréal: Presses de l'Université de Montréal, 1978), 19.

34. Charles Baudelaire, *Œuvres complètes* (Paris: Robert Laffont, 1980), 807.

35. Carassus, *Le mythe du dandy*, 47.

36. Ibid., 48.

Conclusion

1. Baudrillard, *De la séduction*, 9.

2. Bernard Guyon, *La pensée politique et sociale de Balzac* (Paris: Librairie Armand Colin, 1947), 349–50.

3. Béatrice Didier, introduction to *Le meunier d'Angibault*, by George Sand (Paris: Librairie Générale Française, 1985), 10–11.

4. Honoré de Balzac, *Physiologie du mariage*, in vol. 10 of *La comédie humaine*, Bibliothèque de la Pléiade (Paris: Gallimard, 1950), 634.

5. M. Fournel, *Traité de la séduction, considéré dans l'ordre judiciaire* (Paris: Demonville, 1781), 8.

6. Peter Trachtenberg, *Le complexe de Casanova: Les séducteurs impénitents et les femmes qui leur succombent* (Paris: Les Editions de l'homme, 1990); Claudine Mosson, Isabelle Multon, Christian Auzanot, and Thierry Mosson, *Séduction: Mode d'emploi* (Paris: Éditions KEOPS, 1990); and Christophe Leroy, *Draguer et séduire aujourd'hui* (Paris: Auto édition, 1993).

7. Didier Derlich, *Séductions*, Editions Jean-Claude Lattès/Carrère Editions 13 (Paris: Livre de poche, 1993).

Bibliography

Un ami de Cythère. *L'art de faire la cour aux femmes et de s'en faire aimer; ou, Conseils aux hommes pour réussir en amour selon les caractères, les rangs, et les classes, soit à la ville ou à la campagne.* Paris: Terry Editeur, 1837.

Armstrong, Nancy. *Desire and Domestic Fiction: A Political History of the Novel.* New York: Oxford University Press, 1987.

L'auteur de la "Biographie dramatique." *L'art de réussir en amour, enseigné en 25 leçons; ou, Nouveaux secrets de triompher des Femmes, et de les fixer.* 2nd ed. Paris: La Librairie française et étrangère, 1826.

Balzac, Honoré de. *Béatrix.* In vol. 2 of *La comédie humaine.* Bibliothèque de la Pléiade. Paris: Gallimard, 1976.

———. *L'elixir de longue vie.* In vol. 11 of *La comédie humaine.* Bibliothèque de la Pléiade. Paris: Gallimard, 1980.

———. "La femme comme il faut." In *Les Français peints par eux-mêmes, encyclopédie morale du dix-neuvième siècle.* Paris: L. Curmer, 1841.

———. *La fille aux yeux d'or.* In vol. 5 of *La comédie humaine.* Bibliothèque de la Pléiade. Paris: Gallimard, 1977.

———. *Illusions perdues.* In vol. 5 of *La comédie humaine.* Bibliothèque de la Pléiade. Paris: Gallimard, 1977.

———. *La peau de chagrin.* In vol. 10 of *La comédie humaine.* Bibliothèque de la Pléiade. Paris: Gallimard, 1979.

———. *Le père Goriot.* In vol. 3 of *La comédie humaine.* Bibliothèque de la Pléiade. Paris: Gallimard, 1976.

———. *Physiologie du mariage.* In vol. 10 of *La comédie humaine.* Bibliothèque de la Pléiade. Paris: Gallimard, 1950.

———. *Un prince de la Bohème.* In vol. 7 of *La comédie humaine.* Bibliothèque de la Pléiade. Paris: Gallimard, 1977.

———. *Les secrets de la princesse de Cadignan.* In vol. 6 of *La comédie humaine.* Bibliothèque de la Pléiade. Paris: Gallimard, 1950.

———. *Splendeurs et misères des courtisanes.* In vol. 6 of *La comédie humaine.* Bibliothèque de la Pléiade. Paris: Gallimard, 1977.

———. *Traité de la vie élégante.* In vol. 12 of *La comédie humaine.* Bibliothèque de la Pléiade. Paris: Gallimard, 1981.

Barbéris, Pierre. In *Balzac, une mythologie réaliste.* Paris: Librairie Larousse, 1971.

———. *Mythes balzaciens.* Paris: Librairie Armand Colin, 1972.

Barthes, Roland. *Le plaisir du texte.* Coll. "Tel Quel." Paris: Seuil, 1973.

Bataille, Georges. *L'erotisme.* Paris: Editions de Minuit, 1957.

———. *La part maudite*. Paris: Editions de Minuit, 1967.

Baudelaire, Charles. *Le peintre de la vie moderne*. In *Œuvres complètes*. Paris: Robert Laffont, 1980.

Baudrillard, Jean. *De la séduction*. Paris: Galilée, 1979.

Beizer, Janet. *Family Plots: Balzac's Narrative Generations*. New Haven, CT: Yale University Press, 1986.

Benjamin, Jessica. *The Bonds of Love: Psychoanalysis, Feminism, and the Problem of Domination*. New York: Pantheon Books, 1988.

Bernheimer, Charles. *Figures of Ill Repute: Representing Prostitution in Nineteenth-Century France*. Cambridge, MA: Harvard University Press, 1989.

———. "Prostitution and Narrative: Balzac's *Splendeurs et misères des courtisanes*." *L'Esprit Créateur* 25 (1985): 22–31.

Bertrand, Michèle. "La séduction dans la littérature psychanalytique." *Etudes freudiennes* 27 (1986): 129–58.

Bossis, Mireille. "*Manon Lescaut – Leone Leoni*: La passion au masculin et/ou au féminin." In *Le récit amoureux*, ed. Didier Coste. Seyssel: Editions du Champ Vallon, 1984.

Bourdieu, Pierre. "La domination masculine." *Actes de la recherche en sciences sociales* 84 (1990): 2–31.

Bricard, Isabelle. *Saintes ou pouliches: L'éducation des jeunes filles au XIXe siècle*. Paris: Albin Michel, 1985.

Brooks, Peter. *Body Work: Objects of Desire in Modern Narrative*. Cambridge, MA: Harvard University Press, 1993.

———. *The Novel of Worldliness: Crébillon, Marivaux, Laclos, Stendhal*. Princeton, NJ: Princeton University Press, 1969.

Burchill, Louise. "Either/Or: Peripeteia of an Alternative in Jean Baudrillard's *De la séduction*." In *Seduced and Abandoned: The Baudrillard Scene*, ed. André Frankovits, 28–44. New York: Semiotext(e), 1984.

Carassus, Emilien. *Le mythe du dandy*. Paris: Librairie Armand Colin, 1971.

Cazenobe, Colette. *Le système du libertinage de Crébillon à Laclos*. Oxford: Voltaire Foundation, 1991.

Chastain, James. *Encyclopedia of 1848 Revolutions*. June 6, 1997. http://www.ohiou.edu/~Chastain/index.htm (accessed August 5, 2003).

Chaussinand-Nogaret, Guy. *La noblesse au XVIIIe siècle: De la féodalité aux Lumières*. Paris: Librairie Hachette, 1976.

Citton, Yves. *Impuissances: Défaillances masculines et pouvoir politique de Montaigne à Stendhal*. Paris: Aubier, 1994.

Clark, Priscilla P. *The Battle of the Bourgeois: The Novel in France, 1789–1848*. Paris: Didier, 1973.

Collingham, H. A. C. *The July Monarchy: A Political History of France, 1830–1848*. London: Longman, 1988.

Crébillon fils. *Les égarements du cœur et de l'esprit*. Coll. Folio. Paris: Gallimard, 1977.

Crecelius, Kathryn. *Family Romances: George Sand's Early Novels*. Bloomington: Indiana University Press, 1987.

Czyba, Lucette. "La femme et le prolétaire dans *Le compagnon du tour de France*." In *George Sand*, ed. Simone Vierne. Paris: C.D.U. et SEDES réunis, 1983.

Darrow, Margaret. "French Noblewomen and the New Domesticity, 1750–1850." *Feminist Studies* 5 (1979): 41–65.

Daumard, Adeline. *Les bourgeois et la bourgeoisie en France depuis 1815*. Paris: Aubier-Montaigne, 1987.

Davidson, Denise Zara. "Constructing Order in Post-Revolutionary France: Women's Identities and Cultural Practices, 1800–1830." Diss., University of Pennsylvania, 1997.

Delumeau, Jean. *La peur en Occident (XIVe–XVIIIe siècles): Une cité assiégée*. Paris: Fayard, 1978.

Derlich, Didier. *Séductions*. Editions Jean-Claude Lattès/Carrère Editions 13. Paris: Livre de poche, 1993.

Didier, Béatrice. Introduction to *Lélia*, by George Sand. Vol 1. Meylan: Editions de l'Aurore, 1987.

———. Introduction to *Le meunier d'Angibault*, by George Sand. Paris: Librairie Générale Française, 1985.

Dorey, Roger. "La relation d'emprise." *Nouvelle Revue de Psychanalyse* 24 (1981): 117–39.

Durkheim, Emile. *Socialism and Saint-Simon*. Yellow Springs, Ohio: Antioch Press, 1958.

Felman, Shoshanna. "Rereading Femininity." *Yale French Studies* 62 (1981): 19–44.

———. *Le scandale du corps parlant: Don Juan avec Austin ou la séduction en deux langues*. Paris: Seuil, 1980.

———. *What Does a Woman Want?* Baltimore: Johns Hopkins University Press, 1993.

Forest, Jean. *L'aristocratie balzacienne*. Paris: Librairie José Corti, 1973.

Fortassier, Rose. "Echos des 'Liaisons dangereuses' dans 'La comédie humaine.'" In *L'Année balzacienne*, 277–81. Paris: Garnier Frères, 1976.

———. *Les mondains de La comédie humaine: Etude historique et psychologique*. Paris: Klincksieck, 1974.

Fournel, Jean-François. *Traité de la séduction*. Paris: Demonville, 1781.

Fraisse, Geneviève. *Muse de la raison: La démocratie exclusive et la différence des sexes*. Aix-en-Provence: Alinéa, 1989.

Frappier-Mazur, Lucienne. "Code romantique et résurgences du féminin dans *La Comtesse du Rudolstadt (Consuelo)*." In *Le récit amoureux*, ed. Didier Coste, 53–70. Seyssel: Editions du Champ Vallon, 1984.

———. *L'expression métaphorique dans la "Comédie humaine": Domaine social et physiologique*. Paris: Librairie C. Klincksieck, 1976.

Freud, Sigmund. "The Economic Problem of Masochism." In *General Psychological Theory*, ed. Philip Rieff, 190–201. New York: Macmillan, 1963.

———. "On Narcissism: An Introduction." In *General Psychological Theory*, ed. Philip Rieff, 56–82. New York: Macmillan, 1963.

Gallop, Jane. *The Daughter's Seduction: Feminism and Psychoanalysis*. Ithaca, NY: Cornell University Press, 1982.

———. "French Theory and the Seduction of Feminism." In *Men in Feminism*, ed. Alice Jardine and Paul Smith, 111–15. New York: Methuen, 1987.

Genevray, Françoise. "Le personnage de Don Juan dans *Lélia* et *Le Château des Désertes*." *Présence de George Sand* 10 (1981): 26–31.

Girard, René. *Des choses cachées depuis la fondation du monde*. Coll. Le Livre de poche biblio essais. Paris: Editions Grasset & Fasquelle, 1978.

———. *Mensonge romantique et vérité romanesque*. Coll. Pluriel. Paris: Bernard Grasset, 1961.

Gnüg, Hiltrud. "The Dandy and the Don Juan Type." In *European Romanticism: Literary Cross-Currents, Modes and Models*, ed. Gerhart Hoffmeister, 229–46. Detroit: Wayne State University Press, 1990.

"La grande dame de 1830." In vol. 1 of *Les Français peints par eux-mêmes, encyclopédie morale du dix-neuvième siècle*, 162–68. Paris: L. Curmer, 1841.

Green, André. *Narcissisme de vie, narcissisme de mort*. Paris: Editions de Minuit, 1983.

———. "Un, autre, neutre: Valeurs narcissiques du même." *Nouvelle Revue de Psychanalyse* 13 (1976): 37–79.

Guyon, Bernard. "Le 'Don Juan' de Balzac." In *L'Année balzacienne,* 9–28. Paris: Garnier Frères, 1977.

———. *La pensée politique et sociale de Balzac*. Paris: Librairie Armand Colin, 1947.

Higgs, David. *Nobles in Nineteenth-Century France: The Practice of Inegalitarianism.* Baltimore: Johns Hopkins University Press, 1987.

Janin, Jules. Introduction to *Les Français peints par eux-mêmes, encyclopédie morale du dix-neuvième siècle*. Vol. 1. Paris: L. Curmer, 1841.

Kelly, Dorothy. *Fictional Genders: Role and Representation in Nineteenth-Century French Narrative*. Lincoln: University of Nebraska Press, 1989.

Khan, M. Masud R. "Entre l'idole et l'idéal." *Nouvelle Revue de Psychanalyse* 13 (1976): 259–64.

Kierkegaard, Søren. "The Seducer's Diary." In *Either/Or: A Fragment of Life*, trans. Alastair Hannay, 243–376. London: Penguin Books, 1992.

Kofman, Sarah. *L'énigme de la femme: La femme dans les textes de Freud*. Paris: Galilée, 1980.

Kohut, Heinz. *The Analysis of the Self*. New York: International Universities Press, 1971.

———. "Forms and Transformations of Narcissism." In vol. 1 of *The Search for the Self: Selected Writings of Heinz Kohut: 1950–1978*, ed. Paul H. Ornstein, 427–60. New York: International Universities Press, 1978.

Lacan, Jacques. *Ecrits*. Paris: Seuil, 1966.

———. *Le séminaire de Jacques Lacan: Livre XX, "Encore," 1972–1973*. Texte établi par Jacques-Allain Miller. Paris: Seuil, 1975.

Laclos, Choderlos de. *Les liaisons dangereuses*. Coll. Folio. Paris: Gallimard, 1972.

Laden, Marie-Paule. "The Pitfalls of Success: Jacob's Evolution in Marivaux's *Le paysan parvenu*." *Romanic Review* 74 (1983): 170–82.

LAMI. *L'art de rendre les femmes fidèles*. Paris: Chez l'éditeur à la librairie française et étrangère, 1828.

Landes, Joan. *Women and the Public Sphere in the Age of the French Revolution*. Ithaca, NY: Cornell University Press, 1988.

Laplanche, Jean. *Vie et mort en psychanalyse*. Paris: Flammarion, 1970.

Laplanche, Jean, and Jean-Bertand Pontalis. "Fantasme originaire, fantasmes des origines, origine du fantasme." *Les Temps Modernes*. 19, no. 215 (1964).

Lemaire, Michel. *Le dandysme de Baudelaire à Mallarmé*. Montréal: Les Presses de l'université de Montréal, 1978.

Lemoine-Guéry, Nadine. "La femme froide chez Honoré de Balzac et George Sand." *Présence de George Sand* 14 (1982): 46–52.

Leroy, Christophe. *Draguer et séduire aujourd'hui*. Paris: Auto édition, 1993.

Lewis, H. D. "The Legal Status of Women in Nineteenth-Century France." *Journal of European Studies* 10 (1980): 178–88.

Mandrell, James. *Don Juan and the Point of Honor: Seduction, Patriarchal Society, and Literary Tradition*. University Park: Pennsylvania State University Press, 1992.

Marceau, Félicien. *Balzac et son monde*. Paris: Gallimard, 1970.

Marivaux, Pierre Carlet de. "Le cabinet du philosophe." *Journaux et œuvres divers*. Paris: Bordas, 1988.

———. *Le paysan parvenu*. Coll. Folio. Paris: Editions Gallimard, 1981.

Martin-Fugier, Anne. *La vie élégante ou la formation du Tout-Paris, 1815–1848*. Paris: Fayard, 1990.

Massardier-Kenney, Françoise. "L'espace du féminin dans *La marquise*." *George Sand Studies* 10 (1990–91): 28–33.

Matlock, Jann. *Scenes of Seduction: Prostitution, Hysteria and Reading Difference in Nineteenth-Century France*. New York: Columbia University Press, 1994.

M. G***. *L'art de connaître les femmes*. 2nd ed. Paris: Chez les marchands de nouveautés, 1821.

Milner, Max. *Le romantisme*. Paris: Arthaud, 1973.

Mosson, Claudine, Isabelle Multon, Christian Auzanot, and Thierry Mosson. *Séduction: Mode d'emploi*. Paris: Éditions KEOPS, 1990.

Mozet, Nicole. "Coquetterie et pouvoir dans les romans sandiens du Second Empire." *Revue des Sciences humaines* 226 (1992): 193–209.

Naginski, Isabelle. "Les deux *Lélia*: Une réécriture exemplaire." *Revue des Sciences Humaines* 226 (1992): 65–84.

———. "From Melancholy to Ecstasy: *Lélia* and Sand's Feminine Sublime." *George Sand Studies* 11 (1992): 3–13.

———. *George Sand: Writing for Her Life*. New Brunswick, NJ: Rutgers University Press, 1991.

———. Preface to *La marquise*. In *Nouvelles*, by George Sand, 35–44. Paris: Des femmes, 1986.

Nesci, Catherine. *La femme mode d'emploi: Balzac, de la "Physiologie du mariage" à "La comédie humaine."* Lexington, KY: French Forum Publishers, 1992.

Pacteau, Francette. "The Impossible Referent: Representations of the Androgyne." In *Formations of Fantasy*, ed. Victor Burgin, James Donald, and Cora Kaplan, 62–84. London: Methuen, 1986.

Pasco, Allan. *Balzacian Montage: Configuring "La comédie humaine."* Toronto: University of Toronto Press, 1991.

P.C. and A.L.R. *L'art de briller en société, ou manuel de l'homme du monde*. 3rd ed. Paris: Terry Editeur, 1829.

Petrey, Sandy. "George and Georgina Sand: Realist Gender in *Indiana*." In *Textuality and Sexuality: Reading Theories and Practices*, ed. Judith Still and Michael Worton, 133–47. Manchester: Manchester University Press, 1993.

———. *Realism and Revolution: Balzac, Stendhal, Zola, and the Performances of History*. Ithaca, NY: Cornell University Press, 1988.

Phillips, Adam. *On Flirtation*. Cambridge, MA: Harvard University Press, 1994.

Plant, Sadie. "Baudrillard's Woman: The Eve of Seduction." In *Forget Baudrillard*, ed. Chris Rojek and Bryan S. Turner, 88–106. London: Routledge, 1993.

Prasad, Pratima. "Uncovering Narrative Convention in Sand's *Lélia*." *George Sand Studies* 20 (2001): 7–20.

Prendergast, Christopher. *The Order of Mimesis: Balzac, Stendhal, Nerval, Flaubert*. Cambridge: Cambridge University Press, 1986.

Rea, Annabelle. "The Mid-Life Rebirth Journey in *Isidora*." In *The Traveler in the Life and Works of George Sand*, ed. Tamara Alvarez-Detrell and Michael G. Paulson, 140–50. Troy, NY: Whitson Publishing Co., 1994.

Reichler, Claude. *L'age libertin*. Paris: Editions de Minuit, 1987.

———. *La diabolie: La séduction, la renarderie, l'écriture*. Paris: Editions de Minuit, 1979.

Rétat, Pierre. "Ethique et idéologie dans *Les égarements*." In *Les paradoxes du romancier: Les "égarements" de Crébillon*. Grenoble: Presses Universitaires de Grenoble, 1975.

Riggs, Larry W. "Class, Gender and Performance in George Sand's *Leone Leoni*." *George Sand Studies* 10, nos. 1–2 (1990–91): 50–59.

Rivière, Joan. "Womanliness as a Masquerade." *International Journal of Psychoanalysis* 10 (1929): 303–13.

Rosolato, Guy. "Le narcissisme." *Narcisses: Nouvelle Revue de Psychanalyse* 13 (1976): 7–36.

Roussel, Roy. *The Conversation of the Sexes: Seduction and Equality in Selected Seventeenth- and Eighteenth-Century Texts*. New York: Oxford University Press, 1986.

Saint-Amand, Pierre. *Séduire ou la passion des lumières*. Paris: Méridiens Klincksieck, 1987.

Saint-Ange, Louis de. *Le secret de triompher des femmes et de les fixer*. Bruxelles: De la société typographique, 1825.

Salomon, Pierre. "George Sand et Don Juan." *Présence de George Sand* 11 (1981): 47–48.

Sand, George. *Adriani*. Paris: Editions France-Empire, 1980.

———. *Césarine Dietrich*. Paris: Calman Lévy, 1897.

———. *Le Château des Désertes*. Meylan: Editions de l'Aurore, 1985.

———. *Le compagnon du tour de France*. In *Œuvres complètes*. Vol. 12. Paris: Perrotin, 1843.

———. *Consuelo*. Vols. 1 and 2. Meylan: Editions de l'Aurore, 1983.

———. *Consuelo – La comtesse de Rudolstadt*. Paris: Garnier Frères, 1959.

———. *Correspondance*. Paris: Garnier Frères, 1964.

———. *Horace*. Meylan: Editions de l'Aurore, 1982.

———. *Indiana*. Coll. Folio. Paris: Editions Gallimard, 1984.

———. *Isidora*. Paris: Michel Lévy Frères, 1880.

———. "Lavinia." In *"Leone Leoni" et autres grandes histoires d'amour*. Paris: J'ai lu, n.d.

———. *Lélia*. 2 vols. Meylan: Editions de l'Aurore, 1987.

———. *Lélia*. Ed. Pierre Reboul. Paris: Garnier Frères, 1960.

———. *"Léone Léoni" et autres grandes histoires d'amour*. Paris: J'ai lu, n.d.

———. *La marquise*. In *Nouvelles*. Paris: Des femmes, 1986.

———. *Œuvres autobiographiques*. Ed. Georges Lubin. Bibliothèque de la Pléiade. Paris: Gallimard, 1970–71.

———. *Œuvres de George Sand: "Teverino," "Leone Leoni."* Paris: Michel Lévy Frères, 1861.

———. "Pauline." In *Nouvelles*. Paris: Des femmes, 1986.

Sansot, Pierre. "Une question ontologique: La séduction; Séducteurs, séduisants et amants." *Traverses* 18 (1980): 119–34.

Sartre, Jean-Paul. *Baudelaire*. Coll. Folio. Paris: Gallimard, 1975.

Schneider, Monique. *Freud et le plaisir*. Paris: Denoël, 1980.

———. "La séduction comme parure ou comme initiation." *Traverses* 17 (1979): 31–44.

Schor, Naomi. *George Sand and Idealism*. New York: Columbia University Press, 1993.

Sclippa, Norbert. *Texte et idéologie: Images de la noblesse et de la bourgeoisie dans le roman français, 1750 à 1830*. New York: Peter Lang, 1987.

Sedgwick, Eve Kosofsky. *Between Men: English Literature and Male Homosocial Desire*. New York: Columbia University Press, 1985.

Sibony, Daniel. *L'amour inconscient: Au-delà du principe de séduction*. Paris: Bernard Grasset, 1983.

———. *Le féminin et la séduction*. Paris: Editions Grasset et Fasquelle, 1986.

Simmel, Georg. *On Women, Sexuality, and Love*. Trans. Guy Oakes. New Haven, CT: Yale University Press, 1984.

———. "Psychologie de la coquetterie." In *Philosophie de l'amour*. Rivages Poches. Paris: Petite Bibliothèque, 1988.

Simon, Ernest. "A Tradition of the Comic Novel: Sorel, Scarron, Furetière, Sterne, Diderot." Diss., Columbia University, 1963.

Simons, Madeleine A. "Le génie au féminin ou les paradoxes de la princesse de Cadignan." *L'Année balzacienne* 9 (1988): 347–66.

Stendhal. *Armance ou quelques scènes d'un salon de Paris en 1827*. Paris: Garnier Frères, 1950.

Szabó, Anna, ed. *Préfaces de George Sand*. Debrecen, Hungary: Kossuth Lajos Tudományegvetem, 1997.

Trachtenberg, Peter. *Le complexe de Casanova: Les séducteurs impénitents et les femmes qui leur succombent*. Paris: Editions de l'homme, 1990.

Vannier, Bernard. *L'inscription du corps: Pour une sémiotique du portrait balzacien*. Paris: Klincksieck, 1972.

Vermeylen, Pierre. *Les idées politiques et sociales de George Sand*. Bruxelles: Editions de l'Université de Bruxelles, 1984.

Virey, Julien-Joseph. *De la femme, sous ses rapports physiologique, moral et littéraire*. Paris: Crochard: 1825.

Walton, Whitney. *Eve's Proud Descendants: Four Women Writers and Republican Politics in Nineteenth-Century France*. Stanford, CA: Stanford University Press, 2000.

Wyngaard, Amy. "Switching Codes: Class, Clothing, and Cultural Change in the Works of Marivaux and Watteau." *Eighteenth Century Studies* 33 (2000): 523–41.

Index